On the Road
in South Korea

On the Road in South Korea

An Enlightening, Offbeat 5,000 Mile Odyssey through an Ancient Land

Copyright © 2016, 2022 by Mark A. Dake

On the Road in South Korea first published as *South Korea: The Enigmatic Peninsula* by Dundurn Press Limited, Canada. This edition published by Hollym Corp., Publishers in arrangement with Dundurn Press Limited.

All rights reserved. No part of this publication may be reproduced or utilized in any form, without prior written permission from the copyright holders.

Developmental editor Hahm Minji
Designer Lee Hyehee, Jung Deunhae

First published in 2022
by Hollym Corp., Publishers, Seoul, Korea
Phone +82 2 734 5087 **Fax** +82 2 730 5149
www.hollym.net **e-Mail** hollym@hollym.co.kr

 Hollym

서울시 종로구 종로 12길 15
전화 02 735 7551~4 전송 02 730 5149
홈페이지 www.hollym.co.kr 전자우편 hollym@hollym.co.kr

ISBN: 978-89-7094-071-7 03910

On the Road
in South Korea

An Enlightening, Offbeat 5,000 Mile Odyssey through an Ancient Land

Mark A. Dake

 Hollym

To my father, who would leave the sports section of *The Globe and Mail* on the breakfast table in the winter for me when I was a kid so I could read about my beloved Toronto Maple Leafs.

To my mother, who loved reading epic novels and introduced me as a boy to quality fiction and non-fiction.

Contents

Map of South Korea

NORTH KOREA

EAST SEA
(SEA OF JAPAN)

Dokdo
Ulleungdo

SEOUL

INCHEON

GYEONGGI

GANGWON

NORTH
CHUNGCHEONG

SOUTH
CHUNGCHEONG

NORTH
GYEONGSANG

Panmunjeom

Ganghwado

Suwon

Icheon

Anseong

Pyeongtaek

Dangjin

Seosan

Cheonan

Jincheon

Eumseong

Chungju

Danyang

Gongju

DAEJEON

Gyeryong
Mt.

Nogeunri

Sangju

Mungyeong

Andong

Bohyeon
Mt.

Baegam

Hupo

Pohang

Wonju

Pyeongchang

Yeongwol

Taebaek

Uljin

Doma

Gangneung

Donghae

Samcheok

Yangyang

Sokcho

Seorak
Mt.

Eulji Observatory

Haean
(Punch Bowl)

Inje

Taebaek Mountains

Sobaek Mountains

Charyeong Mountains

Gwangju Mountains

Han River

North Han River

Imjin River

Han River

Geum River

Nakdong River

Anmyeondo

Cheonsu
Bay

NORTHWEST

CHAPTER 1

Panmunjeom: "The Most Dangerous Place in the World"

"This is the most dangerous place in the world," half-joked our Korean guide over the loudspeaker. Our tour bus was approaching the Demilitarized Zone (DMZ) in Panmunjeom. "Are you ready?"

Contrary to our guide's statement, more hazardous places do exist than the four-kilometer-wide, 250-kilometer-long DMZ. Syria, Sudan and Afghanistan come to mind. The militarized border has divided South from North Korea since the Korean War ended in a ceasefire with the signing of an armistice at Panmunjeom on July 27, 1953.

Thousands of incidents have occurred along the DMZ, many in Panmunjeom, the only place along the entire border where soldiers from South and North Korea face each other. Many conflicts have been minor: North Korean People's Army (KPA) soldiers spitting on the shoes of opposing soldiers, name-calling, guns going off. In 1974, after KPA lieutenant Pak Chul was prevented from taking a photo of a visiting ranking U.S. officer, Pak kicked a U.S. soldier in the groin.

But deadly incidents have also happened. More than 90 Americans, 500 South Koreans and 900 North Koreans have been killed along the North-South border since the truce was signed. On July 11, 2008, fifty-three-year-old South Korean housewife Park Wang-ja was on a popular government-run group tour just north of the DMZ on the east coast. The region is renowned for its plethora of towering, steeple-like granite peaks known collectively as the Geumgang, or Diamond Mountains. Ms. Park's tour group was staying at the Mount Geumgang Resort. In early morning on July 11, she took a solo stroll from the resort but mistakenly wandered off the ascribed route into a restricted military zone. A North Korean solider in a guard tower ordered her to halt. She panicked and tried to bolt. The soldier shot her dead. Due to the death, South Korea suspended the joint tour project and it has yet to be restarted. More recently, two Republic of Korea (ROK) soldiers on patrol in the DMZ in Paju near Panmunjeom lost their lower legs after stepping on land mines.

Our bus — with about forty mostly foreign tourists on board — had departed Seoul sixty kilometers southeast in the morning. After a stop for lunch, then a tour into the First Infiltration Tunnel — hollowed out by the North under the DMZ and discovered by the South in 1974 — our next stop was the DMZ and the Joint Security Area (JSA). In the JSA are belligerent and unpredictable KPA soldiers who eat iron for breakfast, ore for lunch and steel for dinner. With the luck of a middle-aged Canadian buttercup like me, a vengeful North Korean soldier might kidnap me and whisk me to one of his country's remote gulags, where I'd spend the rest of my sad existence hoeing desiccated fields of shriveled potatoes with a small trowel. I didn't like the prospect of this — not at all.

Things can and do go wrong in the JSA. Take, for example, on November 23, 1984, when a group of Russian students attending Kim Il-sung University in Pyongyang was bussed to the JSA for a tour. One of the students was a young Russian named Andrei Lankov – today a professor at Kookmin University in Seoul. Through Lankov, I gleaned details of what had transpired.

Lankov's classmate was twenty-two-year-old Russian Vasily Matauzik, who that morning was taking photos standing in North Korea a few meters from the Military Demarcation Line (MDL) separating the two countries. "Matauzik suddenly dashed across the line into the South," recalled Lankov. "A KPA solider raced after him, then all hell broke loose." More than a dozen KPA soldiers equipped with Kalashnikov automatic rifles sped out in hot pursuit from Panmungak – the North's main building just meters from the MDL.

"Twenty to thirty KPA guards opened fire and ran across the MDL in an effort to prevent the defection," wrote Wayne A. Kirkbride in *DMZ: A Story of the Panmunjeom Axe Murder.*

In response, United Nations Command (UNC) Security Battalion soldiers – comprising American and ROK troops equipped with heavy weapons – dashed out from a building in the DMZ. Ironically, the Korean War armistice stipulates soldiers in the DMZ must use only minimum force and be armed with non-automatic weapons. Both sides ignore the rule.

"For twenty minutes, bullets were flying everywhere," said Lankov, who had sprinted into Panmungak to escape the hail of gunfire.

In the melee, one ROK and three KPA soldiers were killed, five injured. Matauzik made it safely into the South. Lankov referred disdainfully to Matauzik – the son of a ranking Russian officer – as a "spoiled brat, directly responsible for the deaths."

Several hundred meters south of the JSA our tour bus stopped at Camp Bonifas, base of the security battalion, comprising approximately 600 soldiers – 60 percent ROK, the others American. (Confirming precise numbers in this high-risk security area is a challenge.) The battalion provides protection to visiting military officers, government officials, guests and, most importantly, daisies like me. The soldiers are in a constant state of military readiness.

The Washington Post once described Camp Bonifas as a "small collection of buildings surrounded by triple coils of razor wire, just 440 yards south of the DMZ." Minus minefields and soldiers, it "resembled a big Boy Scout camp."

Camp Bonifas's main gate is utilitarian, like entering a cut-rate summer camp that your parents would send you and your sister to as kids. A young U.S. soldier – our security escort – stepped onto our bus and walked slowly up the aisle, handing us identification tags. His name tag read Sergeant Naumenkof. He was a wholesome-faced, sleepy-looking young man who spoke in a slow midwest American drawl. I envisioned Naumenkof laboring on a Kansas farm rather than defending South Korea from the enemy.

"These ID tags must be prominently displayed on your jackets at all times," he ordered. "There'll be no flash photography. Turn off your cell phones." Naumenkof handed each of us a sheet of paper. "This is a visitor's declaration page that you all must sign," he said.

I noted one paragraph in particular: "The visit to the Joint Security Area at Panmunjeom will entail entry into a hostile area and possibility of injury or death as a direct result of enemy action."

We had no choice but to sign it if we wanted to tour the JSA. We all did, thus releasing the South Korean government from any liability if a KPA guard decided to use me as a punching bag or for target practice.

Naumenkof escorted us off the bus into nearby Ballinger Hall, a small auditorium named in honor of Robert M. Ballinger, a U.S. Navy commander who died along with an ROK soldier in an explosion in the First Infiltration Tunnel on November 20, 1974.

We took our seats in the hall. Naumenkof strode onto the stage, and announced, "Did you guys read the waiver you just signed? If something happens to you, it's not our fault!" We all laughed.

"What does the waiver say?" he called.

A fellow in our group declared no photos were allowed in the DMZ. Naumenkof confirmed this. Another person hollered there was to be no fraternization with North Korean guards.

"No fraternization," echoed Naumenkof.

I thought that if someone in our group was daft enough to approach an enemy guard and drape an arm around him for a selfie, the moron deserved to wind up on a permanent vacation at a North Korean gulag.

"No gestures, no pointing," offered another tour member.

"No pointing," reiterated Naumenkof.

"Stay in your group," someone called.

"Stay in your group," the soldier agreed.

"Follow instructions."

"Absolutely."

"Don't defect to the North!" I blurted.

The audience guffawed but Naumenkof stared at me with a decidedly unkind gaze I deciphered was either half-restrained humor or a desire to deliver a taekwondo kick my way. Fortunately, witnesses were on hand to deter such unnecessary action.

"Do not defect to North Korea — that's the number one rule around here," Naumenkof repeated dryly. "The biggest thing is, this area we're going to go up to is dangerous. As recently as three weeks ago, we had incidents up there. It's important that you follow instructions, your safety does depend on it. Most importantly, do not point, do not wave, do not gesture to the North Koreans; these are violations of the Armistice Agreement."

Naumenkof surrendered the stage to a young UNC U.S. soldier who began a speech providing insight into the DMZ. Not just any speech though. This was the world's fastest, with not a single pause, delivered non-stop in nine minutes and forty-seven seconds. (I timed him.) A side benefit of being stationed at Camp Bonifas is apparently soldiers have plenty of down time to memorize speeches.

The soldier concluded, speaking rapidly: "Your-tour-group-will-be-escorted-into-Panmunjeom-by-soldiers-of-the-UN-Security-Force-who-are-above-average-aptitude-of-normal-soldiers."

What a relief knowing we'd be accompanied by university Ivy-Leaguers.

After the speech we were back in front of Ballinger Hall to transfer onto a military bus to head to the nearby JSA. En route, Naumenkof announced that off to the side was the village of Daeseong-dong, population 250. Through a retinue of trees I could make out a tightly grouped handful of homes and little farms. "Daeseong-dong is the only village permitted by South Korean authorities to be in the DMZ," Naumenkof said. Only people who grew up here or are direct descendants are permitted to reside in it. It is afforded twenty-four-hour military protection. In evenings residents must be in their homes, windows and doors locked until morning.

Our military bus stopped at the JSA checkpoint entrance. We disembarked. Heavy sheets of rain that had accompanied us from Seoul had dissipated to a minuscule drizzle, though low, dark ominous cloud cover remained. Two Korean UNC silent, buff Arnold Schwarzenegger-like guards joined us.

"They have black belts in karate," said Naumenkof. I made a mental note to stay close to the duo, to guarantee my safety.

We strolled into the JSA, a lonely, desolate, peaceful looking square of utilitarian gray concrete seemingly no larger than a football field. We were observing a microcosm of the DMZ's other 249 kilometers stretching west and east, guarded by a ten-feet-tall chain link barrier and rolls of coiled barbed-wire, watchtowers every few hundred meters, floodlights shining into no-man's land.

In the center of the JSA is a row of seven low, barrack-style buildings referred to as Conference Row. Several units belong to the North, several to the South. Directly north of Conference Row, in North Korea, is formal, white three-story Panmungak, where Andrei Lankov took refuge in 1984. Behind us in the South is large steel-and-glass Freedom House for proposed North-South family meetings. A total of twenty-four mostly small, low buildings are in the JSA.

"UNC soldiers are hidden in some units," Naumenkof announced. "They can be outfitted in full combat gear and ready to fight in just ninety seconds. That's really fast!"

Our group stood next to Conference Row at the Military Armistice Commission building, where meetings between North and South officials took place. A narrow alley between the building and another unit is the access point to both countries. At the alleyway's midpoint is the MDL dividing line. At the far end of the alley, fourteen meters away in North Korea, stood a KPA guard. His short, slight frame was enveloped by a brown-green uniform. He wore a tall, Soviet-style wide-brimmed hat. He was so light and unimposing that a stiff gust of wind might have blown him away.

Next to us, a helmeted ROK soldier stood ramrod straight, feet apart, arms by his side, as if about to draw his pistol holstered to his waist. His muscular chest and ample biceps were evident through a tight-fitting, short-sleeve shirt. His stare was locked on the North Korean guard across the MDL.

We entered the long, narrow, spartan Military Armistice Commission building. Windows afford a view out to the adjacent alley and dividing line. In the center of the room to the side are a wood table and a few chairs. Half the table is in the South, the other half in the North. Stand on one side of the room, you are in South Korea. Cross to the other side, you are in North Korea. Two countries for the price of one!

My two ROK bodyguards accompanied us, and one positioned himself against the near wall, the other at the far door that opened to North Korea.

"Do not interfere or touch the ROK guards – they will physically stop you if you cross in front or behind them," warned Naumenkof. "Do not go near the door to the North. Two KPA guards are standing outside it. There have been incidents where tourists and ROK soldiers have been pulled through the door and brutalized."

Naumenkof said that in 2002, U.S. President George W. Bush and South Korean President Kim Dae-jung were in this room when two KPA guards barged in. "One removed the American silk flag and polished his shoes with it while the other took down the South Korean flag and blew his nose on it." Not wanting a repeat, the South had the silk flags replaced with plastic ones.

We exited, boarded the military shuttle bus, and rode a few hundred meters on a lonely road through woods to remote UNC Checkpoint 3 on the border. We disembarked, and were greeted by a young, enthusiastic Korean soldier surnamed Han, who gleefully announced that the North was monitoring our group this very moment from KPA Checkpoint 5 in close proximity.

"Their radio tower is jamming our hand phone signals," Han said. "If you try to use our phone, it won't work. Go ahead," he dared happily, "try."

Our view north over the DMZ into no-man's-land was limited by a soupy veil of white mist hugging the ground, reducing visibility to a hundred or so meters. On a clear day we'd be able to see the sparsely populated terrain of foothills and brush north of the DMZ and low, steep hills on the horizon.

"Can you see the A-frame building out there," Han asked, pointing to the DMZ.

Through thick mist, all I could make out was the vague outline of woods. "It's the North Korea Peace Museum, it holds the two axes North Korean soldiers used to kill two U.S. officers in 1976," he said. The murders almost brought the two Koreas to the brink of conflict. The killings occurred near where we now stood close to the Bridge of No Return. On this bridge, Korean War prisoners on both sides crossed to return to their respective nations. Some North Korean soldiers made the difficult decision to stay in the South and not cross back to their homeland, knowing they'd never see family and friends again. We strolled down to the long-abandoned, single-lane bridge, its concrete darkened and weathered over time. It crosses to the North over a creek overgrown with bush. Up until 1976, it was the only land route linking the two countries.

Two towering poplar trees once stood next to the bridge, the trees' branches periodically partially blocking the view of UNC guards – who would have stood at nearby UNC Checkpoint 3 – out to the North's checkpoint. UNC work crews occasionally trimmed the trees to ensure an unobstructed view.

On the morning of Wednesday August 18, 1976, a modest security team and work crew led by Captain Arthur G. Bonifas and First Lieutenant Mark T. Barrett motored out in a truck to trim the poplars. Three of the crew, armed with axes, climbed ladders into the tree. Within minutes, nine KPA guards, and Senior Lieutenant Pak Chul – the same who'd kicked a U.S. officer in the groin in the JSA – were racing across the bridge to the poplar.

Pak ordered Bonifas to cease cutting. Bonifas told his crew to continue. Pak became incensed and threatened to kill Bonifas. He called for reinforcements. Ten minutes later, about thirty KPA soldiers were massed under the tree.

Pak slipped off his wristwatch, wrapped it in a white handkerchief, put it in his trousers pocket and shouted, "Kill the U.S. aggressors!"

Pak pounced on Bonifas, struck him in the back and knocked him to the ground. Five KPA guards joined the attack and beat Bonifas to death. Barrett was separated from the others and bludgeoned to death with an axe. Four U.S. enlisted men and four ROK crew were injured. The melee lasted about four minutes, only stopped when the truck driver positioned his vehicle over Bonifas's mutilated body. The entire incident was captured on video camera from the nearby UN checkpoint. Film clips were shown on television news programs, still frames printed in newspapers and books. Bonifas, a West Point graduate, had volunteered to be sent to Korea. He was scheduled to return home to New York to his wife and three young children in two weeks.

The next day, U.S. President Gerald Ford approved a massive military plan called Operation Paul Bunyan – a direct response to the murders. Readied for action in South Korea were the ROK's 600,000 soldiers and 37,000 U.S. troops, including special forces, UH-1 Huey and Cobra attack helicopters. Sheridan tanks were positioned near Panmunjeom. Squadrons of F-111 and F-4 Phantom fighter jets, and B-52 bombers, were put on high alert. The U.S. aircraft carrier USS Midway stood by.

Two days later, backed by this massive amalgamation of firepower, sixty-four ROK Special Forces, and engineers equipped with chainsaws, entered the JSA to cut down the two poplars. Had the KPA in the JSA resisted, war would have likely resulted. The trees were felled without incident.

Due to the murders changes came to the JSA. Once free to wander the entire compound, soldiers on both sides were now restricted to their own halves. The Bridge of No Return was closed as well.

The military bus returned us to Camp Bonifas. We transferred onto our tour bus to head back to Seoul. Our probe of the JSA hadn't seemed that perilous – I hadn't been manhandled, bullied or ridiculed by North Korean soldiers. That was the main thing.

Not far south of Panmunjeom, we shuttled over Freedom Bridge, crossing the wide, formidable west-flowing Imjin River. The Han River moves northwest through Seoul, converging with the Imjin River, the result a single river emptying at the Yellow Sea. For security reasons, no vessels ply the Imjin River in this area and civilian vehicles aren't allowed north of here.

An hour later, we were back in Seoul's mass of concrete, steel and low mountains. Our tour concluded where it had begun this morning: at Camp Kim, at the U.S. Yongsan garrison in central Seoul. Sixty minutes later, after riding two subway lines, I was back in southeast Seoul at my small flat in Myeongil-dong.

In contrast to Panmunjeom — "the most dangerous place in the world" — Seoul seemed as safe as a new-born babe in its mother's arms.

CHAPTER 2

Hello, South Korea!

I'd been living in Seoul for more than a decade when my Aunt Irene in Toronto sent me as a gift, the book *In a Sunburned Country*, about writer Bill Bryson's travels through Australia. I'd never heard of Bryson. But when I read his comic narrative of his fascinating trip Down Under, I was immediately smitten, and realized why millions of readers were similarly hooked on this best-selling author.

I got to thinking Bryson was needed to trundle through South Korea, to put it on the map by way of another literary travel hit. Other than China and Japan — accounting for about 60 percent of approximately 15 million tourists who annually visit South Korea — the only country outside Asia with a slim inflow of tourists into the country is the U.S. The rest of the world seems to have little interest to visit.

It might not come as a surprise, but many people know little about Korea. Actually, a number of Americans, I have noted, know a minimum of their own country, let alone other nations. Even my people, Canadians, seem ill-informed. When I'm back in my hometown of Toronto, and mention I live in Korea, I'm sometimes asked "North or South?" As if foreigners are permitted to visit North Korea.

I'd love to reply that I was North Korean leader Kim Jong-un's personal assistant but never do.

Koreans living in Canada have told me with a sigh they're sometimes asked if they're from North or South. Of the more than two million Koreans living in the West, only a tiny handful are from the North. Chances are virtually nil that the Korean you run into at a shop in your neighborhood in North America will be North Korean.

On hiatus from South Korea and temporarily residing in the small city of Brockville, east of Toronto on the shore of the St. Lawrence River, I walked into the local post office to mail a parcel to South Korea. "Can I check the postage cost, please?" I asked the middle-aged female clerk.

The woman found a booklet under the counter on which were listed names of countries, and announced with a puzzled look, "There are two Koreas."

No shit, Sherlock Holmes.

"Which Korea is it going to?" she asked.

"It can only go to one ... mail doesn't go to the other," I replied politely, hoping by simple deduction she'd figure the correct country. She didn't.

"So, which one?" she asked again.

"To South Korea," I replied. "You can't get in or out of the North. There's no international mail delivery there."

She looked surprised, and said, "Oh, I didn't know that!"

Well, read a newspaper then. Read something, anything ... please.

Even people who do read and watch TV news and documentaries, like my mother, can be rather clueless about South Korea. My mother was a school librarian in Toronto for many years. I'd have thought in her downtime, she might have wandered over to the East Asia section and taken a peek at material on South Korea, considering I was living there.

Just prior to my parents visiting me in Seoul in fall 2000, my mother phoned from Toronto, asking worriedly, "Should we get inoculated for disease?"

Of course, mom. We all suffer from dengue fever and typhoid in South Korea.

Next, she innocently wondered, "Should we bring purification tablets to put in drinking water?"

I sighed, shook my head, and answered, "Mom, South Korea's not a third-world country." Upon arrival in Seoul, she looked around at the multitudes of high-rise apartments, and remarked with surprise, "I didn't think there'd be so many buildings." Had she been expecting mud huts with straw roofs?

Familiarity with the peninsula was markedly worse in previous times. In a television documentary I'd seen on the Korean War, a U.S. soldier who'd arrived in South Korea in 1950 sent a letter to his wife back in America, asking that she mail him a world map so he could figure out where the country was. In 1888, Lillias Stirling Horton, an American missionary doctor who became the personal physician to Empress Myeongseong, wrote in her book, *Fifteen Years Among the Topknots*, "People back home have never even heard of Corea."

It wasn't always that people weren't curious about the country. It was also simply there was also little if any literature available on it. Between 1894 and 1897, British traveler Isabella Bird Bishop trekked through Korea on four different occasions, describing her adventures in *Korea and Her Neighbours*. The day Bishop's book was published in England in 1898, a run of 2,000 copies was immediately sold out, and in America, five editions had to be printed to satiate public demand.

Heck, it wasn't until 1882 that Korea, for the first time in its history, officially opened its borders to foreigners. During the conservative, Confucian-based Joseon Kingdom's reign, beginning in 1392, the country kept itself cloistered and sequestered, zealously guarding against encroachment by foreign devils. When thirty-six survivors of the Dutch ship *Sparrow Hawk* – shipwrecked in 1653 off the south coast – sought to leave the country to return to the Netherlands, the kingdom refused their request. Thirteen years later, eight of *Sparrow Hawk*'s crew sneaked aboard a boat and escaped to Nagasaki and onward to the Netherlands. Crew member Hendrik Hamel described the tribulations in *Hamel's Journal and a Description of the Kingdom of Korea, 1653-1666.*

Only in the past few decades, has there really been a reason to visit the country for leisure and pleasure. From 1910 to 1945 it was a Japanese colony. Between 1948 to 1988 were a series of authoritarian, military-backed regimes. From June 1950 to July 1953, the county was ravaged by the Korean War. In recent years, young international backpackers have ventured to the peninsula, though it's not always an easy country to journey through. Language is but one issue, and amenities and accommodation haven't really been adopted to fit North American and European vacation lifestyles. While Southeast Asian neighbors such as the Philippines, Thailand, Indonesia and Vietnam offer modestly-priced beachfront motel rooms and cottages with a hammock and maybe a kayak, you won't find similar facilities in Korea. Koreans and Westerners have differing views of vacationing. The latter might prefer nature and aesthetics, a week or two at a pleasant country cottage. Koreans gravitate to short group package tours to popular tourist destinations.

***

On the afternoon of June 1, 1995, I departed Los Angeles International Airport, and 10,000 kilometers and twelve hours later mysteriously arrived in South Korea on the afternoon of June 1. The plane touched down at Gimpo International Airport, northwest of Seoul. Flying low, peering out the window, the day clear and sunny, I marveled at the city's rugged beauty of craggy, low granite mountain ridges in full bloom of green woods, contrasting with innumerable clusters of white, high-rise apartment buildings. I'd never seen so many blocks of apartments – seemingly a million of them. Splitting the city into north and south halves was the wide, brawny Han River. The juxtaposition of nature versus concrete, of two dominant and vivid colors – bold green and white – was visually stunning. It was my first time in the country. I immediately liked it.

My job in Seoul was to teach English language to young Korean students at a unique staple of Korean society called *hagwon*: private, after-school academies. There are 25,000 *hagwon* in Seoul. Nationally, three out of four Korean students ranging in age from pre-kindergarten through high school, study at them. Predominant subjects are English, science and math. There are also *hagwon* for taekwondo, piano and art. Many Korean students daily attend public school and *hagwon*, often on weekends too. Exhausted kids sometimes don't return home from academies until late at night.

I'd been employed at various jobs in Canada – many intermittent and temporary – before signing up for Korea. I'd spent most summers coaching tennis. There were also brief stints as a sports writer at the *Tahoe Daily Tribune* in Lake Tahoe, California, and at CBC-TV in Toronto. Construction and taxi-driving were jobs I'd worked at after high school. I had itchy feet, liked to move around, and didn't stay in one place for too long. Long, cold eastern Canadian winters of ice and snow weren't endearing, and I tended to avoid them. I bled the blue and white of my hometown Toronto Maple Leafs' ice hockey team, but even it couldn't tempt me to spend winters there.

In spring 1995, living in Long Beach, California, and in need of employment and funds, I spotted ads in the *Los Angeles Times* announcing lucky applicants could be teaching English in South Korea in a matter of weeks. Teaching experience wasn't needed. A university degree was. I'd somehow managed to get one of those, competing on the tennis teams at Anderson College in South Carolina and at Illinois State University. Something good must be happening in South Korea, I decided. I applied. My interview was with a vivacious Korean woman at an office on the second floor at a rather seedy mini strip mall on the coastal highway south of Los Angeles. "You'll love Korea," she gushed. "You can make a lot of money. You'll teach at an academy, but in your free time you can teach privately. Many Koreans want English lessons. If you want, you can be busy all day teaching."

I was sold. In Canada, I'd never been able to string together much in the way of savings, mainly because accumulating money wasn't a priority, but also because I was often between jobs. High taxes and rent and living expenses made saving difficult too. I was now thirty-seven and having only a few spare bucks in my pocket was wearing thin. Steady work and a regular paycheck seemed propitious. The Korean woman was so positive about my future that I signed the contract on the spot. Several weeks later, I was on my way to a country where national pastimes include singing karaoke, playing video games, mountain hiking and drinking an alcoholic firewater called *soju*. I had no attraction to any of these four activities, so I'd need to find other activities to keep me occupied.

Upon landing at Gimpo International Airport, I was met by my *hagwon* manager, Mr. Lee, who was so pleased to see me that he took my hand in his walking through the airport. The only other time I'd held a fellow's hand was when I was nine. I'd been arguing with my table-mate at breakfast prayers at a summer church ranch outside Toronto that my parents had forced my two sisters and me to attend. As punishment, the preacher ordered the other lad and me to hold hands for two hours walking through the camp's grounds. In the 1960s in Canada, boys didn't hold hands. The practice in Korea shows friendship. My academy was in Myeongil-dong, on the periphery of southeast Seoul, on the top four floors of a commercial building. A total of 1,000 elementary, middle and high school students studied at Wonil Academy. Of thirty teachers, I was the only foreigner.

I taught classes Monday to Friday between 2:00 and 11:00 p.m., to bright, boisterous, funny students in air-conditioned classrooms. At the end of each month the academy owner, Mr. So, presented me with a thick envelope bulging with 10,000 won bills totaling 1.5 million won, equivalent to almost $3,000 Canadian dollars. I'd never seen so much money at one time. With free accommodation and just three percent income tax, I was able to save and kicked myself for not having come to Korea ten years sooner.

I hadn't experienced a city like Seoul nor a country like South Korea before. My global travel hopping had included North and Central America, Europe and the Middle East. Lining Seoul's streets were four-and-five-floor commercial buildings plastered with neon signs. Bright green, orange, red and yellow neon lights flashed on buildings and lit up the night, advertising coffee shops, cafés, restaurants, pocket ball halls and PC-*bang*, the latter a large dark room with rows of computers where mostly male school students played military-themed video games. The neon lights were a visual smorgasbord. Across the city at night, numerous crosses blazed in red neon light atop small churches. As far as I could tell, Koreans were a godly people who loved *soju*.

Seoul's sidewalks teemed with crowds of young adult women decked in the latest fashion — often miniskirts and high heels. School children in smart uniforms strode to and from school and *hagwon*. Housewives were out shopping and socializing with friends. Citizens didn't seem to sleep much. Even well past midnight, they were out and about. Roads were crammed with city buses, cars and taxis, horns honking. Buses screeched to loud halts at bus stops, then roared back into traffic, engine noise a constant. A cloak of diesel exhaust floated low in evenings over Myeongil-dong's main street busy with buses. The haze was visible under the dull, yellow illumination of street lamps.

I wasn't used to so much energy, to this mass of humanity. Where I come from in Don Mills — a quiet, conservative, predominantly white middle-class suburb of Toronto — few people walk the streets. Almost everyone drives. In Seoul there are about ten million people — more than the population of many countries. About twenty-six million citizens — half the nation's total populace — reside in the Seoul capital area, including the port of Incheon and assorted satellite cities, replete with armies of high-rise apartment buildings.

I was overwhelmed by the dynamism, spirit and collective sense of unity. The country is magical and safe. One can walk through any city at any time of the night and not have to worry about being held up or attacked. The worst thing to happen might be encountering a happy, drunken group of men leaving a bar at night. Thankfully, federal law ensures owning a gun is a near impossibility. A good thing, because with Koreans' quick temperament combined with their love of potent *soju*, if purchasing a firearm was as simple as applying for a library card in America, the peninsula would resemble the 1800's American wild west, and not many South Korean males would remain.

In Canada, and the U.S., bylaws keep suburbs free from commercial enterprises such as shops, the closest ones often a mile or two from residential areas. (No wonder everyone drives.) No such rules exist in South Korea. Neighborhoods and small districts typically comprise two-or-three-story, condominium-like housing (or *jutaek*) and apartment buildings, and are independent and self-contained. Everything one needs, including convenience and hardware stores, take-out restaurants, laundry shops, *hagwon*, doctor's and dentist's offices, churches, saunas and spas, are in every district.

For reasons I couldn't explain, the homicide rate in Korea seemed a highly guarded secret. I wasn't able to find the statistic in the newspapers. Curious as to what it was, I asked my good friend, Heju, if she could find it. She visited a police station in her hometown, Daejeon. An officer told her, "We can't give out the number. You'll have to fill out a form and send it to a government agency to get it." Maybe to the "Shady and Secretive Department of Not-To-Be-Divulged Homicide Rates." It wasn't until later I learned about 300 homicides a year occur in the country. More than I expected, but with a population of fifty-two million, obviously a few bad apples exist.

Historically, Korea was a peace-loving country. Unlike a number of Western and European nations, who colonized other countries and pillaged natural resources, Korea never sent its armies to neighboring Japan or China, probably because Korea never really had an army to send. China rampaged through Korea a number of times in their long histories. Japan attacked in the sixteenth century, and also governed the country as a colony from 1910 to 1945. For the longest while, Korea was an international outcast, like a school loner who sat off to the side and kept to himself. Maybe it was a national collective lack of curiosity, perhaps a lackadaisical sense of adventure or fear of the unknown that kept Koreans at home, but if other nations had engendered a similar inward-looking ethos, North America and Australia might to this day remain unsettled. Koreans rarely ventured far from their own little corner of the world.

***

After reading Bryson's *In a Sunburned Country* and hungrily devouring his other hilarious books, it occurred to me it was unlikely he'd find his way to Korea to pen a bestseller. If he wasn't going to, then by golly, it left only me, by default, to try to scrape together a few pages to hopefully resemble a book. I planned to take a trip through this ancient land and write about it.

South Korea isn't very large — just 38,750 square miles — about 500 kilometers long and 250 kilometers wide. Thirty-seven of America's fifty states are bigger. Nevertheless, a pan-national tour wasn't as simple as I imagined. Seventy percent of the country is mountainous, and there are 17,268 kilometers of undulating, indented coastline, and over 3,000 islands off the west and south coasts.

Mountains are everywhere. Paralleling the east coast is the steep, 1,500-meter-tall granite Taebaek Mountain range. Branching west from the Taebaeks, sweeping north of Seoul, is the low Gwangju range. Splintering from the Taebaeks, moving south of Seoul, is the low, well-worn Charyeong range. The kings — the Sobaek Mountains — are a brawny, broad stalwart amalgamation of eminences averaging 900-plus meters underpinning the center of the peninsula. They reach from the Taebaeks in the north to the south coast. The short Noryeong Mountain range breaks off from the Sobaeks in the southwest and runs to the west coast. Other areas boast eminences too. No matter where one stands on the peninsula, some hill, mountain, ridge or peak is almost always in view.

It would be helpful to first learn a bit about the country prior to embarking on the trip. I began to frequent new and used English-language book stores in Seoul, and bought up any title I could find on Korea's history, geography, geology, culture, notable people and architecture. There were many books on the Korean War and on the country's economic miracle. I joined the Korean branch of the Royal Asiatic Society (RAS) in Seoul, and from its small library, purchased esoteric books on things Korean. There were also twice-monthly RAS lectures to attend on Korean topics.

I ordered home delivery of the three local English-language daily newspapers: *The Korea Times*, *The Korea Herald* and *Korea JoongAng Daily*. There was also the Asian edition of the *International Herald Tribune* (today the international edition of *The New York Times*). Nightly, I zealously read each, trying to discover unique sights to see and sites to visit. I don't mean to disparage Korea – God knows the last century alone has been difficult enough – but the papers seemed to serve up a steady diet of novel forms of social oddities – and sometimes just plain weird stuff.

Take, for example, the story about a thirteen-year-old boy named Kim Sung-ho, who for twelve hours was trapped in his bedroom under mountains of test papers, notebooks and textbooks. Sung-ho's mother had him enrolled in nine different academies, his bedroom stacked ceiling-high with papers and books. One evening, Sung-ho accidentally nudged a tower of books over and everything came crashing down. His mother, unable to open his bedroom door, called the police, who broke down the door with an axe. It took thirty minutes to get to the boy, and fifty garbage bags to carry out the junk.

There were plenty of newspaper stories about some corporate scion, or some chairman of some major domestic corporation, or a politician involved in embezzlement of company or public funds or tax evasion or stock price manipulation. There were photos of annual National Assembly brawls with opposing political parties squaring off in the chamber and engaging in half-nelsons and jabs.

To undertake my journey solo would be folly. My ability to speak and understand Hangeul, the Korean spoken language, was poor, comparable to the English spoken by an elderly Chinese shopkeeper at a market in New York's Chinatown. "Fruit good ... you buy mister!" To capture the unvarnished heart, soul and spirit of Korea and its people mandated I be accompanied by someone to translate so I could understand what was being spoken.

Hangeul was invented in 1443 by a team of educators assembled under Korea's cerebral King Sejong. The language, designed to be fundamental and scientific, has fourteen consonants and eleven vowels. Hangeul, largely bereft of romance, poetry and aesthetics, instead is dominated by short, staccato-like bursts with plenty of hard kk, jj, ss and hh sounds. The French language may be whimsical and fluttery, Italian infused with long, lovely rolling Os, but Hangeul has neither. I'd been in Korea long enough that I should have learned it. My bad. There was only one real choice for translator – my good friend of several years, Kim Heju. I'd met Heju – four years younger than I – traveling on the south coast in Yeosu in South Jeolla province. Six months earlier, her Canadian husband had sadly died of cancer. He had been a teacher. He and Heju had lived in Canada, Japan, China, Australia and South Korea.

Heju was born in Daejeon, about 160 kilometers south of Seoul. As a kid she was a tomboy and played outdoors with boys. She attended a Daejeon private school run by German nuns and learned to speak English well. She didn't enjoy school much and dropped out of university. She likes to read, particularly history, and enjoys yoga and travel. She believes in karma, fate, feng shui, Eastern medicine and aliens. Unlike the majority of her country's citizens, she has little ambition to accumulate great wealth and doesn't automatically ascribe to the theory that Korea is the center of the universe. She is impulsive, impractical and gregarious and marches to the beat of her own drum. She is also bossy and didactic. There is little I can do about that. Every Korean female, age three to 103, is headstrong and commanding. It's a Korean thing – hardwired in the genes.

Heju was teaching English to Korean kids at a *hagwon* in Daejeon. I asked if she'd like to join me on the three-to-four-month-long excursion.

"You won't have to pay a cent. I'll pay for accommodation, travel and food," I declared, and it wasn't every day that the son of a Scottish mother and Dutch father acted so benevolently.

Heju, non-committal, hemmed and hawed.

I sweetened the pot. "I'll give you a percentage of book royalties. If I sell a lot of books, you could become rich!" I announced, though there was no guarantee that I'd finish the trip, let alone a manuscript.

Despite Heju's normally buoyant outlook – like many of her fellow people – she was imbued with a healthy dose of skepticism. "How much could I make from royalties?" she asked doubtfully, in jest, I think. After months of indecision, she finally agreed to join me.

Choosing the right season to undertake the expedition was important. Winters are too cold. Summers, as I immediately discovered upon arrival in Seoul, are sweltering, the air saturated with heated water and like being in a sauna, barely survivable. Springtime in March was the best time to begin. March is a transitional month when winter's sometimes bitterly cold, dry air – often conceived in Siberia – sweeps south over the peninsula and finally loses steam, defeated by warm air flowing north from the South China Sea.

Heju arranged for a four-month leave of absence from her academy in Daejeon. My one-year contract teaching at a local elementary after-school program in Seoul ended in February. Two years after first reading Bryson's book, we began the trip, spending the first three weeks exploring Seoul in cool, blustery March.

Seoul was the country's vortex of power, Korea's capital since 1394. It houses palaces from the last royal Joseon Dynasty, which ruled from 1392 to 1910. We took guided tours of palaces and of important historical sites in and around the city. We had a one-day tour of Panmunjeom. We didn't particularly relish guided tours, but they are the most efficient way to learn about places of interest.

We took a tour of Seodaemun Prison. During Japan's colonization of Korea from 1910 to 1945 an estimated 40,000 Korean political prisoners and criminals were interned there by the Japanese. Some convicts were tortured and executed. We embarked on a guided excursion up Bugak Mountain — the dominant, 300-meter-tall ridge rising in central Seoul behind the presidential Blue House, or Cheongwadae (Pavilion of Blue Tiles). On Bugak's peak we were afforded marvelous panoramic views over Seoul's impossibly busy core and surrounding mountains. Seoul is both rugged and cosmopolitan.

One bleak, chilly afternoon, Heju and I wandered through old, isolated, desolate Yanghwajin Foreign Missionary Cemetery on the Han River's north shore in far west Seoul. The plot of land had been a gift in 1890 from King Gojong to the foreign community, comprising mostly North American and European Protestant missionaries.

We crouched low in front of each of nearly 600 headstones, many worn with faded engravings, and carefully read each inscription. Most graves were from the late 1800s and early 1900s, some grim reminders of how fickle life was then — children of missionary parents often the victims of typhoid, cholera and tuberculosis. Seoul's unhygienic conditions were notorious.

"I thought when I saw it that the Chinese town of Shanghai was the filthiest place human beings live on this earth, but Seoul is a grade lower," wrote Edward Bickerstet, bishop of the Church of England, upon his arrival in Seoul in 1887.

In the 1890s, Isabella Bird Bishop described Seoul's quarter of a million inhabitants residing in a labyrinth of alleys beside foul-smelling ditches, where solid and liquid waste from houses was emptied. "For a great city and a capital its meanness is indescribable," she penned.

The headstones marked a number of Western missionaries.

One grave was of Henry Gerhard Appenzeller, a Methodist from Pennsylvania, who arrived in Korea in 1885 and was only forty-four when he drowned in 1902, trying to rescue a Korean girl. In the cemetery's back corner was the plot of the Underwood clan – Korea's most renowned missionary family. Horrace Grant Underwood – of the Underwood Typewriter Company – was a Presbyterian missionary who arrived in Korea in 1885 and taught and preached and initiated projects to build schools and hospitals. Four or five generations of Underwoods followed Horrace living in Korea. Near the Underwood's grave site on a slight knoll was a headstone curiously listing the names of three family members – a mother and two young boys – who perished on August 12, 1985. What had caused their sad demise that day? I later learned that on that date, Japan Airlines Flight 123 crashed into a mountain west of Tokyo, killing 520 passengers. Had the trio been on the flight?

After three and a half hours in the cemetery, darkness upon us, I scribbled the last headstone inscription into my notebook. I couldn't feel the fingers of my right hand anymore – cramped from writing and cold.

***

After three weeks of daily bopping through Seoul, transported to our destinations by subway, bus and on foot, we were itching to get on the pony and begin our pan South Korea journey. Our pony was a 1994, red Hyundai Scoupe, purportedly designed as a quasi-sports car I'd recently purchased for $1,500 at a used car lot. The Scoupe's two salient features were bucket seats and ample leg room. I'd initially sought a compact car but soon realized such Korean models were designed for Little People, not six-feet-two, 240-pounders like me. I tried squeezing my ample carcass into a Little People's driver's seat at the car lot and very nearly didn't make it out alive. My knees were scrunched under the dashboard, my left elbow pinned against the door, my neck bent forward against the low roof, like being compressed in a broom closet.

The Scoupe's downside was its shock absorbers. They were kaput. And facing any mildly challenging hill, the motor quickly overheated, the engine temperature needle racing to "Extremely Dangerous" territory, the dashboard's red-lit letters screaming: "BAIL!" I only needed the car for a few months. Hopefully, it would last into summer.

I don't like driving in South Korea. I don't like cars much. Vehicles pollute, are noisy, fuel prices – at about $2 per liter – are expensive and people die in road crashes. The country is notoriously full of drivers in a hurry. When electric cars become the norm, maybe I'll buy one. Until then I'm content to get around by foot and bike and on longer hauls by bus and train. Amazingly, more than twenty million vehicles ply the nation's roads. Seven million autos are registered in Seoul alone. Ireland, just a bit smaller than South Korea, has only 2.6 million vehicles. The latter's domestic public transportation system of subways, short and long-distance buses and trains, is excellent. Cars aren't even essential, but Koreans are madly in love with their automobiles. For Heju and me to reach our many varied destinations – particularly off the beaten path – trains and buses weren't going to expediently get us there in limited time.

We loaded the Scoupe's trunk and back seat with cardboard boxes containing hundreds of Korea-related clipped newspaper articles, travel brochures, maps, newspapers and books, and stuffed sundries and clothes into bags. Heju's bags seemed to contain a high percentage of skin cream, ointments, lotions and potions. I had with me a list summarizing in chronological order the hundreds of sites we planned to stop at on the way. There wouldn't be time to take in everything, but we'd try.

Heju didn't drive — she stressed easily. I'd drive slowly, purposefully and assiduously, like a retired fellow navigating a Winnebago. We didn't want to miss out on local scenery and points of interest. Bill Bryson may have zipped 900 unfettered kilometers in a single day from Daly Waters to Alice Springs in Australia's Northern Territory — equivalent to driving the length of South Korea twice. If we attempted a similar marathon, not only would we complete the entire trip in two days, we'd bypass everything.

Our planned route was from Seoul west to the coast, south down the west flank, east along the south coast, north up the east shore and finally west along the border to Seoul. The peninsula isn't wide; we could easily sneak inland to visit places of interest.

When it came time to depart, our stuff was scattered haphazardly in the back seat and around Heju's ankles. We were traveling in a virtual market on wheels.

"We're finally ready to go!" I announced triumphantly.

Heju looked at the overstocked Scoupe, sighed, and replied skeptically, "It looks like we're homeless and living out of the car."

Her pessimism sometimes aggravated me, but it was too late to replace her. On a more positive note, we were finally ready to rock 'n roll. It was April 7.

CHAPTER 3

Ganghwado: A Bullied Island

Just seventy kilometers downstream from Seoul offshore of the Han River estuary, Ganghwa Island has been privy to some pretty remarkable history. In times past — had a foreign ship needed to reach Seoul upstream on the Han River — it would have had to sail past Ganghwado.

For the first eight centuries after Christ, the island was considered a simple prefecture before being upgraded to a fortress. "The first outpost to be attacked and the most important to be defended in case of invasion by sea," wrote Mark Napier Trollope, a British chaplain and bishop in Korea from 1911 to 1930.

When the Mongols invaded Korea in the thirteenth century, they attacked Ganghwado. To cross the fast-moving, dangerous, kilometer-wide Yeomha Channel separating the mainland from the island, they commandeered Korean vessels, then set Ganghwatown's buildings and fort on fire.

In 1636, when the Manchu-dominated Chinese Qing Dynasty

assaulted Korea with 120,000 soldiers, the Korean king and his entire court fled to Ganghwado. In the last millennium, the island served in times of trouble as a refuge for royal families, governments, dethroned monarchs and disgraced officials.

In October 1866, the French Far Eastern Squadron, seeking retribution for the execution of four French priests proselytizing Catholicism in Korea, sailed up the Yeomha Channel and bombed Ganghwado's coastal fortifications, then burned much of Ganghwatown to the ground. Five years later, the U.S. Asiatic Squadron anchored in the same channel and pounded the island's coastal forts with shells. The squadron's marines moved onto land and massacred 243 Korean soldiers, in what's known as the Sinmi Invasion. Ganghwado has seen its share of hurt and pain.

From Myeongil-dong in east Seoul, we drove west on Olympic Expressway 88, skirting the south bank of the Han River. In far west Seoul, we exited onto a winding country road that headed northwest through the wide, expansive Gimpo Plain to Yeomha Channel. An hour later we stopped at the channel, looking west across to Ganghwado's northeast shore rising slightly to a wooded knoll. The morning was gray, light rain falling in early spring chill. Muddy banks and drab gray woods lined both shores, spring's deciduous trees not yet in bloom, only coniferous pines green. Not a village, boat, car or person was in sight on either shoreline. Except for the channel's swirling gray-brown waters, nothing moved. Everything was quiet and peaceful, as if time stood still.

Most of the country's inhabited islands have ports to shelter fishing trawlers. Not here. The lack of human activity and amenities isn't surprising – North Korea is just 1.6 kilometers north of the island. South Korea prohibits boats and fishing in these waters. ROK troops on Ganghwado are in a constant state of readiness.

We drove across Ganghwa Bridge, ripples and eddies swirling

below in the channel's strong current. Twice daily, the Pacific Ocean thrusts vast quantities of water into the shallow Yellow Sea basin and sucks it out, resulting in the world's second-highest tides of up to nine meters on the west coast. The rapid tide fluctuations creates powerful currents sweeping along at seven and eight knots, making local waters hazardous. Tides enter the channel from the south and recede from the north.

Over the bridge is Gapgot — a former historic town, a four-lane stretch of road running past it. Several months earlier, Heju and I had attended a national tourism exhibition in Seoul, and at the Ganghwa Department of Culture and Tourism booth a youthful, friendly employee named Gu Yun-ja, who spoke excellent English, insisted we contact her when we visited.

We phoned Yun-ja, and she arranged for us to tour Ganghwa War Museum, near Gapgot, at 10 this morning. At the museum we met her and a middle-aged female museum guide who didn't speak English. The four of us moved slowly through the spacious, well-appointed and handsome interior.

In one large glassed-in exhibit, large G.I. Joe-type figures represented American and Korean soldiers who fought in the June 1871 Sinmi Invasion at Ganghwado's main citadel. I noted something amiss about the soldiers' positioning. I whispered to Heju, "What a bunch of BS," because I knew our stern, serious museum guide wouldn't take kindly to hearing Korean history being challenged.

The Americans were in blue uniforms and black leather boots but incorrectly in positions of submission, six supine and very dead, several more on the ground being impaled by Korean soldiers' swords. Koreans had on straw shoes and baggy white cotton and hemp pants and shirts — rather like judo attire — and were vanquishing the enemy, not a single Korean on the ground, injured, dying or dead. The actual battle was a massacre in favor of the Americans. Koreans were only armed with slow-loading matchlock muskets, swords and spears. The 650 American marines were equipped with lightweight carbine rifles. Just three Yanks died that day; 243 Koreans killed. I'd seen graphic photos of the carnage, U.S. soldiers standing over bedraggled Korean bodies lying in the dirt where they'd been shot.

"It was a useless slaughter, one from which no good results ensued, and of which we have not since been proud," wrote Horace N. Allen, a Protestant missionary and doctor who arrived in Seoul from Ohio in 1884, in his 1908 book, *Things Korean*.

Museum visitors with no rudimentary knowledge of Korean history might wrongly conclude it was the Americans who'd been walloped. As I would discover at museums across South Korea, patriotism sometimes obfuscates fact.

Farther along on the wall hung *sujagi*, a fifteen-feet-wide beige and yellow cloth flag, featuring two huge, black Korean Hangeul letters representing the name of a general killed in battle. The Americans captured the flag and hung it in Annapolis, Maryland. It was returned to South Korea in 2007.

As we strolled the museum, I took copious notes and asked numerous questions. Heju translated my queries into Korean, answered by the guide in Korean, transcribed by Heju back to English for me. Understandably, this slowed proceedings down. When our museum guide didn't know the answer to a question, Yun-ja voluntarily phoned her office in Ganghwatown to get answers. What normally would have been a ninety-minute tour took about twice as long. It wasn't until about one thirty that we finished.

We thanked our guide and Yun-ja, who'd made a half-dozen calls on our behalf. "Sorry we took so much of your time," we said.

Yun-ja replied enthusiastically, "I loved so many questions. I learned so much today!"

After grabbing bowls of *ramyun* at a food stall at the front of the museum parking lot, Heju and I drove the short distance west to Ganghwatown — one of two towns on the island. Ganghwatown is situated at a long bend on the island road where the pavement widens to six lanes, cars noisily motoring by. Like most towns across the peninsula, this one too wasn't what you'd call pedestrian-friendly.

"If I were mayor, I'd reduce the number of lanes from six to two, and the speed limit to thirty kilometers per hour," I griped. "It feels like we're on a motorway."

We parked and walked on the main street sidewalk past nondescript old shops appearing as if they'd been slapped together with tin and concrete. I'd wrongly envisioned Ganghwatown to be similar, say, to a historic and attractive 250-year-old Massachusetts colonial town.

Mark Trollope, the Anglican bishop in Korea who explored the island in 1902, described its four pavilion gates, bell-kiosk and structures as "empty and ruinous public buildings for which there is no further use, and present a sad picture of decay. Monuments, in a land where the most usual material for architecture is timber rather than brick or stone, have a way of not lasting." Trollope wondered why Koreans, who were excellent masons, hadn't used stonework.

My *Lonely Planet Korea* guidebook was rather uncomplimentary: "The tourist literature and some guide books to Korea go on at some length about Ganghwado's attractions, giving you the impression that the island is littered with fascinating relics and ruins. To a degree it is, but you have to be a real relic enthusiast to want to make the effort."

After some time strolling, in evening we returned to the car and drove a few hundred meters up the road to West Gate Inn, an ordinary, three-floor "love motel." When my parents visited me in Korea, I'd checked them into a love motel, the only available accommodation close to my flat in Myeongil-dong. "Why's our bed heart-shaped," my mother asked.

"Because love motels are for couples," I replied simply.

In West Gate Inn's small lobby, the middle-aged female clerk was seated in a tiny narrow cubicle, her face hidden behind a pulled-down shade. The visages of most love motel clerks are obscured behind window shades, so visual recognition can't be made between clerk and customer, ensuring anonymity. Imagine the scandal if a mayor's wife checked in for a get-together with the town's treasurer, and the motel clerk put names to faces!

"Will you be staying for two hours?" the clerk inquired, the same question love motel clerks always asked us.

"No, overnight," we replied. We needed the room for a good night's sleep, not a nap.

Our room had the usual well-stocked assortment of toothpaste, toothbrushes, hairdryer, hairbrush, comb, razor, shaving cream, aftershave, cologne, moisturizer, shampoo, soap and condoms. A small fridge offered complimentary juice. TV cable programming provided oodles of channels. The only drawback was there wasn't a bedside reading lamp. Love motels never do provide one; reading isn't their purpose.

***

Back in the car in late morning, a shining sun was a welcome reprieve from spring's gray and chill. The brightness improved the look of Ganghwatown somewhat — though not entirely it still appeared dusty and crumbly.

Heju wanted to return to the Ganghwa War Museum to view a Catholic shrine she'd noted there yesterday. She regularly attends Sunday mass. Her Catholic name is Catherine, adopted when she and her sister were students at Catholic St. Mary's Elementary School in Daejeon. Few Koreans could afford private school then, but Heju's father was a banker, a position near the top of the economic ladder. Of Heju's three sisters and brother, two went to private school. Heju recalled fondly, "We had servants, and they walked me to school and did my homework for me."

In the museum parking lot, we counted twenty-one school buses, with groups of noisy young students piling off. Spring is school field trip season. We walked behind the museum and up a slight knoll to the Gapgot Catholic Martyrs' Shrine, to a statue of Mary. Heju stood before it and bowed.

"Bow to Mary," she instructed me.

I wasn't religious. "I'm not Catholic," I sputtered.

"It doesn't matter, it shows respect — bow!" she ordered.

"I won't," I said, and I didn't.

The modest shrine honored Korean Catholics beheaded during religious persecutions between the 1790s and 1871. Christianity began in earnest in Korea in the 1880s when its borders opened for the first time. Missionaries mainly from the U.S., Canada and Europe arrived to introduce Christianity. (Buddhism had arrived in the fourth century.) In the seventeenth and eighteenth centuries, Catholic literature was sneaked into the country by Koreans traveling in China, encountering Franciscan monks. But the ultra-conservative Korean Joseon state viewed Christianity and organized religion as a direct threat to its rule. Public executions were its way to intimidate the population into rejecting the church.

There were four major religious purges. One of the first executions was in 1801, after a Korean Catholic sent a letter to Peking seeking Chinese soldiers to ensure freedom to practice Catholicism. In the mid-1800s, a small number of French Catholic priests arrived to proselytize. The year 1866 was particularly brutal, some 8,000 Catholics and eight of twelve French priests beheaded or strangled to death. Severed heads were displayed on poles in public, including at Gapgot on Ganghwado — then a ferry terminal for passengers traveling between Incheon and Seoul. Seoul's two main execution sites were on the Han River's north shore at Jeoldusan Martyrs' Shrine near Yanghwajin Foreign Cemetery, where Heju and I had visited a couple of weeks earlier. The other was eight kilometers upriver at Saenamteo.

On the shrine in front of us was a plaque on which was written that a Catholic father and son duo had gathered the remains of the executed and given them proper burials. The father did so in 1839, the son during the 1866 exterminations. The son — Soon-jib (Peter) Park — witnessed 150 executions. When he died in 1911, at eighty-two, he was buried in his hometown of Incheon. Later, his remains were transferred to Jeoldusan Martyrs' Shrine in Seoul, then to Ganghwado in 2011.

At the top of the knoll we looked east over Yeomha Channel. Immediately adjacent was the single-lane, lonely, long-abandoned Old Ganghwa Bridge built in 1969, the island's first road link to the mainland. When the nearby New Ganghwa Bridge was built downriver in 1997, the original Ganghwa Bridge was permanently closed to traffic. The channel was gray-brown. The only sound was birds chirping in trees.

A score of meters away on the edge of a patch of woods was a small wood cabin. A plaque on the house read a Catholic priest resided here. A skipping rope hung on the wall on the front porch. Apparently, men of the cloth exercised just like us laymen.

We returned to the museum parking lot where ten young Korean marines in green fatigues stood silently in marching formation behind their leader. We approached the marines' young leader, Song Samoon, his name, stitched on his uniform. From Samoon's implacable, stern expression, it appeared he didn't suffer fools gladly.

"Excuse me, can you tell us how many soldiers are stationed on

Ganghwado?" we asked Samoon.

He turned and stared icily. "About 20,000," he said.

"Can a North Korean submarine navigate the channel?" I continued.

"No, it's too shallow."

"Which areas of Ganghwado have soldiers?"

Samoon looked chagrined and muttered, "Ganghwado's entire north coast, and the west coast of Gimpo have barbed wire. There's no access for citizens there."

Sensing he was itching to march his troops, Heju tugged at my arm and whispered urgently, "Let's go!"

I'm not the sharpest tool in the tool shed, but even I wasn't so obtuse that I didn't get her point. We thanked the soldier, and he abruptly marched his squad across the lot, in search of, I supposed, North Korean spies.

We drove south on the island road, paralleling the west bank of the channel, and about halfway down-island stopped on the side of the road, our map indicating an old sentry post, or *dondae*, was here. Inland, across the road is a wide shallow pond sectioned by narrow earthen walking paths rising a foot or two above the water line. An elderly farmer was standing on a path in the pond. We trudged over to him and introduced ourselves.

He gave us a big smile, exposing front teeth generously lined with so much silver, if he extracted them and melted them down, he could take early retirement.

"I've been farming here for fifty years," he said.

We asked about the pond's water source, and he said that every spring he dammed the area, which was supplied with water from a nearby small river flowing from inland to the channel. He also said that prior to the Old Ganghwa Bridge, built in 1969, the only mode of transportation to and from the mainland then was by a large skiff rowed by an oarsman across the turbulent channel.

We crossed back over the road. Next to the Scoupe was a parked van, two men preparing fishing rods.

"Fishing in the channel?" I asked one of them.

"No, over there," he answered, pointing across the road.

"Oh, in the dammed pond," I said.

"No, it's the Han River."

It wasn't the Han; its mouth is northeast of Ganghwado. This inland pool was a glorified frog pond. "The farmer said the pond is a local stream," I said.

"No, no, no, no, no, it's the Hangang!" he declared.

In good conscience I couldn't possibly let such an egregious error slide. I relayed that the pond was water from the local river.

"You sure?" he asked.

"Yes."

"I didn't know that."

"Why did you think it was the Han?" I queried.

"I was just guessing," he said.

I present the quintessential Korean male, so confident in his abilities, so supremely sure and self-possessed, that the mere thought he could be wrong, ever, about anything, wouldn't enter his consciousness.

Heju and I walked up a low, wooded hill to the sentry post overlooking the channel. The *dondae* was large and circular, built of thousands of piled small rocks. Within its low walls was enough space for a hundred men. It had a sense of gravity.

We returned to the car and headed a few kilometers south to Gwangseong Garrison, where the 243 Korean soldiers had died in the 1871 battle. We popped our heads into the small tour office at the garrison entrance. It was 4:30 p.m., the office closing in thirty minutes. "Is it possible to get a short tour?" we asked a guide.

"It's busy this time of year," said a weary-looking guide, Lee Nam-sook, who hesitatingly agreed to accompany us. "We get up to 2,000 visitors a day." Ms. Lee led us up the path, to the impressive, dominating fort originally constructed in 1656 and refurbished in 1977. It stood high on a broad promontory jutting far into the channel. The grand front gate was massive; above its thick granite blocks rested a heavy, traditional wood and tiled arched roof, curving sharply up at the corners.

We continued walking along the dirt path high above the channel, the path lined with beautiful pine trees, their roots exposed from the erosive action of rain and wind. We soon came to a clearing called Sinmisunuichong, translating to "A Tomb for Those Who Died Righteously During the Year of the Sheep." Seven gravestones honored the Koreans killed in the Sinmi battle. A small stone monument honored two generals — brothers killed in battle. Although 243 men died in the massacre, the ashes of only fifty-three men remained. There were no names of dead soldiers, only referred to as "Nameless Heroes."

"Why didn't they list the names of the dead?" we asked Ms. Lee.

"Because many of the soldiers weren't professional military men," she said. "They were peasants or servants of the lower class, and many didn't have names. Some bodies were too mangled to be identified. And families didn't come to search for their kin because they probably lived too far away."

Ms. Lee returned to her office, and Heju and I continued down the path to the water to a low stone rampart, where three cannon were aimed at the channel. The cannon had likely been fired at the American navy ships in 1871.

We trundled onto the flat, tree-lined earthen spit protruding into the channel, the only ones here. It was deathly still, the only sound being a flock of squawking geese flying north low overhead in V formation. It was low tide. The channel's murky brown water was shallow and only half a kilometer wide, flowing swiftly in the middle. Moss-laden boulders were on the shore. The approaching dusk sky was gray.

I trained my binoculars across the water onto the mainland – a military zone and off limits to citizens. I spotted a small village devoid of inhabitants, and barbed wire running atop a chain-link fence partially hidden by woods. At regular intervals were tall floodlight posts. Camouflaged guard posts poked up through trees.

We returned to the car and headed in the darkness to Ganghwatown. We stopped on the main road in town at a plain but popular, brightly-lit restaurant offering inexpensive meals for thrifty diners like me. Heju and I took seats at a table in the busy, bustling place. At the next table sat two older gentlemen, one reminding me of the famous late U.S. television news host, Larry King, if Mr. King were Asian. His pal was about ten years his senior, wearing a wrinkled green sports coat, listening with rapt, earnest attention to his friend.

I couldn't understand the man's soliloquy. It seemed fascinating. I asked Heju if she could listen in. "Maybe I can use in the book what he's saying," I said.

"I don't want to," she replied, not wanting to get involved in strangers' matters.

"What they're saying could be very important!" I pressed.

Heju reluctantly acquiesced and quietly, unobtrusively listened. A few minutes later she relayed the conversation: "The younger man's saying, 'I'd like to live with a Japanese woman. I don't like Korean women, they're too tough, they try to control you all the time. Japanese women are softer.'"

"Is it true Korean women are tough?" I asked Heju, though I already knew the answer.

"Yes," she readily agreed, "most Korean women like to argue."

A short time later the Korean Broadcasting System's nine o'clock news appeared on the television screen on the wall, and I asked Heju if she could translate the lead stories. Intensely ingesting noodles from her bowl, without looking up, she replied, "I can't ... I'm eating."

"Come on!" I pestered.

But she wouldn't budge, and I was relegated to watching the screen and creating my own plot lines for the news videos. When Heju was distracted, I surreptitiously added a sprinkle of arsenic into her noodles.

After dinner, the phone rang on the cashier's desk, and the restaurant owner, a woman about fifty, picked it up, listened for a moment, then shouted angrily into the mouthpiece: "You brought me old seaweed. It falls apart when I roll it. Bring me good seaweed tomorrow!" She slammed down the receiver and threw her plastic gloves onto the table. The restaurant deliveryman was next in her sights, and she yelled at him: "What happened to the lid for the rice bowl?" Wisely wanting no part of the battle, he silently slipped on his motorcycle helmet and hastily exited through the front door.

In Dr. Allen's book, *Things Korean*, he wrote that when Korean women were "pressed too far, they will turn and the fury into which they then work themselves is something awful to contemplate." More than a century later, the same still seems true.

※※※

In the grayness of a late-morning mist, Heju and I returned to Gwangseong Garrison. Its parking lot was jammed with almost forty school buses, hundreds of elementary school students disgorging in class-friendly, color-coded tracksuits, carrying lunch boxes, being shepherded by teachers.

After a brief look into the fort itself, we drove south on the island road, to Ganghwado's southeast tip to Choji Fort, where U.S. marines came ashore in 1871. The parking lot was packed with tour buses and school kids. In the large square were gift shops selling tacky back-scratchers, toy bows and arrows. Masses of chattering elementary school kids were loitering.

We approached Korea's future leaders for informal interviews, and asked a group of tykes: "What have you seen on Ganghwado so far?"

"I don't remember," one replied.

We tried speaking to two other students, but they defiantly refused to grant us an interview and huffed off.

"Did you see Gwangseongbo Fort?" we ventured to another bunch of kids. One lad thought about it a moment and complained wearily, "I got tired walking from the bus to the fort."

We strolled over to the hard-clay shoreline strewn with rocks. Just down-river, imposing Choji Bridge crossed to the mainland. Next to us on the shore a smattering of visitors were looking out to the channel. Then a group of five elderly female friends wandered up to the water's edge beside us.

"Hello," I said, "where are you from?"

"Seoul," one replied.

"Have you had a chance to visit Gwangseong Garrison yet?"

There were puzzled looks all round. One of the ladies queried, "Gwangseong what?"

"Gwangseongbo ... the fort," Heju explained.

The woman shook her head. "We didn't go to that university!" she irritably stated. Her friend chimed in, "I don't live in Gwangseong ... I live in Seoul."

We tried a new tack, asking if they knew about this fort. We explained that U.S. marines came ashore here in 1871.

The ladies were unimpressed. "We don't know about that. How would we know, we weren't alive then. Maybe eighty-year-old people would know what happened then!"

We bid goodbye to the historically-challenged group and walked up a rounded slight hill, atop it the rudimentary circular stone fort, crowds of noisy, hyper-active school kids buzzing about, teachers exhorting, "*Pali! Pali!*" (Hurry! Hurry!) It felt like a carnival so we quickly retreated to the car, then drove inland and southwest to 470-meter-high Mani Mountain, the tallest peak of the island's five low mountain ranges. Atop Manisan was a stone shrine said to be 5,000 years old, with special significance for Koreans. Five millennia ago, the first Korean state, Gojoseon — comprising today's South Korea and a vast area of North Korea and beyond — was formed under the leadership of Dangun, a mythical god credited with forming the Korean race. Or so legend has it.

We drove through a swath of agricultural plains, past a few concrete farm shacks with galvanized tin roofs, past a handful of rusting, low old apartment buildings, by a smattering of small industrial units. Alongside a narrow, shallow river dam were several men fishing. It was late afternoon when we parked at the base of Manisan — plump, broad and swollen with green-gray woods. A wide path moved in front of a souvenir shop and restaurants and on up the mountain. We began trekking the path, no one going up or coming down. The woods were quiet and serene, the air fresh, a creek flowing alongside. Typical of most woods in Korea, tree trunks and limbs are of slight to modest proportion. Most forests on the peninsula today are new growth planted in the 1970s, the land then largely bereft of trees.

After twenty minutes we approached a small clearing, the trail turning narrower and slightly steeper, though still not a difficult ascent. Chirping birds, gently rustling tree branches, and the distant barking of a dog were heard. A trailside sign boasted that Manisan is among the top-ten energizing sites on the peninsula, a reference to feng shui and geomancy, the Asian philosophy espousing Earth as a positive energy life force.

"I feel great from the mountain's energy. That's why I'm not tired!" Heju, a fervent believer in feng shui, enthused. She regularly laments though about various aches and pains, perceived blood clots, stiff muscles, palpitations and headaches. No western doctor can find anything wrong with her, but Korean eastern medicine practitioners prescribe herbs and potions that she steadfastly believes alleviate her symptoms.

"I feel like shit and my thigh muscles ache," I moaned sullenly. Manisan was obviously capricious about to whom it dispensed fortuitous feng shui. My idea of fun isn't lugging 240 pounds of flesh and bone uphill.

"Hurry up. We'd better be off the mountain by dark," Heju urged impatiently. "I can't see the path at night."

About three-quarters up to the summit was a small clearing affording a slim view north. We gazed over the alluvial plains far below, divided into thousands of small, orderly rectangular agricultural plots and bordered by tall wooded hills. Ganghwado had once comprised four separate islands, but over the eons, millions of tons of silt and mud were deposited to the coast via the Han and Imjin Rivers. The spaces between the four islands were filled in, forming singular Ganghwa Island, thirty kilometers long and fifteen kilometers wide. The narrow plains scattered between the five low mountain ranges contain rich soil.

The hundreds of rectangular plots and hills below expose the incongruence of trying to wander across the Korean peninsula. Draw a line between any two points almost anywhere on a map, and I'd argue it is near impossible to walk a straight line for long between them. You'd run into agricultural plots, roads, buildings, villages, steep, insurmountable abrupt knolls, humps, hills, mountains and peaks, sometimes all of the above. In his book, *Notes From a Small Island*, Bryson describes rambling comfortably mile after mile on earthen paths across rolling meadows and hills in the English countryside, minor obstacles being an occasional low stone fence. Good luck attempting a similar cross-country amble in Korea. Virtually no meadows remain — all long ago transformed to rice paddies and agricultural plots. There are many magnificent areas to hike though mostly the vertical and not horizontal sort.

We reached Manisan's summit. Surprisingly, there was a helicopter pad. A cold, stiff southerly wind was blowing in our faces and bending tree boughs. A deep purple dusk sky was rimmed by the setting sun's silvery outline. The arresting, haunting view was south over an expansive vista extending thirty kilometers to a shallow leaden sea and great wide mudflats interspersed with gray hazy islands. About 1,800 square kilometers of mud and tidal flats are exposed at low tide on the west coast.

I peered through my binoculars, spotting a Korean Air passenger jet on its final approach to Incheon International Airport on Yeongjong Island on Incheon's coast fifteen kilometers south. The plane seemingly hung motionless in the sky as if suspended in mid-air.

My thermometer read nine degrees Celsius, but a biting wind and the start of slanted shards of rain made it feel much colder. Heju was morose, her usual exuberance replaced by silence. She removed a thin wool shawl from her backpack and wrapped it round her head.

"You look like an Afghan nomad," I kidded.

She replied despondently, "I'm going down. I can't see at night," and she started down the trail.

"Hey, wait for me. We'll go together!" I called, but she was already disappearing behind a large boulder on the path.

I walked along the ridge, to the reported 5,000-year old shrine, Chamseongdan, roughly translating to "An Altar to Worship the

Stars." The size of a small house it was larger and more impressive than I expected, replete with thousands of small rocks carefully piled to form a circular wall and roof. It has a graceful symmetry. A wire fence encloses it. Twice yearly, on January 1 and in the fall, officials open the gate and permit visitors to enter. There is debate about whether the shrine was constructed 5,000 years ago — as some historians contend — or more recently.

As I began to make my way down the path, my phone rang, and I dug through my waist pack — stuffed with a wallet, notebook, mini tape recorder, camera, compass and the kitchen sink — to retrieve it.

Heju was on the line. "Are you coming?" she asked impatiently.

"No, I'm going up."

"Be careful — the rocks on the path are slippery."

"I know."

"I don't care about you. I just don't want my camera to get damaged," she deadpanned.

"Don't worry, I tied it to my ankle. It's dragging along."

"Hurry up," she demanded, brushing aside my attempts at humor. "I'm waiting."

Yes, milady. I'm a mere plebeian at your beck and call, my life's mission to nobly serve you. I trekked as fast as I could without slipping, and about a third of the way down, caught up with Her Highness, sitting on a stone step on the path in dark gray light. We made it to the car in about forty-five minutes, darkness enveloping us, and drove to Ganghwatown and the motel.

Relaxing in the room and discussing tomorrow's itinerary, Heju suddenly let it be known that the journey — all three days on the road thus far — wasn't all roses. "It's work, boot camp, it's not travel!" she contested hotly.

I was vexed. "Are you kidding?" I replied. Real work constituted physical activity, I said, like a construction worker lugging sheets of plywood on a worksite, or a factory worker stacking heavy boxes all day onto a skiff on a loading dock. Sitting in a car being ferried about and translating didn't seem like hard labor to me.

"It IS work!" she retorted, then added defiantly, "And we're spending too much time on Ganghwado. At this rate, we'll never finish the trip on time!" She had a point.

In the following weeks, Heju occasionally reminded me the endeavor wasn't something she was entirely relishing. She suggested I was better suited to a profession such as commanding a Roman slave ship. Now, that was real work!

CHAPTER 4

More Ganghwa Island

We began our fourth day on Ganghwado treating Yun-ja, the exceptionally kind Ganghwa tourism employee, to lunch at a restaurant in town. Yun-ja was phoning us daily, inquiring if there was anything she could assist us with.

Seated at the restaurant table, she remarked admiringly, "You've stayed on Ganghwado for three days. Most Koreans visit one day, then leave."

"Because there's so much to see!" I replied, the honest truth.

After lunch, Heju and I drove along main street, and stopped in front of the utilitarian Incheon Ganghwa Police Station. I wanted to ask the police about a newspaper article I'd read some time ago, noting the tragic drowning of four young students on Ganghwado's mudflats.

Behind the station desk were two officers, Jang Bu-gun and Choi Kyung-ju, who I mentioned the drownings to.

"Yes, I remember it," said officer Choi. "A group was on a church outing collecting shellfish on Dongmak Beach. The tide rushes in quickly there. It's dangerous, so no one's allowed to swim. When the tide came in, the girls panicked and got stuck in the mud. After the tide went out, people found their bodies. Locals don't go out to where the girls went; they use boards instead to catch shellfish on the mudflats."

I'd seen a TV program about Korean coastal villagers who collected shellfish in deep soft mudflats, leaning their weight on wide wood planks, so as not to sink. Later on the trip, near the southwest coastal city of Gunsan in North Jeolla province, Heju and I were out on the tidal flats, and I sank up to my shins in the goo. The mud acted like a powerful suction cup, tightly gripping my feet. The more I shimmied to try to extricate myself, the deeper I sank. Finally, I had to slip out of my shoes to escape, then reach deep into the mud to pull out my stuck shoes.

"How do you get out of the mud if you're stuck?" I asked the officers.

"If you panic, your legs sink deeper," one replied. "If you stand, it's easy to sink. So lie down, and when the tide comes in, let the water float you out."

Easier said than done, I thought.

The following day on Ganghwado's west shore at the tiny village of Oedo, we chatted with a local police officer named Kang Chang-seob, who gave a different account of the drownings. "Three boys and a girl," Kang said. "They were out on the mudflats. The tide was coming in and the water was shallow. When they were walking back to shore, they accidentally stepped off the mud into a deep rift and drowned." The officer's version seemed more plausible than getting stuck in mud and the tide sweeping over them.

After half an hour at the Ganghwa Police Station, through the front door entered an officer, accompanied by a slight man and a much larger fellow, the two with grim countenances. The smaller man was a taxi driver, the other his passenger the previous night. The passenger had been drunk and they had a punch-up.

"They're here to work it out," the officer said. The pair didn't seem overly conciliatory. "When Koreans get drunk, they become very emotional, and it's easy to get in a fight." Drunken fights, minor thefts and traffic accidents are the most common issues police deal with on Ganghwado, he said.

Before fists started flying we took our leave and drove along a quiet back street with old dwellings on it to the Goryeo Palace site. Goryeo was the royal dynasty from AD 918 to 1392. Goryeo Palace was constructed in 1232 as a refuge for the royal court during the 1231-1259 Mongol siege. The Mongols destroyed the palace in 1259. During the 1636 Manchu invasion, royalty moved to Ganghwado and several new buildings were erected to house them. After the royal family departed Ganghwado, the buildings were later converted for government use.

A library was erected on the site in 1782 to hold a surfeit of royal books permanently stored at the royal library at Changdeok Palace in Seoul. About 4,000 books, referred to as *Uigwe* (Royal Protocols), recorded daily occurrences of kings' lives during Joseon, the pages containing beautiful hand-drawn illustrations of events such as weddings and funerals, court performances and palace construction. In 1782, about 300 of the 4,000 Royal Protocol volumes were transferred to the Ganghwa Library, or Oegyujanggak (Outside Buildings for Writings by Important People).

When the French attacked Ganghwado in 1866, they set fire to the library and town walls and hauled away cannon, 8,000 muskets, boxes of silver and gold, jade, paintings and the Royal Protocols. Fast forward to 1973 when a Korean citizen in Paris discovered the 297 pilfered *Uigwe* volumes in storage at the Bibleothèque Nationale de

France. In the following decades, Korea pushed France for the books' return. In 2011, Presidents Nicolas Sarkozy and Lee Myung-bak signed an agreement and the treasures were returned to Korea.

The Goryeo Palace site was reconstructed from scratch in 1976. Its architecture mimics the original palace, a substantial stone wall surrounding the grounds and a traditional front gate with two mammoth, thick vertical wood pillars supporting a heavy, arched tiled roof. We entered through the gate to a modest field of grass which I was delighted to walk on. Grass is a rare find on the peninsula.

Off to the side in the front corner of the grounds are several single-story wood government buildings, including the royal library, rebuilt from scratch in 2003 — its wood so dry, its paint so faded, the structure could have passed for centuries old. The main building is L-shaped, its foundation granite stone, its black shale-tiled arched roof extending far over the front wall. A series of faded green shutter-like doors stretch along the front wall. Vertical wood beams support the roof with a porch underneath. The courtyard comprises dry earth. After exiting, we drove a few hundred meters along and came to what looked like a vacant lot with a ruinous low rock foundation. Officials believe this to be part of the original Goryeo Palace site erected in 1232.

In our Ganghwado brochure was a photo of nearby Ganghwa Anglican Church constructed in 1900 under the guidance of Charles John Corfe, the Church of England's first bishop in Korea. Corfe was posted in the country from 1889 to 1905. When Anglican missionaries first arrived in Korea in the late 1800s, to integrate themselves into society, they erected several churches in traditional Korean architectural style. Ganghwa Anglican Church was the first such type.

Bishop Corfe wasn't enamored with his time here. Educated at Oxford, he served twenty years as a Royal Navy chaplain prior to arriving in the country at age forty-six. He thought Korea and the people backward and he missed England. Recounting his years in the new land he wrote the book, *The Anglican Church in Corea.*

The church is atop a slight hill near the Goryeo Palace site. We pulled the car in front of the grounds. Refurbished in 1984, the building is a mix of western and Korean architecture with Buddhist elements. Rust-colored brick comprises the lower exterior walls, with vertical, deep-red inlaid wood beams. Above is a row of wood-shuttered windows painted turquoise. The roof is traditional Korean, massive and double-tiered with gray-tile shingles. Wood rafters are light green-blue.

At one end of the building is a row of four faded turquoise wood doors. We popped our heads in to find several women cleaning. "Are you open?" we called.

"No, only on Sundays," one answered.

Today was Friday. "Is it okay if we come in and look around?" we asked.

"Yes, come in."

We took off our shoes and entered a godly place. We were instantly transported back in time, to what seemed like Victorian England, enveloped by sumptuous dark redwood. Nine floor-to-ceiling vertical beams, each a foot thick, ran lengthwise on each side supporting the weight of the second-floor wood walkway and roof. Above the walkway stretched a row of windows. Nine large horizontal beams supported the high roof. Lovely chandeliers, each with six small, delicate white ceramic lamp shades, hung from the ceiling. The walls were white clay framed with wood. The pews were ten rows of redwood chairs. Everything was bathed in a soft golden glow. Artisans who'd refurbished the church were masters. In the back corner were two portable gas heaters to warm the interior in winter. We sat in a pew to soak up the ambiance.

"It's beautiful. I love it here. I could stay all day," said Heju, in a state of ecclesiastical bliss.

Even I was imbued by a temporary wave of serenity.

We asked a woman if the wood floors were polished.

"Twice a year," she said. "But we don't wax them any more. Our parishioners are old and slip if we do."

I envisioned Sunday morning worship with elderly churchgoers taking long runs in stocking feet over ice-like floor beams, whooping and hollering in delight and tumbling like bowling pins.

We'd been sitting for about half an hour when two foreign men entered and sat in front of us. We exchanged salutations. One man had a German accent. He said he was employed as a choir composition teacher at a university in Seoul. His brief answers to my questions indicated he wanted quiet, and he sat trance-like, absorbing the ethereal ambiance. Later, I discovered he'd been the music director at the Spandau School of Church Music in Berlin.

After an hour, having received ample blessings of good fortune from above, I suggested to Heju it was time to move on. She was obviously contemplating entering the nunhood and permanently residing in the church.

***

We puttered west out of Ganghwatown in the northern quadrant on the island's circular road. We made consecutive brief stops at an insect museum, a hillside crematorium and at a millennium-old dolmen. The latter is a tomb comprising two large vertical megalithic stones supporting a flat horizontal capstone. In the crematorium the manager showed us into a memorial room. Lining each wall, floor-to-ceiling, were hundreds of little post office-type boxes with windows. In almost every window was a photo of the deceased and often a pack of cigarettes. Many photos were of young adult men, most who had died in car accidents, the manager explained. Back on the pavement, a small road sign noted just ahead was a "five-story pagoda."

"Let's see it. It must be huge!" I said. According to my calculations, one story equalled about three meters, so a five-story pagoda would be a whopping fifteen meters tall. We turned the car onto the dirt side road and soon dead-ended at woods. We began strolling on a path through the woods looking for the giant pagoda, but we couldn't find it.

"Where is it?" Heju wondered.

"It's got to be here somewhere," I added, miffed.

About to head back to the car, it suddenly dawned on me that a puny little pile of five small rocks stacked atop each other the height of a child on the path was the five-story pagoda. "You've got to be kidding," I declared. "That's the five-story pagoda?" Heju reminded me that for a Korean pagoda, "one story" equals one small rock.

Back on the blacktop, evening approaching, we swung south, paralleling the island's west coast. A solid range of low, wooded hills blocked our view to the sea. A short way along, in the area of Mangwol, we turned off the main road onto a muddy, rutted side road leading to the sea. Under a dark-gray dusk sky, I switched on the headlights illuminating a vast, bleak expanse of mud and paddies. We reached the desolate coast and emerged from the car, met by a cold, salty wind blowing in off the water. About a mile out a twinkle of yellow lights shimmered in the darkness, their genesis a small village on Seongmo Island. It was low tide, and before us was a vast, exposed deep morass of brown gooey mud with long, wide moats and trenches carved deep in the sludge. The massive ditches are cavernous enough to swallow a small house. I'd never seen such treacherous sinkholes.

"No wonder people drown here!" I said.

Off to the side was Mangwol Dondae, a low crumbling sentry post of small rocks. How exhilarating to imagine more than three centuries earlier, soldiers gazed out on the lookout for foreign vessels.

Back in the Scoupe, we moved south on the island road and soon rolled into the small coastal village of Oepo, at about the island's halfway point. Oepo's "downtown" was a short, narrow section of road minus a sidewalk, lined by brightly-lit fish restaurants. Long aquariums in front were full of fish for sale. Being Friday evening, the restaurants were bereft of customers, but tomorrow they'd be full of crowds arriving by the carload from Seoul.

We entered each of five modern, closely-grouped motels in Oepo to check room prices. All five were identically priced and above market cost. "The Oepo Motel Cartel," I joked to Heju. A stone's throw prior to entering town we'd passed the castle-like, five-floor Ganghwa Haesoo Sauna. We backtracked and pulled into the hotel's parking lot. The place was quiet and dark.

"It's closed," Heju said.

"Let's try it anyway," I replied. We walked into the substantial, utilitarian, dimly-lit lobby, the only people here.

"Hello? Anyone here?" Heju called.

No reply. She tried again.

A few moments later, a woman appeared from behind a door at the front desk. Friendly and engaging, she said rooms were just 25,000 won, a price that pleased me.

With no elevator we trudged up stairs carrying our bags to our fifth-floor room. At each stairwell landing we peered down long, shadowy, high-ceiling corridors with red, musty carpets. The halls reminded me of the ones in the haunted Overlook Hotel in Stephen King's classic horror movie, *The Shining*. Had Jack Nicholson, as the crazed Jack Torrance, stuck his face — hideous, contorted and bug-eyed — out a door and chortled evilly, "Heeerrrrreeee's Johnnnnyyyyyy!" it wouldn't have surprised me.

Our room was worth 25,000 won. Well, maybe 15,000 won. It wasn't dirty, there weren't stains on the walls, but it just felt very worn, as if 10,000 customers had stayed in it before us. It evoked a rooming house feel like in a seedy Los Angeles neighborhood, where a down-on-his-luck detective portrayed in a gritty 1950's film noir would reside.

The only illumination was a single, low watt light bulb hanging from the ceiling, the glass lampshade full of a significant number of long-deceased flies. The large window's thick red curtains were bulky and dowdy. The bed was short and narrow, its pliable mattress the world's saggiest. The ancient television set wasn't hooked up to cable. The phone on the bedside table didn't work.

"What do you expect for 25,000 won," Heju complained, cynically.

Clean sheets and no live bugs scampering about — on those two fronts the room scored ten out of ten.

The room had character and most importantly wasn't a Holiday Inn. Into the TV we inserted a VHS movie tape that we'd borrowed from a stack of tapes in the downstairs lobby and contentedly watched *Basketball Diaries*. If Leonardo DiCaprio hadn't won a best actor award for his stellar performance as a drug addict, he certainly should have.

***

At ten in the morning, Heju was about to dash out of the room to luxuriate in the hotel's ground floor hot tub. She adored saunas. I asked if she could translate a brochure I'd picked up the previous night in the lobby listing the spa's water contents of lithium, iron, zinc, copper, sulfur, chlorine, oxidized silicon, magnesium, calcium, sodium and strontium piped up from 300 meters underground. Lithium is helpful for sufferers of manic depression and psychosis, and strontium assists in healing bone fractures in the elderly, the brochure noted. It seems that many of these minerals in the water can also be found in a bottle of multi-vitamin pills.

After Heju headed downstairs, I was off to the basement sauna's one cold-water and two hot-water tubs. Thermometers in the tubs indicated the less hot one was forty-one degrees Celsius, the hotter tub a scalding forty-five degrees. I tried dipping my toes into the hotter tub and almost had to be revived by medical personnel. Two men submerged up to their necks, basked contentedly like sea lions. I'd seen Korean men relaxing in hot tubs in similar temperatures and I'm convinced that Koreans have developed super-resistant skin cells over the millennia, allowing them to withstand temperatures that would boil most humans alive. I embarrassingly slunk into the forty-one-degree tub, relegated for daisies and buttercups. Soaking in it were two skinny, university-age pals, giggling and splashing each other, so I allotted them a wide berth. Slowly and methodically, inch by inch, (I scald easily) I lowered my body into the water until partially submerged. After ten minutes — my skin red, stewed and shriveled — I dried off.

Heju and I checked out of Overlook Hotel and puttered in the car the two minutes to Oepo's small harbor, then walked along its short concrete wharf. The sky was blue, a fresh warm breeze blowing in off the sea, the first warm day of spring. It felt marvelous to absorb the heat after a cold winter.

It was low tide. Immediately offshore was an expansive mud pudding, the shallow yellowish-brown sea alive and bubbling with currents and tidal movement. About a mile out, Seongmo Island's steep forested mountain slope ran parallel to Ganghwado. A narrow ferry, docked at Oepo's cement pier, was loading a few cars and passengers to be shuttled to Seongmodo. On this Saturday early afternoon, Oepo was springing to life with day trippers arriving en masse from Seoul.

We returned to the car, moved onto the island road jammed with Seoul city-slickers, and crawled south in gridlock, taking more than an hour to reach Jeondeung Buddhist Temple at Jeongjok Mountain in the island's south. Originally constructed in AD 381, Jeondeung Temple is the oldest of more than 3,000 Buddhist temples in South Korea. Between the fourth and thirteenth centuries, Buddhism flourished in the country, but with the adaptation of Confucianism in 1392 by the conservative Joseon Dynasty, the government suppressed and relegated Buddhism to second-class status and even destroyed temples.

Jeongjok Mountain is low, broad and well treed. A wide path — busy with weekend visitors — leads from the parking lot up a gradual incline to the temple. Branches of centuries-old massive pine, cherry and ginkgo trees stretch high over the path creating a great green canopy. We came to a small wood café on the side of the path. In front were three well-lubricated gentlemen friends wearing identical gray windbreakers, "Incheon Airport" stitched on the jackets. The trio boisterously greeted us.

Noting the Incheon Airport crests, Heju asked, "Do you work at the airport?"

"Yes, but we're retired," replied one. Then he looked at me and asked, "Do you work at the airport?"

A strange question, I thought. I replied no. The fellow paused, and with barely contained glee, announced, "Why ... were you fired?" the joke setting the soused threesome into convulsions of laughter. I was glad to have contributed to their merriment. We bade adieu to the comedians and proceeded on.

Jeondeung Temple's entrance is through stately, formal South Gate, an arched tunnel about six meters high, carved from finely cut granite. On the gate's top is a massive, heavy arched roof of black shale tiles set in vertical rows. On each side of the gate reaches out tall thick walls of piled rocks. At one time these walls protected the former fortress. South Gate and parts of the wall were rebuilt in 1976.

We strode along the front wall. On November 9, 1866, 160 French troops, under the command of Pierre-Gustave Roze — leader of the French Far Eastern Squadron — were ambushed by Korean soldiers here. The French had based in Ganghwatown after landing on the island in October. To scout a report of enemy buildup, Roze sent his troops down island. Behind the wall waited hundreds of soldiers. When the French drew parallel, archers rained down a cavalcade of arrows and spears onto the unsuspecting foe. A Ganghwado guidebook put the number of French dead at about sixty. Korean history books more commonly state that three Frenchmen were killed and dozens injured. Three days later, Roze and his troops departed Ganghwado. Koreans consider Roze's departure a surrender, proud of sending the French packing.

We strolled to the end of the front wall, and followed it around the corner and up through woods to East Gate, where we entered the temple grounds brimming with families and kids. The compound is compact with a handful of finely-built small wood buildings with faded rusty red and green colors and great graceful roofs.

The temple was constructed in AD 381 under the auspices of a monk named Ado, who had left China for Korea to spread Buddhism. The Korean queen had presented a gift of a jade lamp to the temple, and henceforth it became known as Jeondeungsa (Temple of the Bequeathed Lamp).

The main hall was rebuilt after a fire in 1621. While not large, its exotic-looking roof flares up to a graceful arch at each corner. The roof's underside was skillfully constructed, with round intricately carved beams extending out. At each corner are small, wood gargoyle-like figures, shoulders and hands seemingly supporting the roof.

We drifted into a nearby small wood hall, its arresting low ceiling carved in ornate detail depicting serpents and birds. A slow but steady stream of women was entering and leaving, and kneeling and bowing low on the hall floor offering prayers to the Buddha statue in front.

Outside the hall, we asked one woman what she'd prayed for.

"For my family and kids," she replied.

After she wandered off, Heju said, "They always say that they only pray for their families."

"They don't pray for world peace, to end poverty, for poor kids in Africa?" I asked.

"No, just always for their families."

Now late afternoon we returned to the road to finally depart Ganghwado after five days. Heju was elated. Numerous visitors who'd spent the day on the island were now departing and returning to Seoul causing serious gridlock, and it took more than ninety minutes to reach the bottleneck at Choji Bridge and cross to the mainland. Under wet skies we slowly paralleled the mainland's coast south on a series of haphazard, isolated, poorly marked country roads, passing the odd factory. At nine o'clock, we finally entered the three-million-inhabitant, blue-collar city of Incheon under a torrent of rain. We'd covered a mere thirty kilometers in four hours.

We slowly navigated through a maze of traffic on a major Incheon city road, lashing rain making it difficult to see clearly out the front window, the Scoupe's windshield wipers laboriously working overtime. Neon lights, blazing brightly on store fronts, morphed into a swirling, liquid kaleidoscope of arresting rainbow colors. Due to the downpour we opted to stay the night at a nearby motel. Tomorrow morning we would take a guided tour in Suwon — forty kilometers southeast — of a renowned walled fort and summer palace.

CHAPTER 5

Suwon: A Palace, Fort and Railroads

Having just arrived in Suwon from Incheon, Heju and I were standing in front of Hwaseong Haenggung (Hwaseong the district name; Haenggung translating to "Visiting Palace"). Visiting palaces were constructed within and outside of Seoul for royalty as a home away from home. Seoul could be highly malodorous during summer, and having an additional palace just forty kilometers south in Suwon allowed kings a reprieve from the city. Shortly after Hwaseong Visiting Palace was built in 1794, its grounds were expanded to include thirty-three buildings — the largest detached palace in Korea, though still smaller than Seoul's five palaces.

King Jeongjo ordered the small village of Suwon, and the palace to be fortified by a surrounding wall. Not just any wall. This one would be imposing and massive, three stories high and six kilometers around. The king's ultimate goal was to move the capital from Seoul to Suwon, but when he died in 1800 his successor opted against it.

A shuttle bus arriving from Seoul stopped in front of the palace, on board about a dozen Royal Asiatic Society members and tour leader Peter Bartholomew. Peter is an American who arrived in South Korea with the Peace Corps in 1968. He is a well-known amateur expert on Joseon architecture and provides annual tours to palaces in Suwon and Seoul and of grand architecture across the peninsula. He was past president of the Korea Branch of the Royal Asiatic Society as well. Peter is talkative, quick to laugh and fluent in Korean.

It was only mid-April, but the morning was already oppressively hot, the sun bright and searing, and my thermometer read twenty-seven degrees Celsius. Combined with the heated, moisture-laden air, the actual temperature was closer to thirty-five degrees. I felt as if a damp, hot blanket had been thrown over me. I didn't do well in such conditions. I removed a tissue from my pocket and wiped away the sweat from the back of my neck. It was going to be a long day.

Peter stood before us equipped with a megaphone and began a passionate diatribe aimed against the Japanese. During Japan's 1910–1945 iron-fisted rule over Korea, the colonizers slowly and assiduously tried to eradicate everything Korean, including its architecture. They destroyed and mutilated virtually every Joseon-era compound of significance – most demolition occurring in the 1930s, Peter said.

"Japan eliminated 95 percent of all grand structures," he continued. Peter defined grand structures as monumental, well-designed and unsurpassed in Asia, built to last many hundreds of years and developed over 2,000 years.

By the early 1900s, about 350 provincial walled towns and administrative centers, and a hundred military compounds totaling between 17,000 and 20,000 structures existed in Korea. "The Japanese demolished every one of them," Peter declared, his voice rising with passion and amplified by the megaphone. "Detached palaces were systematically eliminated too. All but two of approximately thirty buildings at Hwaseong Palace were torn down."

Hwaseong Palace and the fort are prime examples of grand-scale architecture – the last major construction projects of Joseon. In 1996, the government hired experts to rebuild· the palace, and architects started from scratch. The placement of new buildings was pin-point accurate, due to architects unearthing enough of the original stone foundation in the 1980s to provide an exact blueprint. Before us was a virtually rebuilt palace compound. Peter – cynical of past governments' poor attempts to rebuild and refurbish Joseon architecture – offered praise: "They did an excellent job."

We stood at the palace entrance: a row of four heavy, massively wide, tall swinging doors with eight round, vertical, enormous wood posts supporting the wood deck above. Over the deck a huge, black-tiled roof sweeps elegantly above the doors. The palace's low stone walls comprise rows of small, light-colored brick. Inside the grounds, paralleling the front wall, are what look like long barracks commonly used as residences by the royal court, including servants, musicians, scholars, artists, poets and *gisaeng*. The top half of the barracks is soft pink clay bordered by small wooden shutters, the roof modest and tiled with black shale.

We entered the front gate into the grounds of flat stone and hard-packed sandy earth, similar to Joseon palaces. It is austere and stark, not a blade of grass anywhere, and reminded me of a military compound. The main courtyard is rectangular – about fifty meters wide. At the far end are two stately halls with high, heavy, dominating black shale tiled roofs. The king and royal family would have resided there. Peter led us through various courtyards, perhaps fifteen in all, in some, residential barrack-like structures with long covered porches running in front, providing shelter from the sun and summer monsoons. The walls are smooth red clay with green lattice shutters. Some front walls can swing up, held in place by hooks under eaves. "This allowed a breeze to flow through during hot summers," said Peter.

The wood and clay have been exquisitely kept up, colors predominantly rusty red and earthy pink. Clay was laid under the roof tiles for insulation. "Mixed with water, clay forms a dense hard layer and is a superb insulator," Peter said. "It blocks cold winter air and humid summer air."

The courtyards, structures and open spaces were designed in a specific, assiduous symmetry, rather like the precise layout of a German village — every chalet, shop and café spotless, prim and orderly. I longed for something, anything, to be out of place.

During Joseon, choreographed ceremonies were performed in palace courtyards with hundreds of court-appointed singers and dancers participating, everyone set in exact prearranged positions prior to the king's heavenly entrance. A royal birthday, for example, commonly had up to a thousand singers and dancers. All very pompous and stuffy. Had I been king, I'd have eschewed the unwieldy protocol and converted the courtyards into red clay courts to play tennis.

To move from Seoul to Suwon, the king was carried in a palanquin. Royalty was considered mythical — a conduit between heaven and Earth — and rarely ventured into public. Citizens were forced to avert their gazes from kings; it was considered sacrilegious to look directly at deity. Thousands of soldiers, horsemen, bannermen, musicians, dancers, guards and servants, all cloaked in extravagant color, accompanied the king.

In the late 1890s, Isabella Bird Bishop witnessed King Gojong being carried in a palanquin from his palace in Seoul across the city to his ancestors' graves. Bishop estimated more than 100,000 people lined the roadway.

"It was one of the most remarkable spectacles I ever saw," she wrote.

A long mural painted on a courtyard wall in the palace depicted thousands in the king's entourage in transit from Seoul to Suwon.

Back at the palace entrance, we hopped onto the shuttle bus and were ushered into a nearby restaurant for lunch. What a relief to be out of the deadly heat and in an air-conditioned room. We'd completed only half the tour. The second half, a six-kilometer trek around Hwaseong Fortress in the mid-afternoon furnace, awaited.

After lunch we walked from the palace to the fortress's west wall, built on Paldal Mountain – a gently sloping long hill adjacent to the palace. The wall's height varies from four to nine meters. Originally earthen, it was rebuilt with thick granite blocks, many irregularly shaped. Atop are modest-size granite blocks forming parapets with crenels and turrets: small square openings through which to fire weapons.

The Japanese demolished the wall's sentry posts in the 1920s and 1930s. When President Park Chung-hee came to power in 1961, he decreed the walls weren't of value and ordered long sections of two of them razed. In the 1970s, the government undertook a massive repair and reconstruction project of the fort.

At the crest of Paldal Mountain by the wall is a command post and fire beacon. Long ago, smoke messages were quickly relayed the length of Korea using such beacons. Looking from the crest to west Suwon is an airy panorama of flat plains dominated by orderly agricultural fields.

We descended the hill along the wall and near the bottom entered West Gate Pavilion – a mini castle tower of heavy stone, vertical wood beams supporting the roof's massive weight. Reduced to listless rag dolls under the sun, we collapsed on seats in the pavilion.

"It's so cool in here," I said in relief, as if an air conditioner was switched on.

"That's because clay's a great insulator," replied Peter.

After twenty minutes we turned at the wall's northwest corner, continuing along the imperious front to the grand entrance named Longevity and Peace Gate. The castle-like eminence ascends close to five stories — the largest gate of its kind in South Korea, testament to architectural grandeur. Massive gray granite blocks create a soaring arched entranceway. Above is more granite and brick, atop it a long, ornately-carved, two-story pavilion with a black shale roof.

"North Korean soldiers took refuge behind the gate at the beginning of the Korean War," said Peter. "U.S. troops fired artillery shells at the wall to try to dislodge them and blew it to smithereens." He pointed to pockmarks and gouges in the stone. "That's where the shells hit."

At the fort's northeast corner we walked south along the wall, passing more grand architectural structures. It wasn't until late afternoon that our group, exhausted and wilting, finished the circumnavigation. Peter and the RAS members boarded the shuttle bus for Seoul. Heju and I would stay and explore Suwon. We strolled to a local market, refreshing ourselves with a long respite in an air-conditioned ice cream shop. In early evening we drove to downtown Suwon.

In Suwon's city center we approached a huge indoor complex that included the Suwon train and subway stations and two major department stores and hundreds of shops and restaurants. In front was an impossibly busy, vitally energetic multi-lane road. Innumerable pedestrians buzzed about on crowded sidewalks. Multi-story buildings were ablaze in a rainbow of bright neon lights in the darkness, and crushes of cars, taxis and buses noisily jockeyed for position on the wide street.

We parked across from the station at a little park by the sidewalk, where mostly Filipino men and women were socializing on the early Sunday evening, their weekly day off from employment at Suwon factories or as domestic helpers. We sneaked back into a network of old lanes with brightly-lit store fronts, but the shops weren't selling items. Rather, women were standing behind large windows in Suwon's red-light district. On the lane we struck up a conversation with a group of well-tailored, young Pakistani men in their twenties. They spoke English and were employed as laborers at local factories. Heju asked if they had Korean girlfriends.

There were smiles. One of the men admitted they didn't. "Korean women want expensive gifts and to be taken out for meals. We prefer to save our money," he said.

Heju enthusiastically told them she loved Pakistani food. Two of the lads kindly led us via the back lane to the busy main street to a nearby Pakistani restaurant, its front a nondescript windowless brick wall. We entered through an obscure door into Little Pakistan, packed with voluble young Pakistani men — mustached and bearded — smoking cigarettes, the thick, acrid smoke stinging our eyes. The long, large utilitarian windowless room had a concrete floor and long communal tables, dishes of lamb and rice in front of many groups of men. We were shown to a small table at the rear. Behind us, a Pakistani chef was busy cooking in a semi-open kitchen. Heju was the only Korean and female in the place, and I was the only Westerner.

We ordered Basmati rice, lamb in sauce and pita bread and patiently waited with hungry bellies. It wasn't every day that a parsimonious Dutch-Scotsman shelled out at restaurants, where merchandise disappears down gullets never to be seen again.

"I love lamb!" Heju announced, as happy as a child at a birthday party. Her mood always elevated when we dined out. She paused a moment, as if in deep thought, then announced accusingly, "Hey, we hardly ever eat out!"

"Of course we don't!" I replied in mock alarm. "The trip's costing a lot of money. I need to be careful."

We observed a rather touching ritual: pairs and small groups of men arriving and departing, engaging in a lengthy process of shaking hands, hugging, cheek-kissing and waving to almost every other man in the place. It took considerable time for a group to get from their table to the front door and vice versa.

This brotherly love was lost on the kitchen chef — a dark-haired man about fifty-five — his face weathered, his penetrating dark eyes staring intently and directly at me with not a small degree of hostility. Was he offended I was the only Westerner here?

"Heju ... don't look now," I whispered stealthily, "but the chef in the kitchen ... I think he..."

Heju turned to look.

"Not now!" I interjected, muffling a cry.

A few moments later I gave the green light: "Okay ... slowly ... take your time — look!" and she cast an unobtrusive glance in his direction.

"I think he wants to kill me," I squeaked. "He keeps glaring at me."

Heju mulled this over a few moments, then asked solemnly, "Can I have your plate of lamb and rice if he does?"

Ha ha! During dinner I shot frequent furtive glances at my nemesis, who was continuing to eyeball me. I sat poised and alert, ready to leap from my chair and dash out the front door if he rushed me.

The lamb was marvelous — succulent and tender, the Indian rice fluffy and tasty (Korean rice is sticky and glutinous), the naan bread delectable. My only complaint was there wasn't enough food on the table, a fundamental problem at restaurants, it seemed to me. I was often relegated to begging for scraps from Heju, who thankfully ate like a bird, and usually couldn't finish her meal. I got her leftovers.

Only partially satiated, our clothes reeking of cigarette smoke, we exited to the bustling sidewalk and bright lights. I warily glanced back at the restaurant to ascertain if the chef was following us. "Just making sure he's not after me," I said to Heju, who thought me bonkers.

Early the next afternoon, we drove the twenty or so kilometers north to Uiwang to the Korean Rail Museum. A sign in front of the gated museum read, "Closed Mondays." Today, of course, was Monday. So instead we spent a leisurely day sightseeing on the outskirts of Suwon, taking in a tour of a Buddhist temple and strolling a park housing the tomb of King Jeongjo, who died in 1800.

Late the following afternoon, we were back in Uiwang at the rail museum. In its ample concrete front grounds were about half a dozen old diesel and electric locomotive engines and passenger cars. A plaque in front of one luxury passenger car read that on November 1, 1966, "U.S. President Lydon [sic] B. Johnson" rode this same rail car. At the rear of the grounds was a mangled, rusted train engine. Prior to the Korean War, the same engine had puffed back and forth along sixty kilometers of track between Seoul and Gaeseong, the latter in today's North Korea. Both the track and engine were bombed in the war.

On the ground next to the engine was a short section of narrow-gauge rail line measuring two-feet, six-inches wide. Standard-gauge track is four-feet, 8.5-inches wide. The little track was the kind a choo-choo train slowly tootled along at an amusement park. A train historian told us that during colonization the Japanese built a number of narrow-gauge lines in Korea, all later torn up or altered to standard-gauge. The Japanese constructed the narrow-gauge Suin Rail Line, joining Suwon forty-seven kilometers northwest to Incheon. Sixty more kilometers of narrow-gauge track were added from Suwon east to Yeoju. In the 1970s, these tracks were dismantled.

Touring Incheon a few days later, we stopped at the moribund Songdo Amusement Park on the coast, where a huge Ferris wheel, rides and a mini zoo once thrived, before more modern theme parks began springing up. Two local old-timers employed at the park's front gate fondly recalled riding the narrow-gauge Suin Line in the 1970s. In those days, only the rail line and a dirt road connected Incheon to Suwon, they said. "Each rail car was about eight meters long, so narrow it was tippy. Even a cow looking at the train could tip it over," one joked.

The train wheels caused a racket, the cars slowly bumping and clattering on the track. The rail cars were crowded, noisy and smelly, with farmers toting pigs, chickens, dogs and shrimp to sell at outdoor markets at station stops.

The government demolished the Suin Line in 1995, and what a shame. Imagine the fun families, kids and tourists would have today riding the narrow, clackety cars over rattling rails.

At about four o'clock we entered the spacious rail museum, curiously devoid of visitors. Maybe not surprising, considering it is located in a vast industrial park behind factories and literally impossible to find. The museum was also apparently bereft of staff. As we wandered through, we spotted glimpses of occasional movement in shadows we suspected were employees, but not a single human materialized until closing time.

The history of rail travel in Korea is interesting. In 1897, the country's first rail line was constructed by an American company. The line linked Incheon to Seoul. The Japanese began laying tracks to connect Busan to Seoul in 1900, completed in 1905. A photo depicting the line's inauguration in Seoul shows Japanese officials and soldiers in the forefront, thousands of curious Koreans along the track.

By 1911, a line joined Seoul to Manchuria in northeast China and on to Mukden to today's Shenyang. Japan's aim was to join Busan to China in order to facilitate its future conquest of China.

Subsequent routes were constructed by the Japanese, most on a north-south axis. It was challenging to build west-east, due to the major north-south axis Sobaek and Taebaek Mountains. Even on north-south lines, numerous rail tunnels were needed. On the Jungang Line, marrying Seoul to Gyeongju in the southeast, are forty-two tunnels; four-and-a-half-kilometer Jungnyeong Tunnel is the longest.

Up until the 1960s, rail travel was the only real option for Koreans. Practically no one owned a car, few paved roads existed, and bus transport was in its nascent stage. More than 150 million passengers annually rode the rails.

In the museum were old photos depicting some rail oddities. A 1963 photo showed a section of track on the Yeongdong Line between the east coast cities of Donghae and Simpo, the rail cars being winched up a low, steep mountain slope with passengers trudging alongside. Switchback tracks were built on the section in the 1970s, and winching the cars became obsolete.

At five minutes before six, a sleepy-looking college-aged fellow in a uniform suddenly and conveniently materialized beside us and announced, "Closing time." Finally, a staff member to answer a few of my railroad queries! I put several to him, but to each he replied a listless, "I don't know." I persisted, and he replied curtly, "If you want to get answers ... check our museum website." How daft of me to expect a rail museum employee to know a thing or two about railroads.

Heju and I needed to head back to Seoul. Over the next two days we had several tours lined up in the big city. We pointed the car north on the main, six-lane artery toward the capital of ancient and modern Korea. The busy, wide road was jammed with myriad vehicles, on both sides, never-ending rows of tall, garish white apartment buildings. Our Scoupe was surprisingly popular — most of Greater Seoul's seven million vehicles were accompanying us. We passed the satellite city of Anyang, then near Gwacheon — immediately south of

Seoul — we stagnated in a massive traffic jam. Finally, at nine o'clock, we culminated in Amsa-dong by the Han River near Myeongil-dong. The forty kilometer drive had taken three hours.

Since I was subletting my Myeongil-dong flat to an Australian English teacher while I was on the road, Heju and I checked into a motel in Amsa-dong. At Bali Motel's front office, a female clerk sitting behind a narrow pane of glass, asked, of course, "Will you be staying two hours?"

"No, for the night," we replied as usual.

"Thirty thousand won," she said.

A couple who looked to be in their forties entered the small lobby and waited behind us. The man wore a suit, his female companion — attempting to remain incognito — lurked in the shadows, head bowed. These were the two-hour customers.

Our room was just slightly bigger than a jail cell, on the ceiling dim green and red fluorescent lights, a throwback to the 1960s' hippie era. From the adjacent room came loud expressions from an amorous couple. We decided to leave the motel in the morning.

CHAPTER 6

Seoul: Hiking Bugak Mountain;
Brawling Monks

In mid-morning we puttered in the car across the street to Casa Motel. In Casa Motel's lobby was a small office, against its side wall were multi banks of video monitors, screens displaying live, closed-circuit feeds of halls on the four floors. A husband-and-wife owner team was keeping a keen eye on the monitors.

"You staying two hours?" the man — a short, aggressive type with the disposition of an aggrieved used car salesman — asked brusquely.

"No, for the night," I said.

He wasn't pleased. "Where are you going to park your car then?"

"In the motel lot," I replied.

"You can't! If you do, customers (the two-hour kind) can't get in and out with their cars during the day. If you keep your car in the lot, the room fee will be 30,000 won," he said, tacking 5,000 won onto the original price.

"That's okay," I said.

I parked. Heju and I hauled our bags, containing food, clothes, books, camera, binoculars and newspapers, into the motel lobby.

The owner demanded to know where we were going with all the stuff. Two-hour customers don't bring luggage.

"We're journalists touring Korea, and we've got valuable equipment," I said, exaggerating our status.

"Well, don't leave it in the room when you go!" he ordered caustically. As if we were about to donate it to him.

I waited expectantly at the office window for the room key, but he ignored me. I finally asked him for the key.

"There's no key!" he barked. "What do you need a key for? Customers only stay two hours!"

The man's poor bird-size brain couldn't grasp that patrons existed other than those on short trysts, and he was upset because instead of making 20,000 won for a customary two-hour stay, he'd only be earning 30,000 won for a twenty-four-hour rental.

He grudgingly handed us the key. A real joy of a man.

We entered our third-floor room – the first and second floors were reserved for short-termers. Walking into the bathroom, I promptly banged my forehead square on the top horizontal beam of the door frame. I cussed and rubbed my head. This wasn't the first time I'd thumped my noggin on a low doorway in this country. "Why do they make such short doors?" I bellowed to Heju.

(When Bishop Corfe arrived in Incheon from England in 1889, the tall man regularly hit his head on low overhead beams in his traditional home. To soften the blows he nailed socks to the cciling.)

I found a tape measure in my bag and measured the length of the door frame. "Five-feet, seven-inches! What kind of idiotic motel is this!" I hollered.

We departed Casa Motel at noon and walked to the nearby Amsa Subway Station for our afternoon appointment of a guided hike up to Bugak Mountain's 340-meter crest. Bugaksan is the distinguished, wooded eminence rising prominently in downtown Seoul behind the Blue House – the president's residence.

Once downtown we transferred onto a subway line heading north. We exited at nearby Hansung University Station, then ambled through a busy outdoor market toward Bugaksan's east slope. Once past the market, we were on a dirt path moving through light woods. Off to the side is the quiet, isolated residential neighborhood of Seongbuk, nestled in a long, gradual sweeping wooded valley replete with stately mansions and magnificent, multi-million dollar homes. Seongbuk is the toniest, priciest district in Seoul, home to fabulously wealthy titans of Korean industry. We arrived at the base of Bugaksan's moderate north ascent and waited at a tourist hut with a couple dozen Koreans for our prearranged tour.

In 2007, Bugak Mountain's hiking trails were reopened to the public after forty years off limits. Prior to 1968, the mountain was available for all to enjoy panoramic views from its crest: south over central Seoul, north over the Gwangju Mountains' low granite peaks. On January 21, 1968, a team of thirty-one North Korean special forces commandos dubbed Unit 124 – ordered by Great Leader Kim Il-sung to assassinate South Korea's right-wing President Park Chung-hee – got within 350 meters of the Blue House. The enemy had surreptitiously crossed the border, then scrambled through mountains south to Seoul and down Bugaksan to the Blue House. At a police checkpoint near their target, police chief Choi Gyu-shik grew suspicious and demanded identification. From under trench coats the insurgents withdrew weapons and shot Choi dead. Their cover blown, military guards and police of the heavily armed Capital Garrison Command opened fire, returned by the enemy. Bullets and hand grenades went flying. A bus with civilians on board was caught in the crossfire, killing passengers. More than a hundred people died or were wounded that day.

The North Koreans fled into woods, but over the next nine days, twenty-nine of the thirty-one men were shot dead by ROK soldiers. One commando managed to escape to North Korea to a hero's welcome. The other, Lieutenant Kim Shin-jo, twenty-three, surrendered and made Seoul his home. He eventually became a preacher at a west Seoul church. (We contacted the church to try to arrange an interview, but Mr. Kim declined.) Later, a defector in Seoul who'd fled the North told authorities that as punishment for Kim's surrender, authorities tried Kim's parents and six siblings and executed them.

After the attack, Bugaksan was closed to the public, and a military presence has been deployed on and around the surrounding slopes ever since.

To hike the mountain these days requires taking a government-sanctioned group tour. Individual forays aren't permitted. Heju and I had emailed our identification to the government in advance. Despite my dodgy youthful past that included being consistently late for weekly evening Boy Scout meetings, the feds officially okayed me.

Our group included about twenty mostly middle-aged and elderly Koreans. Our guide was a dour, officious retired man who gravely explained the rules: no smoking, no throwing garbage, stay together at all times, ID cards must be worn around our necks and not removed until the tour's over. Accompanying us for our protection was a young, glum ROK soldier equipped with a rifle, but his sullen and resentful attitude — combined with his weapon — concerned me more than the remote possibility of encountering North Korean commandos.

We headed up a dirt path on an easy, gradual slope through woods to the crest, the mid-April afternoon warm and pleasant. After twenty minutes we arrived on the broad, wooded crest at imposing North Gate, one of four main entrances through the former city wall encompassing old Seoul during the Joseon Dynasty. North Gate comprises granite blocks and is enormous, looming like a castle gate in a *Lord of the Rings* movie. During Joseon, the gate was rarely opened or closed, considered of dubious feng shui quality and more an emergency exit in case a king needed to make a hasty escape. Opposite the gate is the long, gradual downward sweeping slope of gray woods culminating far below at the unseen Blue House.

Reaching out from both sides of the gate on the crest are traces of old Seoul wall's remaining stone foundation. The wall was 18.6 kilometers long and formed an imperfect circle around the city. It ran along, up and down four local mountains: Bugaksan; Naksan just east; Namsan to the south and Inwangsan just west. When the Joseon Dynasty was established in 1392, Seoul was selected as its capital. (Gaeseong, north of Panmunjeom, was the previous capital of the Goryeo Dynasty.) Joseon's first monarch, King Taejo, conscripted 120,000 commoners to construct the first half of the 4.6-meter-tall wall in early 1396. Amazingly, it was completed in just forty-nine days. The summer was given off to the laborers to tend crops, and in the fall, 80,000 men built the wall's second half with four main and four minor gates added.

It must have been quite a scene with 100,000 laborers congregating in Seoul, population 10,000. Earth was initially used for the wall's construction and had to be hauled up hills and slopes. A total of 872 laborers died from exhaustion, ill health and disease. In 1422, 320,000 laborers replaced the entire earthen wall with stone in just forty days.

From North Gate our guide ushered us a few hundred meters west to a clearing on the peak crowded with Koreans on other tour groups busily snapping photos and recording videos of expansive views. Looking south — beyond the downtown core of glass and steel office towers — rises rounded, stalwart wooded Namsan. On its crest is Seoul Tower, 236 meters above sea level.

Far below us is Gyeongbok Palace's spacious grounds and its dominant, massive towering Gate of Radiant Transformation, rebuilt in its original full glory in 2010. In front of the gate, Sejong Street's sixteen lanes were clogged with innumerable cars, taxis, and buses, crawling like ants. To our west is the low but steep Inwang Mountain ridge, its face with large bald patches of granite. Looking north are Gwangju Mountains' rugged granite peaks, including ridges of Bukhan Mountain, not to be confused with Bugak Mountain.

Seoul was selected as the capital for its proximity to the Yellow Sea and for being far enough up the Han River to be protected from Japanese pirates, the scourge of coastal regions, particularly in the thirteenth and fourteenth centuries. The surrounding Han River lowlands are extensive, with plenty of space for citizens to farm. Northwest of Seoul are the fertile, agricultural plains of Paju and Gimpo. Combined with Pyeongtaek's southwest plains, the region would sustain a growing population.

Rice and other goods were transported on flat-bottomed vessels called *hanseon* along the west coast and up the Han River to Seoul. Smaller *hanseon* conveyed supplies such as salt from Seoul farther up the Han to interior villages in exchange for firewood and charcoal. Officials traveled upriver to collect taxes too. In most cases, taxes were paid not in cash but in rice, grain and cotton.

Seoul was favored as a prime location in previous times as well. In Amsa-dong, on the Han River, were discovered pit houses, utensils and other artifacts, dating to 5,000 BC in the Neolithic Age. During the first 700 years after Christ, Korea was ruled by the three kingdoms of Goguryeo north of the Han, Silla in the southeast, and Baekje in the southwest. All three coveted control of strategically important Seoul. Earthen fort walls for the defense of Seoul from that period can be seen today.

In 1394, King Taejo ordered Gyeongbok Palace built in Seoul. Gyeongbok Palace, and Changgyeong and Changdeok Palaces, would form a row. An entire city of roads, shops, markets, residences and government offices was created. A main road was graded through today's downtown Jongno district. Shops supplied silk, linen, hemp, fish, rice, paper, straw-ware and ironware, all regulated by government and taxed.

From the main road radiated a series of minor roads and alleyways, some no wider than a meter. Commoners erected clay *hanok* and mud hovels along them. Even today in some districts of central Seoul one can find narrow alleyways from the Joseon period, with modern buildings built along them. When I arrived in the country, I'd sometimes stroll through the Gwanghwamun district in downtown Seoul, and note crumbling little *hanok* along alleyways. Sadly, modern development has all but erased such vestiges.

Seoul had its essential framework in place by 1420, its population now over 100,000 – the heart and soul of medieval Korea. While political power radiated countrywide, wealth converged in Seoul, and the educated and talented were drawn to the capital.

By 1550, Seoul's five major palaces, and detached palaces and service compounds, formed an almost unbroken line along the wall's west and north quadrants. Palaces were virtual cities with hundreds of structures and mazes of corridors, alleys and gateways. By the nineteenth century, Gyeongbok Palace comprised 150 courtyards and 450 buildings.

When Isabella Bird Bishop gazed down from a hilltop over Seoul in the late 1800s, she described a sea of one-story dwellings with roofs of tile or straw, a city bereft of trees, parks and green spaces. "Not a work of art to be gazed upon," she penned.

Seoul's grand architecture was mostly destroyed by the Japanese during colonization. More than 300 Gyeongbok Palace buildings and its front gate were razed. Joseon government buildings on Sejong Street were replaced with Japanese residences. In 1926, the massive Japanese General Government Building was erected directly in front of Gyeongbok Palace, the former building demolished in 1996. Much of Seoul's wall and its eight arched gates were flattened between 1910 and 1919. Deoksu Palace was reduced to less than a quarter its original size. Changgyeong Palace was converted to a zoo and amusement park in the 1930s and renamed Changgyeong Park, all but five of its original buildings torn down. When Heju was a kid in the 1970s, her parents took her to Changgyeong Park to see zoo animals and ride the rides. In 1983, the animals were relocated. Sections of the palace were rebuilt.

The Japanese sent priceless Korean treasures home to Japanese museums. Some ended up as private collections owned by descendants of Japanese officials. Historian Shinichi Arai at Ibaraki University in Japan studied the removal of Korean cultural assets during colonization, concluding that while many artifacts were returned to Korea, 67,000 known pieces remain in Japan.

Destruction wasn't solely carried out by the Japanese. After liberation in 1945, vigorous expansion was begun by the Korean government, and new thoroughfares were bulldozed through hovels and shantytowns. Traditional compounds were razed too. Since 1960, about 90 percent of Seoul's traditional wood and clay *hanok* homes have been torn down. Peter Bartholomew, who owns a *hanok* in central Seoul, appeared numerous times before Seoul courts in an effort to fight developers' plans to eliminate traditional homes and replace them with high-rise buildings.

"In the 1960s, there were around 250,000 *hanok* in Seoul," Peter said. "Today, there are only about 3,000, and those are disappearing."

Industrialization began in South Korea in the 1960s, with factories springing up around Seoul and surrounding Gyeonggi province.

Millions of young men and women from the provinces flocked to the city in search of employment. It was the beginning of a rapid metamorphosis of Seoul to an urban mecca.

Upon my arrival in South Korea, my English academy put me up in a traditional Korean inn, or *yeogwan* in Cheonho-dong, next to the Han River near Myeongil-dong. About a century old, the inn was on a narrow back lane. It was rectangular-shaped, sealed off by a wall from the hustle and bustle of the city. The entrance was through heavy wood swinging doors, leading to a worn interior, a modest cement courtyard in the center surrounded by a wide veranda running in front of narrow tiny rooms on each side. The rooms had paper-thin walls and a light, sliding glass-wood door opened to the veranda. When rays of sunshine poured into my room in mornings, I slid open the door, shuffled out onto the veranda and basked in the warmth. I slept on the room floor on a thick unrolled bed mat or *yo*. The communal washing room was in an old, small barn-like shed in the courtyard corner. Inside the room was a huge plastic tub I'd fill with hot water and bathe in. Toilets were the old squat kind. On weekends, I threw my dirty clothes into a water-filled big plastic tub in the courtyard, stomped on them with my bare feet, then rinsed and wrung by hand, finally hanging them on the line. Tenants tended to be transient Korean laborers.

Despite the inconveniences, I loved the inn — my own private Shangri-La. After about two months, I was transferred to a basement flat in Myeongil-dong. A couple of years on, strolling through Cheonho-dong, I was shocked to discover the inn replaced by a plain, ugly three-story residential condo or *jutaek*. With foresight, the inn could have been refurbished and used by travelers and guests. Money and modernization had won out. How sad that the government and Koreans have permitted so much old architecture to be dismantled, often in the blink of an eye. Traditional buildings gone forever.

Don't get me started on what transpired in Sangil-dong, the district immediately east of Myeongil-dong, where I resided for most of my years in Korea. Okay – if you insist – I will. From Myeongil-dong I'd look with pleasure east across Sangil-dong – where Seoul ended – to enjoy an arresting, unobstructed view of mountains eight kilometers away. Today, Sangil-dong is unrecognizable. Beginning in 2017, its districts of former markets, shops, homes, *jutaek* and four-and-five-floor apartment buildings, were razed, replaced by scores of ugly, tall white apartment buildings forming a sky-high solid concrete barrier of bland homogeneity. Phalanxes of structures now totally obscure the once wonderful vista from Myeongil-dong to the mountains. Every semblance of Sangil-dong's former character and uniqueness has been erased. The agricultural fields east of Sangil-dong are gone too, developed into numerous apartment buildings. The shortsighted, disheartening destruction and development has been occurring all across Seoul and the country.

Nevertheless, Seoul is a marvelous city of amazing rugged beauty, the only city in the world where within a fifteen-minute walk from its core, one can be hiking mountain trails and ridges. The Han River is striking. During placid evenings, lights from thousands of apartment buildings lining both sides of the river's shoreline, glimmer off its mirror-like blackness. It's an exciting, crowded, bustling metropolis that never sleeps. Seoul was the place to be in 1500. Five hundred years later it still is.

***

On Bugaksan peak, our guide permitted us twenty minutes to relax. Noting two young ROK soldiers armed with rifles, I said to Heju, "Let's see if they know their directions."

I'm sometimes gobsmacked when seeking directions in Korea,

pedestrians occasionally pointing me in arbitrary, random ways, seemingly unaware of north and south. Heju and I approached a soldier, and I pretended to be new to Korea. "Excuse me, could you please tell us which way's north?" I asked.

The young soldier silently gazed north, then west, then south and finally east. He scrunched his face in deep thought. Before he could answer, a nearby elderly Korean man who'd overheard the question, announced in English: "Namsan's south — over there," pointing south, "so North's the opposite way." Correct.

On the other side of the clearing was another young soldier. We we walked over to him, and asked, "Excuse me, do you know which way's west?" He stared at his left hand for some time, as if trying to get his bearings, then at his right hand. Finally he pointed west. Bear in mind, these are trained military men who at a moment's notice must be ready to respond to a North Korean attack. My concern is not if our boys are prepared but if they know which direction to aim their weapons. If the entire ROK military is as muddled about north and south as these two — and mistakenly point their missiles, say, west to China — this could be a very big mess.

Heju and I sat and leaned back against a huge boulder and closed our eyes to enjoy a short siesta. Waking up twenty minutes later, we discovered our tour leader and group were missing. This is a security area. We were now unaccounted for. Had we desired, we could have ostensibly slipped down the face of Bugaksan to the Blue House, broken in and stolen the silverware.

We trekked west from the crest down a steep set of stone steps to street level, exiting at the former wall's minor northwest Jahamun Gate. We walked on a quiet road paralleling the bottom of Bugaksan's south face toward downtown and passed a statue of Captain Choi Gyu-shik, the police officer shot dead by North Korean commandos in 1968. About forty minutes later, we were at the busy thoroughfare in front of Gyeongbok Palace.

On a leafy, fashionable boulevard paralleling the palace's west wall, we strode past fit young secret-service agents in suits, mini earphones in ears, standing at set intervals. At the palace's rear at a traffic circle corner near the Blue House — buzzing with numerous police and agents — we happened upon Korea's most beautiful female police officer. The woman, maybe 30 years old, surely thought me bonkers. I couldn't help but stare.

"She looks dry-cleaned!" I whispered of the immaculate lady to Heju.

Her police uniform comprised black polished shoes, tapered pants, jacket and police bonnet, and collared white shirt and blue tie. Her face was creaseless, liberally awash with foundation and pale blush. Her eyebrows were plucked and penciled in, lips red. Her long, shiny black hair was in a neat bun held together by bobby pins. Her facial expression was frozen in a permanent and wry Mona Lisa smile, as if moving a muscle might crease her mascara. She was so starched, I suspected she'd been dry-cleaned and pressed this morning while in uniform.

We departed Ms. ROK Police Officer and proceeded on the sidewalk between the palace's rear wall and the front of the gated Blue House. The latter's large main residence was simple yet grand, with blue shale roof tiles, the expansive front lawn, manicured grass. Farther along we encountered a second dry-cleaned beautiful policewoman, probably the sister of the original. The hiring manager for Blue House security was definitely male.

It was early evening and Heju was dawdling at a maddeningly turtle-like pace. "Why are you slow today?" I asked.

"My legs ache," she replied in a desultory tone. "We walked a lot today."

We had walked a lot: from our motel in Amsa-dong to the subway station, to Bugaksan, to Gyeongbok Palace and now at the Blue House, maybe ten kilometers total. Later that evening, back at Casa Motel, Heju was soon asleep.

I stayed up. At about 2:00 a.m., I heard voices emanating from the hallway and crept out to investigate. The sounds were coming from a couple amorously expressing themselves in a room. Then I heard the phone ring in my room, and I dashed back in. Heju was sitting up in bed on the phone, staring at me like I'd just stolen her last nickel.

After hanging up, she stated indignantly: "That was the motel owner. He was angry. He wanted to know what you were doing in the hall, in your underwear, listening at peoples' doors!"

Damn, I'd forgotten about the blasted hall cameras. I tried to explain, but Heju was in no mood to listen. She complained bitterly, "I hate it here. It reminds me of prostitution place," and she resumed sleeping.

***

The following afternoon was bright and warm, and we were back downtown, in Jongno-dong, at Jogye Buddhist Temple, the only Buddhist temple in central Seoul. The grounds are just off a quiet, handsome street lined with small shops selling an amazing variety of Buddhist paraphernalia. The temple compound was busy with patrons. To its rear is the massive, box-like temple constructed in 1910. Its exterior walls have a series of immense, wood turquoise doors. The underside of the enormous arched roof is turquoise. Workers in front of the temple in the earthen courtyard were stringing up thousands of candle lanterns on lines of cord in preparation for Buddha's May 19 birthday. Perhaps his 2,644th or so, if one was counting.

In the compound's far corner is the five-floor administrative center, headquarters of South Korea's dominant Jogye Buddhist sect. Jogye's website notes that 3,298 temples across the country belong to the sect. When Japan colonized the nation, Jogye had been long established, but the colonizers imported Taego, a Japanese Buddhist sect. Taego monks are permitted to marry, Jogye monks can not.

About ten million South Koreans practice Buddhism. What a sight when nation-wide, university-entrance exams are held every November for graduating high school students. Hundreds of thousands of mothers flock to temples, to collectively bow and fervently pray so that Buddha will bestow exam success on their sons and daughters. Jogye Temple is also where monks led a mass gathering in 2006, praying that South Korea would be selected as host of the 2014 Winter Olympic Games. Alas, the monks were five years too early; in 2011, the country was awarded the 2018 Winter Olympics in Pyeongchang.

Heju and I weren't at the temple to pray or to seek good grades. We were here to investigate. While on Ganghwa Island, we'd watched a U.S.-produced TV program called *World's Most Shocking Moments*, the video showing monks ferociously battling one another at Jogye Temple in 1998. In one heart-stopping scene, a cherry-picker type crane – the bucket overloaded with five or six policemen – was being raised in front of the administration center. The bucket suddenly tipped, sending the officers plummeting to the ground. Fortunately, no one died.

What transpired on that day in 1998? Inquiring minds wanted to know. We walked across the compound to the administrative center to find out. On the path, a trio of bald monks in long gray cloaks strolled toward us. "Hello," we said, when they drew parallel. "Would you happen to know what happened in 1998 when monks fought here?"

The three looked bemused, and one cheekily replied: "We have so much energy because we're single and can't marry. We use our energy to fight instead, but only during days, because we have no wives to fight with at night."

Good one, Little Grasshopper!

We entered the administrative building, its expansive main floor humming with monks. Standing in the lobby we must have appeared somewhat befuddled. A monk approached us and in excellent English introduced himself and handed us his business card, which read: Venerable Jae-An, Deputy Director, Office of Lay Buddhist Affairs, Jogye Order of Korean Buddhism, Bureau of Missionary Activities. Befitting such a grand title, Jae-An was charismatic, confident and boyish-looking for his forty-one years.

We asked him about the 1998 conflict. Jae-An made light of it. "Fighting among Buddhists is cyclical," he said. "There's 1,000 years of peace followed by short periods of fighting, then 1,000 more years of peace and more fighting and so on." Later, I cobbled together the narrative. Hostilities in 1998 were at a pinnacle due to an escalating feud between rivals within Jogye: progressive monks aligned against the more conservative and entrenched older monks who controlled the organization's ample purse strings. The struggle turned violent and hundreds of riot police were called to Jogye Temple's headquarters. The officers were pelted with debris and projectiles by senior monks holed up in the building and scores of monks were arrested.

There had been bitter clashes previously between Jogye and Taego monks. A particularly bruising one occurred in the 1970s at Younghwa Buddhist Temple, at the base of Acha Mountain in Seoul near the Han River.

Heju and I had hiked Achasan several weeks earlier. Entering Younghwa Temple, we learned from an official that Taego monks occupied the temple in the seventies but Jogye wanted them out.

"Jogye monks confronted Taego monks," he said. "Sticks and clubs were used. Injured monks were taken to the hospital. A court later ruled Jogye was the rightful owner, and Taego monks were evicted."

Historically, Korean monks haven't been averse to battle. During the Imjin War, Japanese soldiers occupied Korean soil between 1592 and 1598, and Korean monks fought bravely against the invaders. These days, Taego and Jogye coexist in brotherly monk love, Jae-An said. "There are no more problems or fighting."

Jae-An abruptly swayed the conversation to my stomach. Without a hint of malice, he asserted, "It's too big, Mark!"

As I always do in public, I was sucking in my gut in an obviously futile endeavor to appear svelte.

"You should meditate to lose fat," he continued. "When I arrived at the temple in 1992, I was fat and had big legs. But we had to kneel for two hours a day. It was very painful but I lost weight. Now I can kneel all day. Some of our monks can stay awake for twenty-one straight days."

I wondered aloud, "Why would anyone want to stay awake for twenty-one straight days?"

"For enlightenment."

"What's enlightenment?"

"Your eyes become brighter, your skin shinier, your body can fly," Jae-An said.

I was satisfied that my eyes and skin are of normal hue. Only in my dreams do I occasionally and happily soar like a bird.

Jae-An then suddenly insisted my calling was the monkhood. "You were a monk in your former life, Mark! You're here today because it's your destiny. You need to live here with me. No more work!"

The "no work" part was enticing, but I couldn't possibly sit cross-legged eight hours a day bowing to Buddha contemplating my sad existence. I'd refuse to shave my head bald and gray robes aren't my forte. I wasn't ready to jettison my freedom and commit to a lifetime of monastic ascetics.

"I need to work to earn money for retirement," I stammered.

Jae-An stated resolutely: "No, your work's over."

"Can I get back to you?" I squeaked.

The Venerable One nodded. Before he had a change of heart and ordered Jogye's orneriest, biggest monk to apprehend me, Heju and I bid a quick goodbye and scampered off the grounds into the safety of the secular world. I made a mental note to never again set foot in Jogye Temple.

CHAPTER 7

Gyeonggido: Persecuted Catholics; North Korean Defector Center

After our near imprisonment at Jogye Temple, Heju and I embarked on a three-day varied sortie through Incheon. We followed this up by entitling ourselves to a day of fun and relaxation at Everland Resort theme park, Korea's version of Disneyland. Everland is east of Incheon near the small city of Yongin, about fifty kilometers south of Seoul.

Everland is owned by Samsung, the global electronics giant. Your guess is as good as mine as to why Samsung owns an amusement park. Korea's major *chaebol*, or family-owned conglomerates, preside over a dizzying array of companies and industries. Samsung's late owner, Lee Gun-hee, who passed away in 2020 as the world's sixty-seventh richest person, was worth $21 billion and owned pretty much all of South Korea. This explains Lee's disastrous business decision in 1994 to establish Samsung Motors, despite every business expert in the country advising against it. Samsung Motors sold its first car in 1998 and almost immediately began hemorrhaging massive losses. Renault was its savior. In 2000, Renault Samsung Motors was born.

Everland is located in rural hilly woodlands amid the low, well-worn rounded Charyeong Mountains, splintering off from the east coast Taebaek Mountains. We entered the park at nine in the morning and traipsed many kilometers through expansive, busy grounds. We toured a zoo and safari park — its poor five-ton Asian elephant, Koshik, chained in an indoor pen. We watched kids being zipped around on amusement park rides. We visited a car museum and art gallery and viewed a parade and a circus performed by Russians and Eastern Europeans. In retrospect, I thank my parents for having patiently hauled me and my two kid sisters around jam-packed Canadian National Exhibition fairgrounds every August in Toronto. As I discovered now at Everland, amusement parks aren't really created for adults in mind. We departed exhausted at 9:00 p.m. and took a room just outside Yongin at the pedestrian Everpark Motel in the nondescript roadside area of Jeondae village.

In the morning, fabulously sunny days continuing, we strolled from the motel on the side of the road to the nearby Seoun Fruit Market — a large outdoor covered stall. A short, wiry man with a brush cut and scar on his face, maybe in his fifties, was sorting fruit. He seemed to be the owner. He looked Korean but had green eyes. Indigenous Koreans don't have green eyes, theirs are uniformly brown or black. The man was the only Korean I'd seen with green eyes, which I found fascinating.

"You see his eyes?" I whispered to Heju, out of his earshot.

"Yeah," she said.

"He's Korean ... right?"

"Yeah."

"Why does he have green eyes?"

"I don't know?"

"Maybe one of his parents is a Westerner. Let's ask about his eyes."

"I don't want to," she wisely cautioned.

What was he going to do: cuss us out? The question would need to be put sensitively, of course. "Just ask real politely. Just say, 'Excuse me sir, but I noticed you have nice green eyes,'" I suggested.

"It's not a good idea," Heju dissented skeptically.

Half a dozen customers were in the stall when Heju approached the man who was tending fruit. She said a few words to him in Korean. Immediately his demeanor altered and his mood darkened. He spat a litany of words, none of which I could understand, but it was obvious he wasn't wishing Heju a nice day. Then he turned his back to her.

"What did he say?" I asked her.

Heju replied stoically, "He told me, 'Don't ask me that fucking question. Why are you asking that fucking question? You ruined my whole day with that fucking question.'" She added pragmatically, "I told you we shouldn't have asked him."

Obviously not. But why did he have green eyes?

East of Yongin, on the outskirts of the nearby city of Icheon, is Chungkang College of Cultural Industries, where I taught English as a second language to students from 1999 to 2001. I wanted to show Heju the campus, so we headed east, cruising leisurely through peaceful, quiet countryside in the broad, green Charyeong hills.

Chungkang College was basically how I left it many years earlier: a handful of red-brick buildings built on the side of a low, rounded green mountain in a pretty wooded area twelve kilometers west of the small, old dusty city of Icheon. Chungkang's earthen soccer field was still there, the site of an infamous soccer match, where our English-language student team suffered a humiliating 17-0 smackdown at the hands of the high-flying, athletic computer science student squad. One of our players, "Charlie," played in heavy construction boots.

At the bottom of the campus is a short, narrow pretty dell replete with numerous rows of rice paddies. The dell dead-ends at a steep hill at Jisan Ski Resort. On the opposite side, over the low mountain ridge, the Jisan Country Club golf course is carved into the side of the surrounding slope. We drove through the dell to the steep road next to the ski hill. The valiant but desperately overwhelmed engine laboriously spurred the auto foot by foot up the steep incline. The dashboard red needle, measuring engine temperature, warned: BAIL NOW!

Finally reaching the crest, we parked at Jisan Country Club's parking lot and walked into its grand, sprawling carpeted clubhouse. Behind the long, wood-paneled front desk, an over-eager but polite, smiling young female clerk greeted us.

"We'd like to inquire about membership," I asked with all the gravitas a person wearing a baseball cap, shorts and sandals could muster. To join a private golf club in Korea about equals the cost of four years' tuition at Harvard.

The young lady took our query seriously. "There's a 300 million won (U.S. $230,000) deposit, plus annual fees of twelve million won," she explained pleasantly. I nodded in sincere understanding. "I'll need a few days to think about it," I replied thoughtfully. She smiled and seemed to believe me.

Hundreds of golf courses dot the peninsula, and young Korean women, in particular, have been dominating world professional golf for years. But playing golf in this country is prohibitively expensive, and nearly all courses, such as Jisan Country Club, are private. Public courses for weekend hackers, costing, say, a reasonable $30 to $40 per round, are rare to non-existent.

I'd read an enlightening opinion piece in the *Korea JoongAng Daily* written by an expat corporate executive in Seoul and avid golfer named Matthew J. Deakin. After participating in corporate golf rounds in Korea, Matthew noted domestic business golf is designed as a feel-good experience, with missed putts, penalty strokes and shanked drives often overlooked and not included on the score card. This evoked memories of my middle school years when my golfing mates and I regularly completed rounds at Toronto's public Don Valley Golf Course's 18 holes with scores of ninety or so — our missed short putts, penalty strokes, lost balls and shanked drives always overlooked.

Matthew wrote that golfers on Korean courses aren't permitted to carry their own golf bags and have to ride carts seating four, generously outfitted with drinks, coolers, balls, tees, markers and first-aid kits. A caddy is also mandatory. These features don't come cheap, and a day on a course for a foursome can cost as much as $1,000. "The Scottish did not invent the game with the intention it would be only available to the richest people," Matthew concluded.

Aye, Laddie!

We slunk out of the clubhouse and strolled to the edge of the par-4, 18th green, where a foursome of businessmen was on the fairway hitting their final approach shots to the green. I focused on the quartet's player wearing a garishly bright and ugly yellow sweater, also the group's worst player. His ball lay 100 meters from the green, and it took him two strokes to reach the putting surface, then four putts to make it over the green's hump, finally sinking his fifth putt. His total for the hole was nine strokes or a quintuple bogey. I'm sure he jotted a one-over-par, bogey-five on his scorecard, as I would have done.

Departing the club we inched the Scoupe down the frighteningly steep slope adjacent to the ski hill, and Heju curiously unbuckled her seat belt and began to open the door.

"What are you doing?" I asked, puzzled.

"I'm getting ready to jump in case the brakes fail," she declared in dead seriousness.

We headed southwest through the greenery of the Charyeongs, a huge, glorious, orange-red sun sinking in the west painting the woods a variety of golden greens. We had the lonely road to ourselves, and I thoroughly enjoyed the decadence of driving under the speed limit, minus pesky, impatient drivers tailing us.

"I love this slow driving," I announced contentedly, just how Henry Ford intended motoring to be.

"At least you're not swearing," Heju said, referring to my penchant for castigating careless drivers daring to navigate too close to the Scoupe.

I had legitimate reason to be wary. Aggressive driving is the norm on roads. When I arrived in the country, road crashes resulted in more than 10,000 deaths annually, on average almost thirty motorists dying daily. Over time the annual road death rate decreased to about 6,000, still a totally unacceptable sixteen people dying per day. I'm adamant I'm not going to be included in this tragic list and zealously guard the space around my vehicle like a mama bear protecting her cubs.

We headed to Anseong County in Gyeonggi province to the Mirinae Holy Site, about forty kilometers south of the golf course. During the four Catholic purges in the 1800s, some persecuted Catholics sought sanctuary in Mirinae. Today, at about forty such holy sites across the peninsula, homage is paid to martyred Catholics. Mirinae is probably the best known. The most notable martyr is a Catholic priest named St. Andrew Taegon Kim, executed at age twenty-four in 1846 and buried at Mirinae. We arrived in Mirinae's general vicinity at dusk and found the secluded Hite Motel on the edge of Gosam Reservoir — a lovely small lake bound by woods.

At about six in the morning — rays of bright sunshine streaming through the motel room's large front window and opaque curtains — Heju woke up and strode to the middle of the room.

"What direction's the bed facing?" she asked me accusingly.

"I don't know?" I said groggily. I wasn't in the habit of taking compass readings in hotel rooms.

"I didn't sleep well," she said sourly, as if it was my fault. She went to the bedside table, withdrew the compass from my waist pack, returned to the center and aligned the needle. "The bed's facing north," she concluded disagreeably. "That's why my body's stiff. I need to sleep with the bed facing east-west."

Feng shui theory has that it's propitious for one's head to face east when sleeping. "I don't want my head facing north again!" Heju continued, aggrieved. "I feel like I have a blood clot. Too bad the bed isn't facing east."

I hoped Heju could hold on for the remaining two months of the trip. Obviously, the stress of traveling with me was having an adverse effect on her. I put my eye mask back on to block out the bright sunshine and resumed sleeping. It mattered little to me if my bed faced purgatory.

In the late morning's heat and mugginess, sky white and hazy, we departed "The Motel of Misaligned Beds" and drove to the Mirinae Holy Site through deathly quiet countryside. We turned off a country road onto a narrow side road moving through a short dell soon dead-ending at a steep low wooded mountain. On one side of the dell is a low, steep escarpment. On the other side is a most incongruent modern tall building resembling a glass pyramid. We parked in a large field among scores of cars and strolled to the building – a church. Today was Sunday and a Catholic service was beginning.

It was wonderfully cool inside; what a relief to be out of the blazing heat. The interior was spacious and quite grand. A soaring ceiling was lined with chandelier, white walls trimmed with wood. Stained-glass windows were high on each side and large, red-brick pillars ran the length of the structure. We sat in a pew off to one side, the place about a quarter full of parishioners.

Directly behind us were a mother and her two young boys — fast asleep. The boys' heads rested on their mother's lap, her head tilted back, eyes closed, mouth agape, dead to the world. Scanning the congregation, I noted many parishioners in similar states of semi-comatose repose. The priest began his sermon, in Korean, of course, and Heju translated. She whispered to me, "The priest's saying: 'I was poor as a kid. Look at my face ... I didn't get enough vitamins and nutrients. It's not healthy. But look at your faces ... they're healthy. Nowadays, people rush and use computers and are busy making money. They ask themselves, 'Do I have more money than my neighbor?' But look at St. Andrew Taegon Kim — he died young, his life was very short, but he was always with God.'"

Numerous times we stood to sing hymns and to pray. This was problematic, because the space between pews was extremely narrow and tight, my knees scrunched against the back of the pew in front. I felt like I was squeezed into an economy-class seat on a fully-booked plane. At the service's conclusion, the priest announced: "The church is a big property and takes a lot of money for upkeep. We're poor and don't have much money. Parishioners don't offer much. Please give generously at the offering."

I decided to investigate which of my neighbors skimped on paying their fair share. Beginning with the last row, parishioners began walking to the front to deposit money into a wood box. When our row headed up, I kept a sharp eye out for who had deep pockets and short arms. The woman on my left dropped in a paltry 2,000 won, and the lady on my right inserted a meager 4,000 won. Heju managed a measly 3,000 won and I sneaked in a negligible 1,000 won. I had an excuse though: I wasn't religious and the trip was expensive. My offering was actually closer to 500 won, after subtracting the cost of the pen I'd inadvertently pilfered from the pew. God have mercy on my soul. Between the four of us we gave an uninspiring 10,000 won. Little wonder the church lacked funds.

After the service, we ascended the stairs to the second floor to view a collection of torture devices used against Catholics during the purges. There was a six-pronged club and a solid oak paddle used to inflict beatings. A thick type of rope-saw would be rapidly pulled back and forth until flesh ripped. "Scissors" was two wooden poles inserted between knees and twisted until bones broke. Beheading by sword was the ultimate punishment. A plaque commemorated three French priests — Bishop Laurent-Marie-Joseph Imbert and Reverends Pierre-Philibert Maubant and Jacques-Honoré Chastan, beheaded in Seoul on September 21, 1839.

We moved outside to the grounds' far corner to a small memorial chapel where a handful of parishioners were waiting in line to be blessed by a priest. When Heju and I came before the priest, he held what looked to be a small musical reed he blessed us with.

"It's a small sliver of Andrew Taegon Kim's toe bone," Heju whispered.

After Andrew Kim was executed in 1846, the state wouldn't permit followers to perform funeral rites. Several Catholics clandestinely carried his body the sixty kilometers from Seoul to Mirinae for burial.

In 1984, Pope John Paul II visited Korea to commemorate the nation's 200 years of Catholicism and canonized 103 Korean martyrs, including St. Andrew Taegon Kim, the first papal canonization outside St. Peter's Basilica in Rome since the Avignon Papacy in the 1300s.

***

South of Mirinae, in Anseong County's bucolic countryside, was our next destination: Hanawon Settlement Support Center for

North Korean Refugees. Hanawon was established by the National Intelligence Service (NIS) in 1999 to help ease the transition for newly-arrived North Korean defectors. Defectors first undergo an intensive one-month interrogation by the NIS – to weed out spies, then spend a mandatory three month orientation at Hanawon.

An *International Herald Tribune* article explained that the facility teaches defectors how to use ATM machines, how not to get conned by online scammers and how to use flush toilets. The latter is an apparent rare commode ... sorry, commodity in the North. During the first decade of the center's existence, 14,247 North Koreans went through the program. Now, the number is about 34,000, despite draconian controls imposed by North Korea's leader Kim Jong-un.

Understandably, authorities aren't keen for the public to snoop around Hanawon, but for a nosy, marauding amateur journalist pair like Heju and me, it was a must-see. Not surprisingly the address isn't readily available on Google. When we departed Mirinae in late afternoon and began motoring through rural backwoods in search of the center, we had only an inkling of its general location and were relying more on serendipity than anything else to find it.

Some miles ahead we pulled into a lonely gas station, the only man-made structure for miles around, and asked the attendant if he knew of Hanawon.

"Just along the road and turn right," he said.

Serendipity!

At a bend on a nearby lonely back road suddenly appeared Hanawon, its tall, red-brick front wall paralleling the road. At both ends, walls ran back and up steep wooded hills. Behind the front wall, we could make out the tops of several red-brick buildings. We stopped at the front gate and approached the guard office.

"We're writing a travel book on Korea and would like to include Hanawon. Is there anyone we can talk to?" Heju asked the guard.

The man got on the phone, spoke briefly, hung up then asked us to wait. About ten minutes later, a Hanawon official whom I guessed was about thirty-five, approached through the gate leading from the inner grounds.

"Can I help you," he asked in English, anxiously looking over his shoulder and eying me with suspicion, appearing fidgety and tense, like he'd just downed three cups of coffee.

I explained the reason for our visit.

"I really appreciate your interest but I can't tell you much," he continued in English. "We're under Blue House and national security rules, and we don't want to cause problems between North and South. North Korean spies can find defectors here, and it would be dangerous for their relatives back home."

Spies attempt to identify defectors in the South and relay the information back to North Korea, where relatives can be punished and sent to a gulag. Of forty-nine North Korean spies detected between 2003 and 2013 in South Korea, twenty-one had arrived under the pretext of defecting.

"I understand, but would it be okay to ask a few questions?" I tried.

The man hesitated but agreed. Suddenly, his gaze narrowed to the front of my shirt where underneath it ran a wire attached from my mini digital recorder in my pant pocket to a tiny microphone under my top shirt button. I recorded dialogue this way to ensure audio transcripts.

"Are you recording this?" he asked tersely.

"Yes, I tape all conversations for the book," I said.

"You need to turn it off," he ordered, obviously a trained professional, the only person I talked with the entire journey to note the microphone.

I complied, extracting a small notepad and pen from my waist pack.

"Are you going to write about this?" he inquired.

"Yes."

"Don't write my name. Don't write it for a newspaper or magazine."

"I won't," I said, my book being neither a newspaper nor magazine. "How are defectors treated in the South?" I asked.

"Lots of people treat them like they're aliens, but they're ordinary people."

"Do they adapt well to life in the South?"

"Ninety percent say they're worried about life here. Kids adapt faster than adults."

"What's the hardest part?"

"For everyone who goes through a new culture it takes time to adapt. It's the same for North Koreans in the South."

In the North's rigidly controlled society, citizens are discouraged to think for themselves. At Hanawon, after three months of structured daily routine, defectors are released into the dog-eat-dog, competitive, fast-paced world of South Korea where they need to think independently and succeed. They often choose to live in hectic Seoul.

The man repeated, "You sure you're not going to write about this for a newspaper, or as a political piece?"

"I'm sure."

"Don't write my name."

"I won't."

Then he abruptly said he had no more time, bade goodbye, turned and walked back through the gate into the facility.

His reticence was understandable — six gulags in the North hold an estimated 150,000-plus political prisoners in ghastly, inhumane conditions with scant chance of release, according to both defectors and a U.S. State Department human rights report.

In the fascinating, jolting 2000 memoir, *The Aquariums of*

Pyongyang: Ten Years in the North Korean Gulag, defector Kang Chol-hwan – with French journalist Pierre Rigoulot – presented a first-hand account of life in the concentration camps and the barbaric cruelty imposed by the dynastic Kim regime. In 1979, Kang was nine when his family was imprisoned at notorious Yodok prison in remote mountains about 120 kilometers northeast of Pyongyang. The family's crime was that Kang's grandfather had been accused of being an agent for the Japanese and the entire family was dragged off.

Kang said his grandmother, mother and sister died from starvation at Yodok. He witnessed hundreds of deaths from hunger, beatings, neglect, disease the elements and execution. Prisoners worked outdoors up to seventeen hours a day. Hunger was a constant, and worms, frogs, salamanders and rodents caught in fields and forests by inmates were eaten to survive. Winters were bitterly cold, prisoners provided meager clothing – mere rags. Once inmates reached teenage years they were ordered to attend executions of those who'd attempted to escape from Yodok. Seventy-six percent of defectors to the South say they've witnessed state-sanctioned public executions. Typically, the North publicly executes "criminals." Kang witnessed fifteen executions at Yodok.

In the book he described one: "The whole camp walked to a bend in a river and sat in front of a huge boulder. Farther away was a small flatbed truck containing the condemned man. He was screaming, 'You bastards! I'm innocent!' Then there was silence. The guards pulled him from the truck to the big boulder in front of the crowd. Mere skin and bones, his hair wild, with bruises, crusts of dried blood and bulging eyes, he resembled an animal. The man's mouth was full of stones: the guards had crammed them in to stop him from yelling. He was tied to a post at eye, chest, and waist levels. From five meters, the first volley of shots killed him, cutting the top rope. The second volley sliced the chest rope. The final one cut the lower rope. The corpse fell forward into the pre-dug pit."

In 1987, now nineteen, Kang was released from Yodok. He reestablished contact with a friend he'd met at camp, whose family was released in 1983. In 1991, the friend's father was accused of criticizing North Korea's Supreme Leader Kim Jong-il, and the family was sent back to Yodok.

Kang escaped North Korea in 1988 by crossing the Yalu River into China and onward to South Korea. When former U.S. president George W. Bush read Kang's book, he asked to meet the author and Kang visited the White House in 2005. The 2012 Asian edition of *Time* lauded Kang a hero. Today, he's a journalist at the major *Chosun Daily* newspaper in Seoul.

Under a setting sun, Heju and I stood in front of Hanawon Center wondering what to do next. Across the road through a narrow crook in the hills was a series of multi-terraced rice paddies reaching far back, and we puttered in the car on the narrow concrete lane, passing rice paddies, stopping at the tiny hamlet of Samjuk about a kilometer from Hanawon. Samjuk has a handful of small dwellings. I positioned the car facing Hanawon, withdrew my binoculars, and began scanning the center. Its outer walls reach back up the hill and disappear in woods. Camouflaged guard towers along the wall are hidden by trees. Inside the compound are low buildings and courtyards.

Suddenly, hundreds of defectors begin streaming out from buildings into a courtyard. Women wore red sweaters with white stripes and black track pants with red stripes. Men had on white shirts and black pants. (Koreans love uniforms.) It was 6:30 p.m. Apparently, North Koreans eat, just like the rest of us.

Heju and I were startled when two village grandmothers quietly walking along the lane from behind suddenly appeared next to the car. Our nerves were on edge. It wasn't every day two average schmucks were involved in international espionage.

We chatted briefly to the ladies. "Do you see North Koreans from Hanawon in Samjuk?" we asked.

"North Korean kids sometimes study at Samjuk Elementary School, but we haven't seen North Korean adults here," said one.

Our cover blown, we had no choice but to immediately terminate the mission. I drove on the lane to the main road, then high-tailed it away from Hanawon. I didn't know the name of the nondescript little rural roadside outpost we stopped at twenty minutes later. I didn't particularly want to know, either. We took a room in a motel on the main street.

"Let's eat in tonight," I said.

"We eat in every night, anyway," Heju replied, which was mostly true.

For dinner we had cans of corn and tuna brought in from the car trunk. I bolted shut the room door and closed the curtains. Spies may have spotted us using binoculars to probe Hanawon. Heju and I were ill-prepared for the possible ghastly demise of two, in-over-their-head gumshoes.

CHAPTER 8

Haengchi: Hometown of Korea's Famous Son

The tiny village of Haengchi should be known to most Koreans – it's the hometown of Ban Ki-moon, the second-most renowned Korean, after the seven lads in the hit boy band, BTS. From 2007 to 2016, Ban was the United Nations' eighth Secretary-General, the first Korean to hold the lofty title.

Ban was born in Haengchi near the small city of Eumseong – where he attended school. Eumseong is tucked away in the northwest corner of land-locked North Chungcheong province. When Ban was designated to succeed Kofi Annan to lead the UN in October 2006, there was so much joy in Eumseong and in the local region that 50,000 citizens celebrated in a soccer stadium in the neighboring city of Chungju.

An *International Herald Tribune* feature I'd read on Ban included the intriguing sidebar that some Koreans believed Bodeok Mountain – the eminence dominating Haengchi village – was of such immaculate feng shui symmetry that its positive life-altering feng shui played no small role in catapulting Ban to his top-gun position. To absorb these positive rays, busloads of Koreans from across the peninsula are drawn to Bodeoksan. I envisioned a one-plus-one deal: scuttlebutt on Ban Ki-moon from Haengchi villagers and eternal prosperity from Bodeoksan's providence.

***

We awoke in the morning. Thank god — considering our close encounter yesterday at Hanawon. Fortunately, we hadn't been poisoned or kidnapped.

We spent much of the day exploring locally, then in early evening navigated south to Haengchi. As the crow flies, Haengchi is only about sixty or so kilometers southeast of Hanawon. But we weren't crows and couldn't fly and the Charyeong Mountains surrounded us. There seemed no such thing as a straight road in these parts. We zigzagged through countryside and finally entered the smooth, lonely, bereft-of-vehicles National Route 37. We passed remote hills and abundant woods moving into North Chungcheong province.

I have no idea why North Chungcheong is referred to as "North." Glance at a map of Korea and you'll note North Chungcheong is predominantly east, not north of its sister province South Chungcheong. When the singular province of Chungcheong was split in two in 1894, cartographers obviously had downed too much *soju*. More than a century later the government hasn't bothered to rectify the error.

North Chungcheong is distinct — the only landlocked province in the country, and home to just 1.5 million people; contrasting to an astonishing 25 million residents in Gyeonggi province, including Seoul and Incheon.

We exited No. 37 to Eumseong in darkness. Like many towns and cities in the country, Eumseong is built on a plain surrounded by hills and low mountains. High in the distance, across the plain, was the genesis of a mysterious, laser-like shaft of bright white light. At a local supermarket, loading up on our daily rations of bread, sliced ham, processed cheese, fruit and orange juice, we inquired about the beam.

"It's from a Buddhist temple on Gaseop Mountain," said the young woman behind the counter of the mountain's 700-meter tall ridge line.

I asked her for directions to nearby Haengchi.

"I don't know," she said. We tried her two co-workers, but they weren't familiar with Haengchi either.

"Ban Ki-moon was born in Haengchi," I mentioned.

"I didn't know that," the woman replied. I found this puzzling. Were I say, a resident of a small town in Canada, and our prime minister was born in the adjacent town, I think I'd know this. I'd erroneously assumed that every Eumseongite would instantly recognize Haengchi as the genesis of the distinguished Ban Ki-moon.

Heju and I checked into a nearby motel for the night.

***

Our aim for the day was to explore Eumseong and Haengchi, but torrential rains limited us to a brief outdoor afternoon stroll. We spent a relaxing day confined to our motel room. We used some of the down time to review newspaper clippings, to learn about forthcoming sites, and some of the time to destroy brain cells, viewing agog, a Korean television staple known as the gag show. Gag shows feature "celebrities" participating in often inane, unscripted activities, who usually spontaneously ad-lib in an effort to produce comedy. More often than not the end result is the only laughs are from the participants themselves. The genre's only purpose seems to be to fill an overabundance of empty television airtime. As we channel-surfed, we noted several celebrities performing on one particular gag show, simultaneously participating on a different gag show on a competing network. On Sunday evenings, airwaves offer live, clearly intelligent and funny comedy sketches; gag shows don't fall in this category.

Under a clear sky, the following morning we puttered through slow, dreary, laid-back Eumseong. Fortunately, we encountered a traditional five-day market, or *jeontong oiljang* – roughly translating to "Going to different towns and coming back every five days." I love outdoor public markets: they are vibrant and interesting, offer fresh produce and varieties of food, and items are below retail price.

Eumseong Market is by a quiet road on the edge of town next to a park. We parked then ambled on the sidewalk to the first vendor, whom I'll refer to as "Birdman." Birdman was a purveyor of more than three dozen cages of birds lining the sidewalk, a plethora of colorful birds' delightful cacophony of chirps and cheeps filling the air.

"The Birdman of Eumseong," I joked to Heju, a pun on the 1962 movie *Birdman of Alcatraz*, starring Burt Lancaster. She didn't get the reference.

Birdman explained that this market was in Eumseong on the 2nd, 7th, 12th, 17th, 22nd and 27th of each month. Today was May 2. Tomorrow, it would be in Wonju sixty kilometers northeast; the next day in Jochiwon sixty kilometers southwest; then in Geumwang, north of Eumseong. It was like a traveling circus. Incredibly, for 600 years, the market has been serving Eumseong and the local region. I'd seen photographs taken in the late 1800s of long-haired, bearded peddlers in grubby white garb, conveying bamboo items piled high on wood A-frames – *jige* – on their backs.

"Do you sell many birds?" we asked Birdman.

"Some days good, some bad," he tersely replied. I suspected this wasn't his best day.

Farther along the sidewalk at a quasi-alleyway were more market stalls and peddlers. Off to the side, a middle-aged female vendor was selling husky-type dogs sitting in large, deep cardboard boxes. We chatted and asked her if her dogs got exercise.

"Of course they do! All my dogs exercise with me every morning," she retorted. But judging from her wide, ample backside resting comfortably on a stool, she hadn't done physical activity since elementary school. I tried another query but was rebuked. "Don't ask so many questions!" she ordered.

Nearby was a three-by-two-feet cage holding sixteen small dogs barely able to move. I didn't like this aspect of the market. Laws protecting animals aren't well enforced in South Korea.

Twelve shivering rabbits sat in a cage two feet long by 1.5 feet wide.

"Why are they shivering?" we asked the owner. It was a sweltering thirty degrees today.

"They're scared," she said, matter-of-factually.

In another big cardboard box were scores of quacking ducks, chirping chickens, roosters and geese, the pungent stench of feces and urine piercing the hot humid air. We moved through the alley passing stalls of plants, dried fish, clothing, spices, cookware and ginseng.

At one stall holding a variety of hats, the engaging and loquacious owner, Eum Doo-hyun, spoke English.

"I've been with Eumseong Market for thirty years," Mr. Eum said. "Before that I worked as a sign painter for movie theaters, but in the 1970s cinemas changed from painted signs to posters and I lost my job."

Mr. Eum's surname was rare, the first I'd heard of "Eum" as a surname in South Korea. There are 286 different indigenous surnames in the country, prominent among them being about ten million Kims, seven million Lees and four million Parks. Koreans often identify themselves by their forefather's birthplace. Ban Ki-moon, for example, is an Eumseong Ban. Heju is a Gyeongju, South Gyeongsang Kim. There are said to be 4,170 places of origin in Korea.

Mr. Eum said, "I guess my name originated about 600 or 700 years ago, at about the time Eumseong Market did." He added jokingly, "Maybe my name is from the Eum in Eumseong?"

Not exactly. After some research, Heju discovered the name Eum originated in China, first appearing in Korea in the Goryeo Dynasty, which ruled from AD 918 to 1392.

Sadly, outdoor markets have been in decline. In 2005, 1,660 markets were running. In 2017, there were 1,450. The reduction correlates to a surfeit of mega-discount supermarket and department store chains that began popping up in the 1990s. Now, when new subdivisions of apartment complexes are developed in Seoul and in other towns and cities, outdoor markets usually aren't in the plans.

"Business isn't so good these days. Politicians don't want outdoor markets anymore," lamented Mr. Eum.

We watched as a frail, severely hunchbacked elderly woman resolutely pushed a rickety old cart full of cardboard past Mr. Eum's stall. It isn't unusual to observe such elderly women in rural areas who suffer from curvature of the spine after decades spent bending over crops.

Mr. Eum sighed and said, "We're the eleventh-richest country in the world, but compared to the U.S., we're so far behind."

We bade goodbye and drove off to find Haengchi. Moving through the center of Eumseong, we passed the main post office, where half a dozen employees were in the rear parking next to a new postal delivery truck, kneeling and bowing on a mat on which were bowls of food.

"What are they doing?" I asked Heju, puzzled.

"They're blessing the truck so it'll be safe to drive. It's an old custom in Korea."

I replied skeptically, "Wouldn't it safer to just drive slower instead of praying?"

A few kilometers southwest of Eumseong at a thin strip of agricultural land running parallel to the road, bordered by a heavily-wooded steep mountain ridge, we pulled onto a bumpy concrete lane, a handful of old country dwellings and farm sheds along it.

A solitary, elderly woman was sauntering along the lane. Through the open car window, Heju called to her, "Excuse me, is Ban Ki-moon's home here?"

The woman turned to us, her expression severe, and muttered, "Up ahead."

We were in Haengchi! "Do you get good feng shui from Bodeoksan?" I announced.

She glared back at me, and commanded darkly, "Just follow the road," and strode off.

The lane dead-ended at a house next to a couple of farm sheds. We exited the car and looked around. Behind the sheds were little dusty plots of earth with red pepper, tobacco and rice growing in them. The village was quiet and still, not a soul around. Haengchi seemed to have seen better days. Bodeok Mountain dominated, its long, high ridge line loomed strikingly even and symmetrical. "It's the shape of a bird spreading its wings," Heju announced admiringly.

"Where are the visitors and buses?" I asked. I'd been expecting an army of bohemian-type people, arms reaching in unison to the mountain, soaking up the rays of prosperity.

Suddenly, a man appeared from behind the shed, and we tried conversing with him, but he uttered only one or two words at a time, and mostly stared silently and intently at us. A few minutes later, a group of about a dozen men came walking along the lane toward us. We exchanged salutations.

"Would you know if anyone in the village is from Ban Ki-moon's family?" we inquired, the men appearing to be in their fifties and sixties.

The fellows looked bemused. One announced brightly, "We're Ki-moon's family ... We're his second cousins!"

Hallelujah! Bodeok Mountain's feng shui did work.

One of the men, Ban Ki-jong, told us, "My father's the twin brother of Ki-moon Ban's father."

The men lived in Eumseong but were in Haengchi to attend a family meeting. "Only about twenty people live in Haengchi now," one Ban said. "About fifty people were here when Ban Ki-moon was a boy." They confessed Haengchi folk are sometimes bothered by out-of-towners arriving at Bodeoksan for its karma. "On holidays, as many as 300 people visit the mountain."

Bodeoksan emitted positive energy, they believed. But Ban Ki-moon's ascension to UN chief was due to perseverance, intelligence and charisma, not feng shui, they insisted. "Only once every hundred years does someone like Ban Ki-moon come along." The men were immensely proud of their cousin.

The fellows were engaging, well-spoken and polite. Real gentlemen. It wasn't difficult to ascertain that Ban Ki-moon is of the same solid pedigree. (The man we'd met a few minutes earlier was also a Ban, but polio had struck when he was a boy and had affected his mind.)

Korean newspapers were fond of reporting Ban Ki-moon was so poor as a kid he trudged ten kilometers daily on foot back and forth to school, where he excelled. "Is it true he walked ten kilometers?" I queried.

The Bans grinned, and one admitted, "Well, maybe closer to three or four kilometers."

After being named UN Secretary General, Ban — accompanied by a large entourage of assistants, staff and press — visited Haengchi. "We met him in here, but he only had time to shake our hands. He had lots of people with him," a Ban said.

The men departed to attend their meeting. Heju and I ambled over to the base of Bodeoksan. On its lower slope is a large landscaped swath of grass with a series of burial mounds, each with a low marble platform. We strolled among the plots, counting seventeen rows of mounds and a total of 131 graves. On one gravestone is the name of the first Ban who'd arrived from China in Korea, buried here in 1643. In South Korea there are only about 4,000 Bans. Ban Ki-moon is an eleventh generation Ban.

Despite standing at the foot of the mountain, we were unable to detect any perceptible positive manifestations from it.

***

Now early evening, we departed Haengchi, proceeding thirty kilometers southwest to the small city of Jincheon. In the passenger seat, Heju was holding up a large calendar featuring twelve color photographs of a dozen small ancient bridges in regions around the country. One photo was of a millennium-old, granite-block foot bridge named Jincheon Nong-gyo (gyo translates to bridge). Jincheon Nong Bridge crosses a minor river in Gugok County just east of Jincheon. We were on our way.

Under a setting sun, we cruised leisurely through picturesque quiet dells, past wooded hills, and alongside a still dark green lake. In a lonely, woodsy farming area in Gugok County — unable to locate the bridge — we stopped on the side of a country road at a small barn, cows being milked by machine. We asked a worker for directions to the bridge, and she pointed up the road. A short way ahead we turned onto a concrete lane that slipped through a tunnel underneath Jungbu Expressway 35. Once through the tunnel, the lane dead-ended at a shallow river with gently sloping muddy banks, a stone bridge spanning the water, woods lining the far bank. We were the only ones here. Heju held up the calendar photo – it matched the bridge before us. At the river bank was a plaque confirming this was Jincheon Nong-gyo – ninety-three meters long, constructed about 1,000 years ago in the Goryeo Dynasty. Large granite blocks spaced about a meter apart in the river supported wide flat stones to walk across the bridge.

In near darkness we ambled onto the stone blocks. About halfway across we were suddenly accosted by a handful of tiny, ravenous flies that obviously hadn't eaten in weeks, their sharp fangs sinking into our soft flesh, removing chunks. The incisions were similar to those of the tiny black fly – the notorious scourge of Canadian woods during spring. Female black flies feed off animal and human blood.

"They're getting me!" Heju cried.

"Me too!" I hollered.

We stood momentarily dumbfounded, frozen to the spot, like a deer caught in headlights. The bugs were signaling to their comrades to join the feast. Suddenly, we were set upon en masse, in danger of being bitten to death. Next-day newspaper headlines would trumpet: "Duo Nipped to Death on Bridge."

We sprinted to the car, appearing like a screaming Tippi Hedren running on a beach road fleeing crazed seagulls in Alfred Hitchcock's famous thriller *The Birds*. We swatted wildly at the blood-thirsty, frenzied insurgents. We flung open the car doors, dove in and slammed them shut. Bugs followed us in. Thousands more massed outside, clamoring to join their brothers and sisters. Having already tasted the sweet, succulent nectar of our hemoglobin, they were in near states of hysteria for seconds.

We spent a few panicked minutes smiting insects dead with rolled-up newspapers. After exterminating them, we finally relaxed a bit. I withdrew my magnifying glass from my waist pack and held it against my driver's side window to examine the critters crawling on the exterior pane.

"My god ... they're aliens!" I exclaimed, the bugs magnified thirty times in size, reminiscent of mutations in a science fiction-horror film, their massive, fierce pincer-like mandibles rapidly opening and closing. Little wonder their bites were so piercing. I'd never seen such jaws.

"Let's get out of here," I declared with some alarm, and started the engine and proceeded through the tunnel onto the desolate country road, our headlight beams cutting through the gray-black darkness. I sped up to try to get rid of the bugs still clinging on to the windows. They hung on with determined resolve. They were definitely Korean.

"I'm going to speed up more," I said, and accelerated to eighty kilometers per hour. The demons wouldn't budge, their feet coated with super glue. "How am I going to get rid of them?" I yelped.

Heju nonchalantly advised, "Just open your window and they'll fall off."

She was a mad-hatter! "If I open it they'll get us!"

She sighed and ordered, "Just open it."

Doing as commanded, I slowly lowered the window and the insects tumbled off. Heju just shook her head.

We puttered west into what I believe was the city of Jincheon. The road atlas indicated it was Jincheon, yet there wasn't a single sign anywhere on the road saying it was Jincheon. We cruised into its small downtown on its main street, shops awash in a multitude of bright neon lights. Spotting a police station on a back lane, I pulled into its parking lot. "I'm going to ask the police if this is Jincheon. If it is Jincheon, I'm going to ask why there aren't signs saying it is," I complained.

We entered the old building and exchanged salutations with several officers behind the front desk. Without further preamble, I asked, matter-of-factually, in Korean, "Is this Jincheon?"

"Yes," replied an officer.

"Well, why isn't there a single sign anywhere on the road saying it is Jincheon? It might be a good idea to put up a sign or two to let drivers know they're in Jincheon. And when we leave Jincheon tomorrow, we'll be heading to Cheonan (the next city west), but there isn't a single road sign in town saying where to exit for Cheonan."

The kindly officers were very apologetic. One magnanimously announced in English, "We'll give you an accord."

"Sorry ... a what?" I asked, puzzled.

"An accord," he repeated.

An upgrade to our lowly Scoupe would be greatly appreciated. "If they want to give us a Honda it's fine with me," I said to Heju.

"He means an escort," she replied, in a tone reserved for those without all their neurons firing. "He's volunteering to give us a police escort out of town."

Oh! You had to love the officers, but I still preferred the Accord. We thanked him but politely declined. Being close to 8:00 p.m., dinner was calling.

We drove on the old main street, parked on the side of the road, and entered Lotteria – South Korea's fast-food burger restaurant chain – bereft of customers. We ordered a couple of burgers.

After dinner, we strolled the sidewalk and sneaked into The Donut – a tiny, independent utilitarian shop. I loved donuts. The owner was a loquacious, twenty-something young man named Yoo Dong-hee, who'd studied in the U.S. and spoke fluent English. It was quickly apparent that Dong-hee was aggrieved.

"I wanted to open a Dunkin' Donuts in Jincheon, but Dunkin' Donuts doesn't permit franchises in towns with less than 100,000 people," he said sourly. Jincheon has under 70,000 people.

He continued vindictively: "But in my shop, I can put donuts out on the shelf any time I want. At Dunkin' Donuts, they have to stop putting out new donuts on shelves in the evening."

"Why?" I asked.

"Because if there are too many donuts on the shelves, customers will think they aren't selling well."

The things you learn.

We found a motel in town. Being early May, and days hot, one would naturally assume indoor heating isn't needed. Our room was stifling, the central heating on, my thermometer recording a balmy twenty-eight degrees Celsius in the room.

We called the manager on the room phone, and asked, "Can you turn off the heat?"

"Our customers like it hot," he answered. We opened the window.

CHAPTER 9

Cheonan: Two Independence-Fighting Korean Ladies

We rolled west from Jincheon, crossing into South Chungcheong province, the late morning dry, hot and thirty degrees. The lonely landscape was sparsely inhabited. The road carved through narrow slices of agricultural plains, interspersed by numerous steep wooded hills. On a lonely, almost unpopulated plain, we came to the Yu Gwan-sun Memorial Hall – a low, formal white building standing alone on the side of a country road. We were in Yongdu in Byeongcheon County – Yu Gwan-sun's birthplace.

Yu Gwan-sun is well-known in Korea due to her heroic opposition to Japanese colonization of Korea. In early 1919 – after nine years of strangulating Japanese laws and decrees – Koreans had reached their collective breaking point and launched a series of nation-wide protests known as the March 1 Independence Movement.

To help contain the uprisings, the colonizers closed schools across the country. Yu, a sixteen-year-old student at Ewha Girl's High School in Seoul, returned to her hometown of Yongdu. On

April 1, she and her father led about 3,000 locals to the local Aunae Market, demanding independence for Korea. Japanese military police reinforcements were called in and opened fire, killing nineteen protesters, reportedly including Yu's parents. The family home was burned to the ground. Across Korea, similar protests were ruthlessly and brutally suppressed, thousands killed.

Yu was arrested and sent to a Japanese military police unit in Cheonan, the nearest city north. At a district court in Gongju, south of Yongdu, a Japanese judge sentenced Yu to three years' incarceration at Seodaemun Prison in Seoul. Yu, Seodaemun inmate number 371, reportedly antagonized her jailers, singing national songs and lecturing them on her country's sovereignty. On September 28, 1920, she died in prison. Unconfirmed reports were she'd succumbed to torture. Yu was seventeen.

At the Yu Gwan-sun Memorial Hall, we walked from the empty parking lot past a solitary shop selling among other things, incongruous black and white masks depicting Edvard Munch's painting *The Scream*. We took seats in a small screening room and began watching rare black-and-white documentary footage of the 1919 Independence Movement protests. We were the only ones in the room.

Soon, a handful of retirement-aged Korean male friends wandered in and took seats. After only a few minutes of viewing, one of the men stood and in an anguished cry, declared, "I can't take this anymore … it makes me too sad," and rushed out.

After the film, Heju and I took a brief stroll through the hall, then we entered the administrative office and spoke to a young, English-speaking employee named Lee Yeong-mi.

"Is it true Yu died of torture by the Japanese at Seodaemun Prison?" we asked.

"No documents exist to prove exactly how she died," Ms. Lee answered. "The Japanese kept records but destroyed them when they left Korea in 1945. We can't really say if Yu was tortured or not. She had a kidney problem which wasn't treated in prison and we think she probably died of that. That's according to witnesses."

Yu's body was retrieved from Seodaemun Prison by representatives of Ewha Girl's High School. An American teacher at Ewha, Jeannette Walker, and Yu's classmates, prepared the body at the school for burial. Her remains were interred at a public cemetery in Itaewon in Seoul. The cemetery was later razed and Yu's remains went missing. In 1962, she was posthumously awarded South Korea's Order of Merit for National Foundation. Every Korean recognizes Yu and her significance to the nation.

During the segment of our trip in Seoul about six weeks earlier, Heju and I had taken a guided tour of Seodaemun Prison on a cool March day. The prison is about a mile west of Gyeongbok Palace near the base of Inwang Mountain's steep granite south face. We strolled the sidewalk alongside a busy road paralleling the prison's tall red brick wall. We entered the facility's front gate into well-appointed spacious grounds. A path connects a series of formidable, red-brick prison blocks with watchtowers and an execution room.

Prior to Japan's colonization in 1910, there was no formal penal system in Korea. Mere straw huts held small-time criminals. In 1908, the Japanese began constructing a national prison system, building twenty-nine facilities, including Seodaemun Prison. Of those twenty-nine, only Seodaemun remains today.

There are no records indicating how many Koreans were interned at Seodaemun. The government estimated about 40,000 independence fighters and political prisoners were locked up along with regular criminals. The former were sometimes held for years without being formally charged, some tortured, some led to the execution chamber and hanged without prior notice.

Our tour guide was Bae Jeong-hee, a serious, officious woman of middle years who had an assiduous nature. Ms. Bae chose her words slowly and carefully in English like a surgeon making a delicate incision. Heju and I were her only patrons this day. The first building we entered was the History Hall, information presented in front of glass displays in Korean only. But the prison is a prominent tourist site visited by various nationalities, so written explanations in several languages seemed logical.

Behind one glass case was a thick, pyramid-shaped straw hat shaped like an upside-down pail. Inmates escorted to Seodaemun by Japanese guards were forced to wear the mask in public as a form of humiliation. Two small slits were for the eyes, the straw reaching down to the shoulders. Also on display was a horse whip used by Japanese guards to punish prisoners.

"Hundreds of new laws were made by the Japanese, including the 1912 'whipping decree,'" Ms. Bae said.

On the wall was a large black and white photo of three Korean men tied to stakes in a field being shot by a Japanese firing squad. "When Korean guerrillas were arrested, they were killed on-site, without trial," Ms. Bae said. Another photo depicted a Korean man without ears and an arm, said to be severed by a Japanese soldier's sword. A drawing illustrated a girl with no hands. "Two Japanese policemen cut her hands off because she carried the Korean flag," our guide said.

I was lobbing queries at Ms. Bae, which flustered her. "If you keep asking so many questions, we'll never finish the tour on time," she rebuked me.

But how were we supposed to learn if written explanations were in Korean and questions weren't encouraged? Korean logic sometimes baffles me.

Entering an adjacent hall, we were met by eerie music coming from loudspeakers. Three narrow, closet-like wood coffins stood upright against a wall, prisoners once wedged into one of these boxes for up to three consecutive days unable to move a muscle. When a poor wretch was released, he might be permanently physically and psychologically crippled. "They sometimes came out crazy," said Ms. Bae.

Each coffin was just five-feet, ten-inches tall, eighteen inches wide and six inches deep.

"Try standing in it," Heju suggested brightly to me.

"No way." I responded. I had an acute fear of tight, closed spaces. Claustrophobia ranks at about the top of my list of fears. Besides, at six-feet two-inches, I'd barely squeeze in. But Heju was only five-feet four-inches and fifty kilograms. Apparently, she wasn't claustrophobic. She voluntarily hopped in and closed the door.

"You okay in there?" I called.

"Yeah," came a muffled response.

About a minute later she emerged. "How was it?" I asked.

"I liked it," she said enthusiastically.

"You liked it?"

"Yeah."

"Wasn't it too small?"

"No, I did a little dance," she said cheerfully.

"A dance?"

"Yeah, I turned around and danced."

"But what if you had to spend three days in there?"

Heju's expression turned dark and she murmured pensively, "I'd go crazy."

"Yeah, just like Ms. Bae said."

Heju wandered across the floor and ducked into a dark waist-high exhibition room. A few moments later, a petrified scream emanated from within. I dashed over and peeked inside to find Heju sitting face-to-face with a life-like male mannequin wearing traditional Korean garb.

We walked downstairs into the shadowy, stone basement-torture chamber. Loudspeakers were broadcasting a continuous loop of anguished cries from Korean mannequin inmates, as Japanese mannequin guards harshly barked orders. On each side of the wide stone hallway is a row of cells, in each a Japanese guard torturing a Korean prisoner.

In one cell hangs an upside-down figure, feet shackled to the ceiling, the guard pouring pepper-laced water into his nose. In another cell a victim's head was being pushed into a tub of water. In a third a woman was sitting on a chair, hands handcuffed in front to the table top, the Japanese officer sitting opposite, thrusting a long needle in and out under her fingernails. Seodaemun management had done a good job presenting the Japanese in the worst possible light.

"What do Japanese visitors think when they see this?" I asked Ms. Bae.

"Some young Japanese say, 'I think this was made up by the Korean government.' Others say, 'Ah ... now I know what real history is — we didn't learn this kind of history in school.' They'd read in their textbooks the Japanese helped Koreans. Older Japanese say, 'We feel very sorry about this.'"

We stepped outside to the grounds, then went in a long, brick prison block once housing male inmates. A spacious, high stone hallway runs down the center of the block. On each side are cells with heavy, thick wood doors. "Prisoners weren't permitted to speak to one another or to guards. They had to push a lever in the cell to trigger a signal to attract a guard," said Ms. Bae. Inmates were sometimes crammed into a single cell forcing them to sleep in shifts.

We entered a cell, and high up on the stone wall is a small square opening with bars. Scrawled on the side wall is graffiti: "Kill the Japanese" and "Japanese should die." Management hadn't bothered to remove it.

Back outside we strolled the path and passed another prison

block once holding inmates afflicted with leprosy and other diseases. "The sick were quarantined but usually weren't given treatment or medication. Many died," said Ms. Bae.

Past a watchtower, in the ground's far rear corner, our guide stopped us in front of a large, innocuous-looking wood-type cabin — the execution chamber constructed in 1923. In front was an old tree.

"It's called the 'wailing tree,'" Ms. Bae said, and suddenly she began wailing in a pitying tone for dramatic effect: "The Japanese didn't announce executions until the last moment," she cried. "The condemned wouldn't know why he was being led outside his cell. Suddenly realizing he'd die, he'd hold onto this tree and cry and cry."

We entered the execution room, uniformed Japanese mannequin officers sitting in chairs on one side, opposite them the condemned mannequin prisoner, noose around neck, secured in a chair above a trap door. To covertly dispose of the bodies, the Japanese had dug a 200-meter-long tunnel under the chamber connecting to a cemetery outside prison grounds. In 1994, the tunnel was discovered when Seodaemun was converted to a tourist site. The Korean government took control of Seodaemun in 1945 and ironically executed convicts here until 1984, when a new penitentiary was constructed in Gyeonggi province.

Ms. Bae led us back to the front office past the meager remnants of the women's prison block where Yu Gwan-sun was held. The tour over, I asked officials if any Korean inmates imprisoned at Seodaemun many decades ago, were still alive.

The ladies kindly made some phone calls. It was discovered that indeed, an eighty-nine-year-old woman, a former prisoner, was living in Seoul. An appointment was made for Heju and me to visit the woman at her south Seoul apartment. What a rare and unexpected opportunity, to meet this apparent last living witness to this salient sliver of Korean history.

A few days later we were in Lee Byeong-hee's apartment. Ms. Lee was a handsome woman, no taller than five feet, of meager weight and unusually young-looking for 89. She was remarkably sharp and alert, with dark penetrating eyes and acute intelligence. Her iron will was tangible. Ms. Lee sat in a wicker chair in a tiny living room — doubling as a bedroom — in the narrow, cramped studio apartment where she lived alone. Her social worker, who visited her daily, sat on the floor with Heju and me. Ms. Lee began recounting her time at Seodaemun.

It was 1935, and Ms. Lee, sixteen, was employed at a Japanese-run garment factory in central Seoul. Her father and mother had moved the family from Daegu to Seoul when she was young. "My parents were hard-core, anti-Japanese activists," she said. "In Daegu, my father placed a bomb in a Japanese bank and was jailed. My brother, cousin and niece spent time behind bars too."

"I grew up hating the Japanese," she said, her eyes piercing. "I learned we had to fight them."

At the garment factory, Ms. Lee organized an anti-Japanese protest and was arrested. Japanese law dictated that prisoners had to be a minimum of seventeen to be incarcerated at federal Seodaemun Prison. Underage prisoners could be held at local jails for only a maximum of twenty-one consecutive days before being released. But the Japanese circumvented this.

"I'd be released after twenty-one days, rearrested the next day, sent back to jail for another twenty-one days, released and rearrested, sent back again and so on. I tried to escape once but the guard caught me. I just gave up. I thought I'd die in the jail."

Ms. Lee spent many months incarcerated at Seoul police station prisons in Seodaemun, Dongdaemun, Namdaemun and Euljiro.

She became most familiar with Dongdaemun Police Station Prison in east-central Seoul. "There were ten cells, ten prisoners in each, women separated from men. Jailers cut off our tie-ribbons from our *hanbok*, so we couldn't hang ourselves with them. There was no heat in the winter – we had to sleep on the floor with only one blanket."

Several women gave birth in jail. Mothers could only keep their babies for six months then had to give them up for adoption. The daily diet was barley and kimchi. No protein, beef, chicken or fish. Prisoners weren't permitted to talk but communicated among themselves using facial expressions and hand signals.

To glean the whereabouts of underground Korean guerrilla ringleaders, inmates such as Ms. Lee were tortured. "Regular criminals were sometimes tortured too, but not to the same extent as independence fighters," she said. "The most terrifying time came when the key turned in my cell door and my name was called. Each time I went into shock. When I was being tortured, I wanted to die. I'd cry, 'Kill me! Kill me!'"

She listed the various punishments. "Airplane" was when a detainee's hands were tied behind the back, hands secured to feet, the person suspended by rope from the ceiling until passing out. "I was tortured this way about thirty times at Dongdaemun Prison. They put a cloth in our mouths so we couldn't scream. It was so painful that each time I passed out after thirty minutes."

Other depravities included hot pepper mixed with water that was poured into a victim's nasal cavity. A cloth was drenched in hot water and placed over the face until passing out. "Chicken Feet" was when fingers and toes were hooked up to electric wires, the current switched on, and appendages curled up like chicken feet. Ms. Lee experienced this too. Heads were submerged in tubs of water, rods twisted through legs of a sitting inmate. "When there was an injury caused by torture, no medicine was given. There were no kind acts at police stations. None," Ms. Lee stated emphatically.

In the late Iris Chang's bestseller, *The Rape of Nanking*, Chang detailed the Japanese army's slaughter and execution of up to 300,000

Chinese citizens and soldiers in Nanking in 1937. My father as a boy, along with his brother, sister, father and mother, were held for about two years until the end of World War II in a Japanese internment camp in Indonesia, where they'd been living as Dutch nationals. My father's mother starved to death in the camp. It didn't surprise me to hear from Ms. Lee about Japanese cruelty. What was startling was her admission that the men who inflicted the torture were Korean!

"Japanese officers watched as Koreans tortured us," she recalled. "I hated the Koreans — they worked for money, they were traitors. The Japanese told us, 'I'm sorry, this is my duty, an order from my government. If you give us the information we need, we won't torture you.' The Koreans said nothing when they tortured us. They were cold-hearted. They didn't care about their own people."

Ms. Lee hated but admired the Japanese. "They fought to the death if they thought they were right. Koreans fought but were opportunistic. They changed sides if it benefited them."

After many months of being locked up at Seoul police station prisons, Ms. Lee turned seventeen. Neither charged with a crime nor told how long she'd be incarcerated for, she was led from Dongdaemun Police Station by foot and streetcar wearing the dreaded straw mask. "I felt like an animal on its way to the slaughterhouse," she said.

After listening to Ms. Lee for about ninety minutes, we asked if she'd like a break, to have a drink of orange juice from a bottle we'd brought. Ms. Lee talked slowly, Heju translating every sentence. The process took time.

"No thanks," Ms. Lee said. "I never got much to drink in prison, so to this day I can't drink much." She wanted to continue; she had the stamina of a horse.

When she arrived at Seodaemun, Ms. Lee was disrobed and handed a blue prison uniform, No. 1009 stitched on it. She was placed in the women's wing in a small cell with eight non-violent prisoners. Thin boards covered the cement floor. A barred opening was high up on the wall. No. 1009 sometimes jumped onto the wall, clung to the bars to peer out at nearby Inwang Mountain. During winter's bitter cold, cell floors would ice over. "Some prisoners died from cold and frostbite," she said.

A bucket of cold water was used to wash. Meager food rations were beans, barley and rice, sometimes accompanied by worms and bugs. Inmates weren't permitted to stand in cells. They were only allowed out to the grounds once a month. A blaring trumpet was their the 5:00 a.m. wake-up call. Ms. Lee often spent days meditating and knitting.

Female guards were both Japanese and Korean. "One Korean guard went to school with me. She told me, 'I'm sorry, you fight for your country, but I work for the Japanese government. My mother's sick. I need money to care for her and my family.'"

Ms. Lee said she heard shrieking when fellow prisoners were taken from their cells to the torture chamber. One woman in her wing had been convicted of conspiring with her boyfriend – the family servant – to kill her husband with whom she had six kids. The pair ran off but were apprehended. A Japanese judge ordered her hanged. When it came time to go to the execution room, the guards placed a hat over the woman's head and tied her hands behind her. "She was screaming," Ms. Lee remembered.

In 1939, now twenty, Ms. Lee's case finally went to trial. About twenty inmates were brought before a Japanese judge. He rattled off the sentences: Prisoner No. 17 ... three years; You ... six years; You ... three years.

"It was a kangaroo court so we threw stuff at the judge, and he had to leave the room. There was no justice. The Japanese had lawyers but we had no lawyers."

Under Japan's National Security Law, Ms. Lee was found guilty and handed a one-year sentence with three years' probation. Since she'd already served four years, she was free to go at midnight. She walked home that night. Not surprisingly, her muscles and joints were stiff and arthritic from lack of use. Her home was empty. Her father, wanted by the Japanese, had fled to China. Her mother had died from starvation and exposure to cold in the house.

"The Japanese guarded the house. They stood by and watched my mother die. They did nothing to help her," she said.

Ms. Lee fled to Beijing, where the Japanese jailed her there for six months, she said. She returned to Korea in 1942 and has remained ever since. She briefly married.

I wondered aloud if she could have taken a Japanese life. "If someone had asked me to assassinate a Japanese general when I was young, I would have, definitely," she said.

I suggested if Koreans had collectively opposed the Japanese, as she had vigorously and patriotically resisted, Korean history might have played out differently. Ms. Lee shook her head. "Koreans couldn't work together — too many were out for themselves," she said disdainfully. "Even some Japanese cared about Koreans, but if Koreans had the opportunity to become rich, they betrayed you. It's the same today."

At a Royal Asiatic Society lecture in Seoul I attended, the topic was the Japanese colonial period in Korea. At the lecture's conclusion, the RAS president, Mr. Jang — in his seventies, always impeccably dressed in a tie and suit — stood and proudly announced to the many attendees that "Korea benefited from Japan during the occupation. Japan helped Korea."

Flabbergasted, I was barely able to stop from standing and asking Mr. Jang what his thoughts were about all those Koreans who'd sacrificed their freedom and lives fighting for independence. Mr. Jang viewed Japanese colonialism through the narrow lens of economic development. The Japanese built railroads, bridges and harbors in Korea, but at the cost of loss of independence and freedom, of commodities plundered, of grand architecture destroyed, of treasures looted, of lives lost. Mr. Jang told me his family had owned a timber mill in Wonju, east of Seoul, during the occupation, and profited under the Japanese. Meanwhile, patriots such as Lee Byeong-hee saw jail time, and Yu Gwan-sun had died.

Over two days, Heju and I spent a total of seven hours at Ms. Lee's apartment, barely time to scratch the surface of her difficult life. Her social worker said Korean journalists sometimes visited Ms. Lee for an interview but only asked a couple of questions then left. "You've stayed for so many hours," she said.

"Because Ms. Lee's life is fascinating," I replied. The indefatigable, courageous woman who was the sole window to a seminal period of Korean history. Her life rightly should have been permanently recorded in a book. What a shame not a single Korean journalist or historian had the foresight to do so. Had I not been involved with the trip, I'd have jumped at the chance.

Lee Byeong-hee sadly passed away four years later. She was ninety-three. I hope she was honored with a venerable funeral she deserved.

***

From the Yu Gwan-sun Memorial Hall it was only a short hop north to Cheonan, to the renowned Independence Hall of Korea. I'd heard the hall was impressive. It opened on August 15, 1987, the forty-second anniversary of Korean independence.

On the periphery of Cheonan we drove to the hall on a long pretty boulevard lined with trees blooming profusely in white and pink spring blossoms. We parked at one of several expansive lots, then strolled on a long path leading to the hall. We walked through two enormous open squares, on each side, landscaped grounds, gardens and large ponds with big gold fish. In one square soars the fifteen-story "Monument to the Nation," resembling two slender arrowheads. At the far end of the second square, named Grand Plaza, rises Grand Hall, looming like a great tribute to ancient Rome. Open in front, the sixteen massive vertical columns support a colossal greenish-blue shale tiled roof. Ground to roof, Grand Hall ascends almost a hundred feet, equivalent to eleven stories, the largest tiled structure in Asia. I paced around a single vertical column and measured twelve meters in circumference. Behind Grand Hall, in the near distance, is Mount Heukseong's long ridge, its slopes blanketed by green woods.

On Grand Hall's back wall rises an enormous, five-story, white granite sculpture — "Statue of Indomitable Koreans" — comprising eight men and one woman resolutely charging ahead, arms pointed forward, representing the country's nine provinces.

How had such a massive sculpture been made? Off to the side of Grand Hall was an information office. Inside we asked a young Korean guide about the sculpture. She phoned her Independence Hall manager, who explained the process to her. After the call she relayed the information to us. A total of 274 wood blocks had been assembled in Grand Hall, forming one massive block. From this block the artist chiseled away creating the sculpture. One at a time, each individually chiseled wood block was transported to a workshop where a corresponding three-to-four-ton granite block was sculpted to the exact same dimension. Then, each finished granite block was hauled to Grand Hall, and placed in the open space where the wood block had been. The process was repeated 274 times until every wood block had been replaced with a granite one. What a Herculean effort! Returning to the sculpture, we examined it closely, detecting the outlines of individual granite blocks.

It was 4:00 p.m., and the hall closed at six, and many large exhibition halls awaited. We wandered into the expansive Hall of National Heritage housing cultural artifacts dating from prehistoric times to the present. A scattering of visitors was present. Moving from glass case to glass case, I got progressively aggrieved. More than a few written statements presented as empirical actually weren't.

One exhibit stated humans first wandered down from mainland Asia to today's Korea between 350,000 and 700,000 years ago. Hold on! Thus far, the oldest proven artifacts unearthed on the peninsula – stone implements found in 1964 by the Geum River in Gongju in South Chungcheong province – dated to 30,690 years old. In caves around Chungju in North Chungcheong province, tools and bones were uncovered by a Korean archaeological professor who claimed they were as old as 350,000 years. But independent testing debunked that assertion, and the find was dated to only several thousand years. At another exhibit was a large antiquated wooden pulley called Geojunggi – once used to lift heavy rocks for construction. Written was that the pulley had been invented by Korean named Jeong Yak-yong. Three weeks earlier in Suwon, tour guide Peter Bartholomew had stated the same pulley – used to build the summer palace – originated in Europe.

At another stop was this: "During Joseon, people were able to enter the political world and govern under kings." Bull! In Joseon, the masses – farmers, peasants, commoners, servants and slaves – were largely poverty-stricken, illiterate and relegated to a lifetime of labor. Unless born into the hereditary noble *yangban* class – constituting just 15 percent of the population – the average Lee stood as much chance of governing under a king as I did of winning the South Korean presidential election.

Such aggrandizement is meant to elevate Korea's standing but in my view it diminishes the integrity of the institute. Just before closing time, back at the information office, we inquired about the origin of the Geojunggi pulley. The same young lady who'd assisted us earlier checked the internet and told us it had been invented in China. Later, after some research, I learned that the Korean, Jeong Yak-yong, hadn't actually invented the pulley but had refined and adapted it to fit local needs. Independence Hall seemed to claim Jeong had conceived the entire pulley system.

There was so much to see and learn at Independence Hall that we decided to stay in Cheonan for the night and return tomorrow.

***

Next morning we were back in a hall viewing a series of poignant black and white photos depicting the Japanese occupation. One photo was of an elderly Korean man wailing and lying on the street in front of a massive Japanese flag raised in front of the colossal Japanese General Government Building, built directly in front of Gyeongbok Palace in central Seoul. Another photo was of Ahn Jung-guen, who shot and killed Ito Hirobumi — serving in Korea as Japan's governor-general from 1905 to 1909 — at the Harbin Train Station in Manchuria on October 26, 1909. Regarded as a hero both in Korea and China, Ahn was hanged on order of a Japanese court on March 26, 1910.

After strolling several hours through halls offering a plethora of information, in mid-afternoon we sought a respite for our weary brains. Venturing outside to an adjacent little park, we sat on a bench under bright, warm sunshine. Across from us on a bench was a couple I guessed to be in their seventies who were visiting Independence Hall.

"Let's ask them about the Japanese period," I said to Heju. I'd observed that knowledge of Korean history was sometimes lacking in the general populace.

We introduced ourselves. The pair said they were from Pyeongtaek, about thirty kilometers northwest of Cheonan.

"Would you know how Queen Min died?" I asked.

Queen Min, officially known as Empress Myeongseong — renowned in Korea — was the wife of King Gojong, who died in 1919. The queen was independent, highly intelligent and she vigorously opposed Japanese efforts to gain a foothold in Korea. In 1905, Japanese agents sneaked over Gyeongbok Palace walls and repeatedly stabbed her to death. The Korean-produced musical, *The Last Empress* — inspired by her life — opened to acclaim in Seoul and was performed at New York State Theater, London's West End, Los Angeles and Toronto.

After hearing my question, the woman defiantly half-shouted, "I don't know how Queen Min died. I don't know about her. I didn't read the explanations in the halls!" I think she was hard of hearing.

I tried another avenue, asking, "Would you know about King Gojong?" This time her husband brusquely retorted, "He was a king. But I don't know about him! If you want to know about Gojong, read the explanations in the hall!"

His combative partner pugnaciously agreed: "Yes, if you don't read the explanations, you won't know!"

I believe the couple was generally fond of telling people off, and I suspected they may have benefited from their own advice to read the information in the halls.

We concluded our visit at the impressive Circle Vision Theatre, where we stood in the center of the expansive circular hall, viewing the enormous IMAX-like 360-degree surround-screen. On the screen was exhilarating footage taken from a fighter jet swooping fast and low over the peninsula's famous landmarks. We were in the cockpit flying the plane, dive-bombing high above mountain peaks. The effects were so realistic I got nauseous.

In late afternoon we finally departed Independence Hall. Over two days we'd spent a total of eight hours here, not nearly enough time to take in its entirety. I'd expected something modest, but everything about the hall was illuminating and grand.

WEST

CHAPTER 10

Gunsan: Japantown

On the southwest coast of the peninsula, in the city of Gunsan, is Japantown. The Japanese built a port in the then small fishing village of Gunsan in 1889, and during colonization, they plundered rice from the verdant west plains and timber and coal from the interior, and shipped the commodities from the port to Japan.

Japanese merchants and officials, settling in Gunsan, weren't thrilled about the local clay, mud and thatched straw dwellings. In photos taken of Gunsan at the end of the 19th century, Korean homes are seen as predominantly mud huts. Japanese architecture was high quality and refined, and the colonizers designed and built their own neighborhood in Gunsan, using high-grade imported materials, and Japantown was born.

From Independence Hall in Cheonan, Heju and I advanced south about a hundred kilometers through South Chungcheong province, passing vast agricultural plains on an almost unbroken flat swath of fertile soil, including the Geum River Basin and Honam Plain. I loved the overall expansiveness — space to breathe and no intrusion of hills or mountains. In the small city of Iksan, inland from Gunsan, we stayed the night in a motel.

In the morning, bright and sunny, we drove from Iksan west to the coast to just north of Gunsan — where the Geum River empties — to tidal flats in Wolpo. The Geum River — at 400 kilometers — is the country's third longest waterway. Like the Han, it culminates at the Yellow Sea, depositing generous amounts of sediment.

We shuttled north on a long, low bridge over the mile-wide Geum River estuary, slow, wide and muddy, reminding me of the mighty Mississippi River. The Geum's source is about a hundred kilometers east, draining Jiri Mountain's north slopes. Immediately west are mountains, so the river flows north in a circuitous route to Daejeon, where the major Daejeon Dam diffuses it into numerous finger lakes. From Daejeon it takes a wide arch west, then southwest to Gunsan.

Once over the bridge past the estuary, we continued north into a dry coastal area on a dusty, isolated backroad paralleling the sea, which was hidden from view. After an hour puttering, we finally stopped in Wolpo and trudged onto the mudflats. The shallow sea was a grayish brown. The mud teems with sea worms, mollusks and crustaceans, in turn attracting migratory birds. In spring, the birds, flying north from Australia and New Zealand to breeding grounds in Siberia and Alaska, stop on Korea's west coast for up to six weeks, fattening up to fly many thousands of kilometers on the second leg of their journeys north. In autumn, on the way back to Down Under, the birds sometimes return here to feed.

On this afternoon, we observed a flock of about a thousand birds, including Grey Plovers, Bar-tailed Godwits and Great Knots, feeding out on the mud. Occasionally, the flock lifted off in massive black swirl of activity, then settled down on the mud again. An ardent bird watcher, viewing with us, recounted once seeing flocks of up to

80,000 birds here. But in 2006, the controversial thirty-three-kilometer-long Saemanguem Seawall — designed to reclaim land — was completed, joining two headlands off Gunsan. The result was some local tidal flats had dried up, depriving migratory birds of natural feeding grounds.

At dusk we departed the coast and cruised south to Gunsan. Reaching its downtown, we entered a concentrated, vibrant, bright entertainment district, replete with night clubs, lounges and motels, not a person to be seen. I'd happened upon other similar entertainment areas, customers typically entering bars and nightclubs via underground parking lots — drinking, dancing and carousing behind closed doors. All very hush-hush. We took a motel room in the district for the night.

Gunsan was bustling and busy as we drove through in mid-morning to the old port area, to Japantown in the west end, where the Geum River estuary meets the shallow, muddy Yellow Sea. Off the main street are several short parallel streets comprising the quiet, concentrated enclave of Japantown. A handful of Korean shops and dwellings on the main street were of cement and cheap metal, seemingly shoddy in comparison to Japantown's architectural excellence. We strolled under a warm sun on peaceful Japantown's residential streets, the only people here. In front of some homes were lovely little landscaped grass gardens and low Juniper trees enclosed by stone walls. The trees' delicate branches grew sideways like gentle waves, birds chirping on them.

The houses are predominately two-and three-stories, with A-shaped roofs, in contrast to Korean-style flat roofs. The homes' facades are striking. One was white clay bordered by wood paneling, with large windows trimmed with artisan woodwork and rafters of brass. Another had white stucco walls and a red-shale roof.

We were admiring one particular dwelling when a retirement-aged gentleman emerged from within and began chatting with us. "I own the house and want to sell it but can't," Yu Sung-gil said. He explained that Japantown had been designated a cultural heritage site by the government in 1989. "The government says we aren't permitted to sell our properties, but they offer us no financial assistance for upkeep," he complained.

Mr. Yu asked if we'd like to tour his house for 10,000 won.

One of the first attributes foreigners note upon arrival in this county is Koreans' wonderful and generous hospitality. Hike a mountain trail, saunter a beach or stroll a park and it's not uncommon for locals to insist that you share with them a taste of kimchi or a shot of *soju*. Compensation is unheard of.

We politely declined his offer. He quickly apologized. "I'm sorry to ask for money, but home maintenance is expensive."

Mr. Yu told us about a unique job he'd held in the 1960s and 1970s with the Peace Salvage Company in Busan, searching for Japanese vessels and submarines sunk by allies during the Second World War off the south coast. When his crew found a submerged craft, divers attached explosives to it and blew up any unexploded ordinances on board.

"We found so many Japanese ships that we lost count," he recalled.

After bidding goodbye to Mr. Yu, we walked across the main street to the quiet old port area. Nearby, we came upon what looked like the bombed-out shell of a large three-story wood building, hints of its former grandeur evident. In front a plaque stated it was once Chosun Bank, constructed by the Japanese in 1917. We entered the long-abandoned structure and climbed a flight of rotted wood stairs, the interior in total disarray, junk strewn everywhere. (Later, the building was rebuilt, transformed to the arresting Modern Architecture Exhibition Hall.)

Farther down the road, at a small square at the port, we came to the august, red-brick Gunsan Customs Building erected by the Japanese in 1899. A plaque stated: "Designed by Germans. Belgium-imported brick; inner walls, wood; roof, slate, copper. This building is a symbol of Japanese Imperialism to plunder rice in Honam region (southwest Korea), a rich agricultural plain."

Next to the structure is the small inner harbor — a short, steel foot bridge connecting it to a series of long, narrow docks, some with small fishing trawlers moored to them. We traipsed over the bridge onto the docks. The sea was a flat, dirty steel-gray, a total blanket of gray clouds hovering low. No boats were in the harbor or at sea.

On one fishing vessel with a long wood bow deck and a powerful inboard engine, a christening to celebrate its launching was being held, a handful of fishermen and their wives indulging in sushi and drinks.

"Come aboard!" one of the fellows called, Korean hospitality unparalleled. We accepted and sat on the front deck, leaning against the railing. At the head of the bow was a boiled pig's head, in its mouth a white envelope containing a traditional gift of cash.

Sitting at the head of the bow was the vessel's luminary, a short, loquacious man, Kim Chong-won, who had an engaging visage of dark circles under his eyes, and no top front teeth, his face flushed from imbibing a bottle of *soju* next to him. He spoke some English but talked non-stop in Korean.

"As a kid I learned English from U.S. soldiers who hung out at Gunsan's bars and nightclubs during the Korean War," Mr. Kim announced with bravado. "I met so many soldiers from the U.S. air force, navy and army, and they gave me chocolates and cigarettes. To this day I still smoke Marlboros."

Mr. Kim loved to hold court, in particular to fondly reminisce about his sixteen-month tour of duty, between 1969 and 1971, as a soldier with the ROK Tiger division in the Vietnam War. South

Korea's participation in the war was a thank you to America for the U.S. having dispatched more than a million troops to fight against North Korean and Chinese soldiers in the Korean War. Returning the favor, President Park Chung-hee sent a total of 320,000 ROK troops to Vietnam between 1964 and 1973. The war was a disaster for the U.S., but earned cash-strapped South Korea hundreds of millions of dollars in mostly U.S. war construction and supply contracts. About 23,000 South Koreans, including 15,000 technicians, were employed by the U.S. in Vietnam during the war.

Gross war revenues accounted for 10 percent of South Korea's foreign exchange earnings in 1966 and about 20 percent in 1967, totaling more than $660 million. President Park reportedly campaigned to have the conflict extended, even as the Americans were pulling out in 1973 — two years before the fall of the U.S.-supported Saigon regime in 1975.

In Vietnam, ROK troops gained a fearsome reputation. On search-and-destroy missions, they'd seal off entire villages and tighten the cordon with special forces plugging holes in the perimeter. Villagers were separated, interrogated and offered rewards for cooperation. A U.S. general claimed Koreans excelled at these operations. Eyewitnesses reported that on some missions, every villager was shot and killed.

"Was Korean troops' reputation in Vietnam true?" I asked Mr. Kim.

"We chased the Viet Cong until we caught them; we never gave up," he replied a matter-of-factually.

The first Korean troops arriving in Vietnam in 1964 were free to marry Vietnamese women, but President Park later ordered a halt to the practice. Mr. Kim rang off a slew of Vietnamese ladies' names he'd befriended there. "The Vietnamese loved Koreans ... they bowed to us," he bragged. He wasn't impressed though with the more recent trend in South Korea of single rural farmers – rebuffed by urban, cosmopolitan ladies for marriage – embarking on marriage-themed trips to Vietnam to search for young brides.

"Men in the Jeolla provinces marry Vietnamese women, but it's not good – Vietnamese women are very lazy," he lamented, shaking his head.

Mr. Kim's extended soliloquies resulted in his mates good-naturedly ribbing him. "We've heard all these stories about Vietnam before – you'll be talking for three days and three nights. We don't want to hear them anymore!" one declared.

Mr. Kim stubbornly countered, "I don't care, I'm going to keep talking!" He was true to his word.

The Viet Cong hid in holes in the ground at night to try to ambush enemy soldiers, he continued. To demonstrate his dazzling fighting prowess, he stood and engaged an imaginary Viet Cong soldier. In rapid succession he thrust out his leg to trip his adversary, threw jabs and drove his fingers into his opponent's eyes. In a mere instant his nemesis was incapacitated and down on the ground. Mr. Kim stood victorious over his vanquished foe, flashing a broad grin. His friends laughed. Mr. Kim was a showman.

After an hour and a half, now early evening, daylight fading, Heju and I bade adieu to our new acquaintances and strolled back to Japantown. We got in the car, found a nearby *yeogwan* and rented a room for the night. In the room, Heju dropped a bombshell: "I'm quitting the trip. I need to take a break. I want to go home tomorrow," she said despondently.

I was gobsmacked. It was true we were on a tight schedule. Heju was weary from translating my English queries into Korean, and the replies back into English for me, for each and every person we spoke to daily. Mental and physical stamina was needed. I tried talking her out of her decision, but her mind was made up. Attempting to sway a Korean woman from an entrenched stance is almost always a futile, losing proposition.

The country's southwest, south and east coasts and north region still needed to be explored. I decided to return to Seoul and find an English-speaking Korean to accompany me.

"I'll drop you off in Daejeon on the way to Seoul. Let's leave in the morning," I said disappointedly.

It was the first week of May. After a total of eight weeks into the expedition – three of those weeks scouting Seoul – Heju and Mark's adventure would be absent half its team. Heju would be missed.

CHAPTER 11

Gongju: Thirty-one Thousand Years of Koreans; A Temple of Pain

On return to Seoul I posted an ad on a website seeking an English-speaking Korean to accompany me on the trip. I received a number of replies, a handful from single females who insisted they'd naturally require their own motel room. Paying for two rooms would double my expenses, which I duly noted in my responses. One woman wanted to join the trip on condition the name of her business be prominently included in the book. A friendly, effervescent young university male student was keen to ride along, though he couldn't speak a word of English.

After about a week in Seoul, I received a promising email from a hopeful-sounding fellow who spoke fluent English and was raring to go. Sung-jai was incredulous I was offering to chauffeur him around the peninsula for free. "Really? You'll pay for meals, motels and gas?" his email read, unaware that the translator's role involved a bit more than relaxing in the passenger seat viewing scenery. "Yes," I answered. Unless he wanted to pay.

We met downtown the following day. Sung-jai was a young-looking thirty-six with a boyish face who could have passed for twenty-six in appearance and manner. "I'm a movie script writer," he said. "Traveling the country will give me ideas for new scripts."

We arranged to depart on the Monday after the coming weekend. On Sunday evening, Sung-jai phoned me and asked worriedly, "I've packed ten T-shirts, ten pairs of underwear and ten pairs of socks. Do you think that's enough?"

It was a long-held tradition in Korea that sons were once considered prince-like, more valuable than daughters. Thankfully, such ethos has all but evaporated. Nevertheless, mothers still sometimes believe their boys shouldn't be burdened with household chores or any type of task at all. Such lads tended to be coddled. From Sung-jai's query, I guessed him to be in this category.

"I think ten pairs of everything might be a little much," I suggested, suppressing the urge to ask if he'd ever packed a travel bag. "Probably five pairs will be fine."

When I picked Sung-jai up in my car Monday morning, he was pulling a modest-sized flight-cabin suitcase on wheels. For this type of journey, lugging wheeled luggage up mountains and on island paths was definitely *faux pas*.

He got in the car and immediately declared, "Hurry, let's go!"

I'd previously explained we'd be on a tight schedule, would sleep in *jjimjilbangs* and long days would prevail. I didn't want there to be surprises for him. No problem, he'd breezily answered. He was ready to rock n' roll.

"It's okay Sung-jai," I said, "we're not in that much of a hurry." I had a bad omen about him.

***

We'd spend our first two days on a military-themed exploration in Gyeonggi province, starting with a visit to Suwon Air Base. The base, off the side of a secondary road in a light-industrial area in Suwon, is administered by the ROK. At the base's front guard post we spoke to a friendly, middle-aged Korean on guard duty, who explained that on site is a battery of Patriot missiles manned twenty-four hours a day, aimed at North Korea, ready for launch on a moment's notice. Information, I thought, perhaps better kept secret.

From Suwon we moved south down the road to the U.S.-administered Osan Air Base and we watched F-16 Falcons and A-10 Thunderbolt 11s roaring overhead and taking off and landing.

Then it was to Pyeongtaek, an old city thirty kilometers south of Osan. In Pyeongtaek, I foolishly drove up to the huge front gate of United States Army Garrison – Humphreys, enclosed by a massive fortress-like wall. Camp Humphreys is America's largest overseas military base, with 5,000 soldiers and a 2.5-kilometer-long runway. A Korean military guard armed with a rifle rushed to my car.

"Back away now!" he angrily ordered. At the risk of my bones being made brittle, I didn't have to be told twice, and I promptly reversed the car from the fort's gate onto the road. We drove the length of Camp Humphrey's side wall – more than three miles – to the rear and exited in a rural area, then peered through the camp's chain link fence at attack helicopters of the U.S. 2nd Combat Aviation Brigade undergoing training maneuvers at dusk. A lot of firepower in South Korea is poised, ready for use against North Korea. Its leader, Kim Jong-un, ought to be careful in dealing with South Korea.

On our second day we sneaked southwest into South Chungcheong province, to Sapgyo Hamsang Park Bay on Asan Bay, and toured a decommissioned warship; inside were tiny narrow bunks and compact living quarters. I concluded I was fortunate not to have chosen a sailor's career. In the evening, we drove to the nearby township of Shinpyeong, a small, featureless roadside village, to find a place to stay. We stopped at a restaurant, sprinted through pelting rain, and sat on the floor at a long, low table — the only customers. From a young waitress, Sung-jai ordered *doenjang-jjigae* soup — a mix of tofu, vegetables and hot peppers. I asked for three bowls of rice. Fifteen minutes later, the waitress returned carrying a tray with the rice and a large steaming pot of *doenjang-jjigae*.

Sung-jai was instantly aggrieved and heatedly complained, "I ordered one small bowl of soup, but you brought a big pot for two people by mistake. The big pot costs 10,000 won, and the small one's 5,000 won. I'm not paying for two. I want to exchange it!"

The timid server, unsure what to do, suggested Sung-jai wait ten minutes until the owner returned to the restaurant.

When the owner wasn't back in the allotted time, Sung-jai curtly announced, "Fuck it, I'm too hungry to wait. I'd be patient if I wasn't starving," and he dug into his chow.

His unnecessary eruption over a minor incident concerned me. After two days with Sung-jai, I'd noticed he was low key, of subdued energy, not one for much conversation. He preferred sitting quietly in the car in glum and brooding silence. The uneasy feeling I had about him continued.

After dinner, we checked into the nearby Shinpyeongjang Yeogwan, rooms a pleasing 25,000 won. The inn's owner, a disagreeable woman of about fifty, showed us two rooms. One had a double bed — too narrow for two adult males to sleep on. The other had no bed — customers slept on the floor on a thick bed roll or *yo* — once a tradition in Korea. "Let's take the room with the bed, and you take the bed and I'll sleep on the floor," Sung-jai kindly offered.

He asked the woman for an extra blanket.

"Why should I give you an extra blanket," she protested curtly. "Just sleep together in the bed."

Sung-jai explained to her the bed was too small for the two of us and that we preferred to sleep separately.

"Take the room with no bed then!" she said.

"But my friend likes the bed," he continued.

The woman repeated that we sleep together, the discussion going in circles. Sung-jai began to lose patience. "Why aren't you willing to give us a blanket!" he stated, raising his voice.

"There wouldn't be a problem if you took the room with no bed. Then I wouldn't have to get you a blanket," she replied. I pitied the woman's poor husband — if he hadn't already left her, which would have been wise.

Sung-jai had had enough. "Why don't you give good service!" he heatedly declared. Turning to me, he announced, "I don't want to stay here any more!"

But I didn't want to search for another *yeogwan* in the darkness and cold lashing rain. I had an idea. Koreans are business-minded. If I asked the owner to return our 25,000 won room fee, I was sure she'd give us a blanket. "Can I get my money back and we'll leave," I told her. She reluctantly strode down the hall, returned a few moments later with two blankets, and handed them to Sung-jai without saying a word.

We walked down the hall to our room, and Sung-jai cursed her under his breath: "What a bitch ... she's so lazy!"

***

I was awakened by what sounded like scurrying mice, but it wasn't mice, it was the TV, which Sung-jai was watching, the volume barely registering. It was 5:15 a.m.

"I couldn't sleep," murmured Sung-jai, sitting up on his *yo*, leaning against the door and gazing at the screen.

I tried to sleep again but, aware that Sung-jai was awake, my slumber was temporary and restless. I arose at 7:30 and we were out the door thirty minutes later.

We cruised south into the west coast Pyeongtaek plains, the landscape an arresting, endless airy oasis of hundreds of thousands of watery, knee-deep, brown-green rice paddies appearing like shallow marshes, flooded by farmers for late spring planting. The overall flatness reminded me of the Netherlands. The occasional farmer was out in his paddies behind what looked like a big, heavy push lawnmower that was automatically planting bunches of little green rice shoots into long rows of muddy water.

We soon turned west and headed to the nearby coastal city of Seosan at wide Cheonsu Bay to view man-made Seosan Dyke. In the book, *Made in Korea: Chung Ju Yung and the Rise of Hyundai*, author Richard Steers explained how Seosan Dyke's midpoint had to be connected to close off the sea in 1984. To block the powerful high tides, Hyundai boss Chung Ju-yung had ordered a huge ship to be anchored lengthwise, where the two lengths of the dyke were to meet in the middle. Scores of dump trucks had been dumping tons of rocks and gravel at the midpoint, but the tides kept sweeping away the fill faster than the dyke could be closed. After several attempts – the ship blocking the tide – the dyke was successfully sealed. The thousands of acres of reclaimed land behind the dyke were owned by Chung. After subsequent years of jettisoning salt from the earth, the area – Seosan Farm – began producing rice. We drove across Seosan Dyke, underpinned by innumerable huge boulders, a freshwater lake inland, the sea on the other side. After crossing we stopped at the south edge of Seosan Farm and looked out over uncountable rice paddies stretching unbroken for tens of kilometers to the horizon.

We departed Seosan and cruised east toward the ancient city of

Gongju in the middle of South Chungcheong province. Gongju was the capital of the Baekje Kingdom, ruling from AD 18 to 660. Baekje comprised the peninsula's southwest from Seoul to the south coast. My guidebook listed a prehistoric museum and ancient king's tomb among Gongju's attractions.

We slowly rolled across coastal plains, soon morphing into the Charyong Mountains' plush, large rounded wooded hills. The winding road for some stretches parallels the wide, meandering Geum River, its slow-moving water carving narrow valleys bordered by beautiful steep green hills. The sun was beginning to set, highlighting surrounding walls of green as we neared Gongju. What a pretty picture.

On the periphery of Gongju, the road moves alongside the Geum River, along the road a few shops and motels, a gas station or two and several low, modern white apartment buildings. Across the river is the hidden, ancient city of Gongju, several bridges spanning the river. On the far bank is a long continuous wall of steep wooded hills, where we could make out the stone remnants of a fourth-century Baekje fortress wall partially hidden behind trees.

We stopped across from old Gongju at a concrete embankment paralleling the Geum River, next to a single-lane, iron-trestle bridge constructed by the Japanese in 1933. A passerby informed us that prior to 1980 – when seventy-two-meter-tall Daecheong Dam was constructed upstream – summer monsoons could raise river levels to higher than the top of the embankment, eight meters above the river.

Monsoons are like no rains I've previously experienced. The water falls in large heavy dollops with thundering intensity. Seventy percent of the rain in the country comes between June and September. In 1940, the heaviest year on record for rainfall in Korea, Seoul received more than two meters. When such precipitation cascades for hour after hour, rivers swell to meters above their normal levels. In narrow mountain passes in South Korea, campers with tents pitched on river banks have been swept away. I'd seen the swollen and flooded Han River in Seoul overflow onto Olympic Expressway 88.

Sung-jai and I trekked down the embankment onto the Geum River's wide, dry silt flats and over to the water's edge next to the old Japanese-built bridge. A few meters upstream a row of small rocks, piled in the water at set intervals, crossed to the far bank. Each rock pile had a stick protruding up.

Back on the embankment, we asked several passersby if they knew of the rock piles' genesis. One woman confidently asserted the rocks had built up naturally over time.

But several minutes later, two elderly women had a different answer. "The rocks and sticks were placed there by people to protect the bridge," they concluded. "When big things float down the river, the rocks and poles catch them. Without the rocks, big things could knock over the bridge. It's not very strong."

Sung-jai, who had the nose of a skeptical journalist, asked the ladies in disbelief, "Those little rocks can protect the bridge?"

Indignant, one replied with total conviction, "Of course they can!"

We drove across the bridge into old Gongju. It wasn't at all what I'd expected, which was a sort of quiet country village, a Main Street, USA, with a library and a grocery and hardware store, a handful of townsfolk greeting each other by first names and inviting neighbors to their homes for Sunday afternoons of home-baked cherry pie and lemon *soju*.

Rather, downtown Gongju is a teeming, mini version of Seoul, a concentrated chaotic hub of human activity. The main road was lined with an assortment of twenty-four-hour convenience stores, mobile phone shops, restaurants, clothing stores and low-rise commercial buildings. Gongju's 115,000 citizens were out celebrating our arrival — jostling for space on sidewalks and clogging the road with vehicles.

We grabbed dinner in a small, plain restaurant, then stole across the street and checked into Gongju Boseok Sauna. A sauna, or *jjimjilbang*, is a type of YMCA/health club/spa/retreat/refugee center rolled into one. There's nothing quite like them anywhere else in the world. For about ten dollars a night, customers get access to locker rooms, showers, hot tubs, sauna, snack shop, TV and a gymnasium-like sleeping area. In the latter, patrons place mats on the floor among other customers and sleep overnight. *Jjimjilbangs* offer professional massages, reclining massage chairs, haircuts and a lounge to sit and relax in.

Shorts and T-shirts are provided, though invariably they are two sizes too small for my frame. Once, a *jjimjilbang* manager insisted I don a uniform, and doing so I appeared like a guy who parades New Jersey beaches in summer in a tight tank-top T-shirt and skin-hugging shorts, portions of his body hanging out.

Jjimjilbangs are almost always efficiently-run, well-organized and clean. They are also sometimes confusingly laid out. Large ones can have up to four or five floors with myriad mysterious stairways and hallways leading to heaven knows where. I've been totally lost in such places and mistakenly entered some room or descended some stairway I shouldn't have. At a massive *jjimjilbang* in Seoul's Itaewon district — once overrun by U.S. soldiers before the nearby U.S. base was moved to Camp Humphreys in Pyeongtaek — I was walking down a narrow, curved flight of wood stairs when I was suddenly startled by a woman's shriek. I'd unknowingly almost entered the women's changeroom. Realizing my error, in mid-step I instantaneously made a 180-degree U-turn and headed back upstairs.

Families and couples patronize *jjimjilbangs* for an entire day or even the weekend. Heju and her mother love them and can spend all day at one. In fact, *jjimjilbangs* once served a more practical purpose for Koreans. Prior to the 1980s, many households didn't have plumbing and hot water, and *jjimjilbangs* offered citizens a place to clean and bathe. I don't quite possess the same passion for them as Heju. I find the sleeping floors unusually hot, and the TVs are usually tuned loudly to annoying dramas. When slumbering, I insert professional-grade silicone ear plugs to drown out the symphony of uproariously loud snoring of fellow sleepers. (Korean men seem to be prolific snorers.)

As I immediately noted upon arrival at Gongju Boseok Sauna, Sung-jai took to *jjimjilbangs* like a bear to honey. First we took long showers. It's quite amazing how much sweat and grime can accumulate on a body from merely sitting in a car for a day. Next we luxuriated in a hot tub, then the sauna. Afterward, pink as piglets, we moved to the sleeping area, threw down mats in front of a big-screen TV, lay down, stretched out and watched television. When the nine o'clock national news appeared, Sung-jai kindly translated for me.

After the news, Sung-jai mysteriously disappeared then materialized thirty minutes later.

"Where did you go?" I asked.

"I had a shower," he said.

I was puzzled. "But you showered before the news."

"I know, but I sweated watching the news," he replied in earnest seriousness.

Koreans are the planet's cleanest, shiniest people. When I'm at a local fitness club or public spa, I'll observe fellows taking long showers collectively lathering into a thick, white froth, systematically scrubbing every pore on their bodies. At saunas, fathers buff with a coarse cloth their elementary school-age sons in a longstanding tradition. The grim-faced boys seem to enjoy it about as much as getting a root canal.

I was in the car in the parking lot at 8:30 a.m., waiting for Sung-jai, who was in the *jjimjilbang*. My cell phone rang and Sung-jai was on the line.

"Where are you?" he asked.

"In the car," I said.

After a long pause, and in an incredulous tone, he inquired, "Are you leaving without a shower?"

Without a shower? I had one twelve hours earlier, and in the ensuing time, I hadn't rolled in pig shit. "I don't need one," I replied. "Where are you?" I asked.

"In the sauna," he said. "I just finished a shower."

If you're counting, and I certainly was, it was Sung-jai's third shower since arriving at the *jjimjilbang*. When he appeared at the car fifteen minutes later, his skin tone was a shade lighter and brighter than twelve hours previous.

We headed to Gongju National Museum in a bucolic area just outside town. The museum is a large, low modern facility that opened to the public in 2004. Our car was the only one in the sprawling parking lot — not surprising, considering it was nine on a Saturday morning and most people were where they ought to be — at home sleeping.

In the museum foyer was a small office where we purchased tickets from a woman of perhaps thirty, sitting behind the window, her nose buried in a book. I assumed she'd gladly respond to a few queries I had about Baekje considering the museum held artifacts from that period. I proffered my first question, and the woman raised her head, fixed me with an expression of irritation, and coldly replied, "I can't answer questions ... I'm reading," and returned to her page.

Perhaps I'm in the minority, but I believe that an employee on the payroll at a publicly funded institution has a civic duty to assist mere proletarians such as me, who contribute to her paycheck via income tax. Not that I actually pay much in the way of income tax as a foreigner living in South Korea. But you know what I mean. I tried a second question, to which she looked up from her book with a look of enmity, and hissed, "If you want to learn about Baekje then visit a bookstore and buy a book on it," and she resumed reading.

To further antagonize her I asked a third question. To get rid of me she reluctantly mumbled a few perfunctory words about Baekje, which didn't explain anything, and continued with her book — hopefully titled: "*Public Service Employees: How to Offer Quality Customer Care and Not Be a Twit.*"

Ancient Baekje ruled the peninsula's southwest; Silla governed the southeast. Silla attacked Baekje in AD 660, resulting in the latter's demise. Almost 1,400 years later, some citizens in the former Baekje region of present-day South and North Jeolla provinces apparently haven't quite forgiven the former Silla stronghold, comprising current southeast North and South Gyeongsang provinces, for the beating. The southwest, some say, still holds a grudge. Adding to the southwest's hurt, beginning in the 1960s, a series of conservative presidents from the southeast awarded the lion's share of industry to their own region, leaving the Jeolla provinces to continue mainly relying on agriculture, farming and fishing, resulting in economic disparity. When presidential elections are held, the rivalry is unmistakable. About 90 percent of Jeolla citizens vote liberal, the same percentage of Gyeongsang people vote conservative.

Between 1927 and 1933 in Gongju, six anonymous Baekje-era hillside tombs were uncovered, another unearthed in 1971. Unlike the first six, the seventh contained a stone tablet, confirming the remains belonged to King Muryeong, Baekje's 25th monarch, and his queen.

The tomb had remained undisturbed since AD 529. More than 2,900 artifacts were recovered from the burial site, including gold diadem ornaments, gilt bronze sarira pots, silver accessories and lacquered wood pillows, many now housed in Gongju National Museum.

We wandered through the museum, viewing arresting artifacts — including exquisitely designed bronze, silver, and gold pieces, and earrings, bracelets, necklaces, bowls, spoons and swords. Baekje culture was renowned for its artisans and beautiful, unique artwork.

Next we drove the short distance to King Muryeong's burial mound and parked beside a small museum and tourist office at the bottom of a gradually rising hill, at the top which is Muryeong's tomb. Now noon, the warm, pleasant Saturday was attracting families — strolling up the path to the several large rounded earthen burial mounds, each about three meters high. A guide in the office had disappointing news: Muryeong's tomb was sealed, closed to public viewing. "The heat from visitors' bodies and from artificial lighting caused condensation to accumulate on the interior walls and resulted in damage," she explained. "We don't have the technology to protect the walls."

We ascended the hill and briefly viewed Muryeong's tomb exterior. We then descended and entered the small museum featuring an exceptionally well-done replica of the original tomb's interior with intricately detailed brickwork in a yellow-gray hue and lotus motifs.

We departed in early afternoon, with plenty of time to reach our next destination — a Buddhist temple-stay about an hour east. Temple-stays permit guests to sleep overnight for a fee. The Temple-Stay Korea Network was established in 2002 by the Jogye Order of Korean Buddhism. Its website states visitors can "sample ordained lifestyle and experience the mental training and cultural experience of Korea's ancient Buddhist tradition."

In the first year, fourteen temples participated. By 2005, there were fifty. At last check, almost one hundred temples were on board. A few days earlier, I'd reserved two spots for Sung-jai and me at Jakwang Buddhist Temple, just west of Daejeon. A temple-stay pamphlet I'd picked up at a tourist booth stated that no payment was required, but "donations were accepted." The word "donations" concerned me. If I didn't leave one, would a very large, surly monk, named Corleone "Big Fist" Kim, rough me up? I'd phoned Jakwang Temple to inquire. A pleasant-sounding fellow, Cedric, sporting a New Zealand accent, answered.

"Everyone asks me about donations," Cedric chuckled. "There'll be an envelope on the floor of your room. If you want you can leave a donation in it without writing your name on the envelope." This pleased me.

We traveled southeast from Gongju toward Daejeon but had difficulty finding the temple in the rural countryside. After phone calls to the temple and an hour searching locally, we finally located it in Hakha-dong in Yuseong County, on a pretty, tree-lined lane not far from steep hills. It was mid-afternoon when we parked in the sun-drenched earthen lot, in front of the ample, stately three-story wood temple. We met Cedric, in his early twenties, an intelligent, easy-going New Zealander who'd been immersing himself in Buddhist study at the temple for four and a half months. The other visitors on this weekend were twelve earthy, bohemian-like young western women and four men.

Cedric led our group through the temple, dispensing bits of Buddhist wisdom as he went. We congregated on the large, spacious upper floor, the large sliding wood doors facing the courtyard, separating the exterior balcony from the interior, bright sunshine flooding through the open doorway. A dog barked in the distance, and nearby, tree limbs rustled in a slight breeze. It was tranquil and quiet.

We sat on mats, and Cedric introduced us to several salient aphorisms of canonical scriptures, or Buddhist Sutra, which to me seemed simplistic and even dotty. He led us in a few chants, then demonstrated traditional Buddhist bows — not simple, dainty bend-at-your-waist type bows that you'd present to Queen Elizabeth. No, these were Marine Corps, body-breaking training bows. From a standing position, we sank to our knees, bent forward from the waist until our stomachs and foreheads touched the floor, arms reaching forward, then we reversed the process and stood. This counted as only one bloody bow!

I don't recall how many bows we performed. I lost count due to being in supreme physical agony. I remember that for about fifteen minutes, we repeated bow after bow after bow. I love exercise, but not repeated calisthenics that reduce one's thigh muscles to quivering bowls of jelly. Buddhist monks in Korea do 108 such bows daily, taking about twenty minutes. On special occasions they'll do 1,080 bows lasting three weeks. (I jest — about three hours.)

Before the trip, I'd picked up a little booklet titled *Everyday Korean Buddha Practices* written by Master Ilta, who claimed that bowing jettisoned negative karma and achieved enlightenment. "The ideal method for lay people to eliminate the 108 mental sufferings is to do 108 prostrations in the morning and chant at nights. Doing so will mean less difficulties and more peace and joy in your life," the master wrote.

Mr. Ilta had it wrong — bowing engendered physical and mental suffering for me.

After completing numerous bows — to atone for my many former sins — more punishment waited. Cedric forced us to sit cross-legged for more than thirty minutes — to pray or meditate or something ... I'm not sure which. The United Nations hasn't yet classified sitting cross-legged for prolonged periods for people fifty-years-old and over as torture, but it ought to. Fellows of my height, weight and age aren't known for subtle flexibility and limberness. Sitting in this position, my legs began to turn to wood, like Pinocchio's, and the blood stopped circulating in my lower appendages. After, it took thirty minutes to re-straighten my legs, to get the blood flowing again. I watch in awe at Koreans sitting cross-legged for hours on the floor at low tables in restaurants. They even seem to enjoy it. I have no idea how they accomplish this feat.

That evening, our group and several monks gathered for dinner in the large basement sitting at a long wood table, with an open kitchen in the corner. Buddhists don't eat meat and there wasn't any. The meal of vegetables, lentils and rice was surprisingly tasty. The gathering was convivial, like a casual Thanksgiving dinner with family and relatives. On my right was a member of our group – a young woman from South Africa who I guessed was a teacher of English as a second language in Korea.

I'm not sure how she got on the topic, but she began a rather pedantic sermon on the evils of money, and how it meant little to her, and how teenagers and young women in Korea – Asians in general – are slaves to money and shop excessively.

"In Singapore, that's all they do is shop," she said grimly. "Money controls them."

I understood her feelings. But having spent more years than I would have preferred in my twenties and thirties living a rather itinerant existence, fretting if I had enough funds to afford a decent meal at a restaurant; after arriving in Korea, and finally being able to save money, something I hadn't been able to accomplish in Canada, I came to understand the importance of having spare funds in the bank. Savings affords one choices, and to a degree peace of mind. What the young woman had conveniently failed to mention was it had required money for her to purchase an air ticket to fly to Korea, to ride the bus from Seoul to the temple, to enjoy the fresh lentils and alfalfa sprouts she surely consumed daily in her vegan diet.

After dinner, we returned to the temple's top floor and viewed a documentary on the Buddhist ethos of harmony, peace and love. The film showed a clip of a street parade in England – with tens of thousands of spectators cheering on victorious British soldiers returning home from Argentina in the 1982 Falklands War. The narrator asked wasn't it unsavory to be celebrating war-time killings? During the short Falklands War, a British submarine fired two torpedoes at an Argentinean cruiser, killing 323 sailors – young men who had mothers, fathers, brothers, sisters, wives, sons and daughters. Yes, I agreed, it was disconcerting, even abhorrent, observing people happily waving flags on the parade route cheering others' deaths.

When the film ended, Cedric asked if we had questions about Buddhism. Someone inquired of Cedric why he'd gotten involved in the faith. He explained: "I was a practicing Catholic in New Zealand, but when I talked to priests to get answers about God, they simply said, 'Have faith.' That wasn't a good enough answer for me."

"Can monks marry?" another asked.

"Yes, but they don't get attached to their partner. If you lose something tomorrow, you won't get upset if you're not attached to it. If your wife died, you'd be upset, but not depressed."

Now hold on Brother Cedric. I've yet to marry, but if I do and love my wife – the reason I'd marry her in the first place – I'd be plenty depressed if she died.

I posed a question: "Monks spend a lot of time doing solitary things, like meditating, chanting and praying, so how do they have enough time to help others?"

Cedric smiled, stared at me, remained silent a few moments, then replied, "I knew you were going to ask that." (How, I had no idea.) He agreed that monks spend a lot of time alone. "But they have time for other things. Here at the temple, they give free English lessons to kids."

It was about ten o'clock when we finally wrapped up. I returned to the somewhat moldy-smelling basement room I shared with Sung-jai, then took a late-night jog on the country lane. The countryside was quiet and desolate, the evening beautiful and warm, a big, bright moon illuminating a black, star-filled sky.

When I returned to the temple, I sat alone on the bench in the courtyard contemplating the meaning of life. I have no idea what the meaning of life is. I concluded though that after more than five decades on this planet, and still not dead, this had some meaning. Karma seems to be on my side.

Our temple-stay brochure stated guests are welcome to rise at 3:00 a.m. to chant and pray. Sleep being integral to my existence, I chose to remain dead to the world and instead rose at a very leisurely 10:00 a.m. I sauntered out to the silent, empty courtyard, shielding my eyes from the sun's harsh glare reflecting off the sandy earth. Cedric was in the courtyard too and we chatted. He recounted an incident illustrating the zeal many Korean parents have for their children's education.

"A mother dropped off her elementary school-aged son at the temple and said she wanted him to stay alone for a week," Cedric recalled. "I asked her, 'Why a week?' She replied that she wanted her son to reflect on life." Cedric shook his head in disbelief, and said, "Reflect on life? The kid was only nine-years-old!"

At about noon, Sung-jai and I jumped into the car parked at the side of the temple. I stuck the key into the ignition and turned it — not a peep from the engine. I tried several more times but discovered the battery was dead. Then karma, a Korean monk, surprisingly one of the few I'd seen at the temple, suddenly appeared in the courtyard. Observing our plight, he stopped to assist. He was no ordinary monk. He was the reincarnation of the 1960s martial arts legend, Bruce Lee. In fact, I think he was the actual Bruce Lee.

Bruce looked to be about thirty, with Hollywood good looks and a chiseled jaw, the top half of his semi-open Buddhist robe revealing a sculpted chest. His thick long black hair flowed down to his shoulders. He could have graced the cover of *GQ* magazine. Why Bruce hadn't shaved his head bald like other Buddhists monks, I couldn't say. He gallantly slid into the driver's seat and waited for Sung-jai and me to push the car to jump-start it. Sung-jai and I positioned ourselves behind the Scoupe and began heaving with all our might. Slowly the auto rolled along the courtyard, Bruce repeatedly turning the key trying to ignite the engine. Not a sound.

We took a breather. Bruce, the strong, silent type, remained behind the steering wheel, patiently waiting for us to resume our labor. We pushed again, but after several more fruitless minutes, it became obvious the car wasn't going to start this way.

"Jump-starting it isn't possible with a dead battery," I informed Bruce. I wasn't sure this was true, but I simply wanted him to exit the car. He was in no hurry to vacate and continued to sit contentedly, perhaps contemplating the meaning of life, or at least, how many calories he was saving by rendering his lazy butt idle. He finally walked away, having not uttered a single word the entire time.

We phoned a local garage, and a kind, young mechanic soon arrived, and charged the battery for just 10,000 won. What service!

I'm embarrassed to admit, but I didn't leave a cash donation in the envelope in our room. I should have, of course. I felt mighty guilty I hadn't, and promised myself if a few of my books sold, I'd donate some proceeds to Jakwang Temple. After we drove off, I phoned Cedric to thank him for the stay and to wish him success.

I'm certain he'd already checked my room, and, realizing the envelope was devoid of bills, had ordered his top monk henchman, Carleone "Big Fist" Kim, to follow me and turn me upside down, and pick up the bills falling out of my pockets. My karma was currently negative.

We headed back to Gongju, to check Paleolithic Stone Age artifacts, housed at Seokjangri Museum in Seokjang village a few kilometers upstream from Gongju by the Geum River. First, though, there's an interesting story about the artifacts I'd like to share.

In 1964, two young Americans from the University of Wisconsin, visiting research students at Yonsei University in Seoul, Korea's premier university, were credited with the initial discovery of Seokjangri Stone Age tools. Albert D. Mohr and L. Laetitia Sample had reason to believe the area of Seokjangri by the Geum River, was a potential site to find ancient tools. The pair strolled the recently-flooded river's banks, their eyes surely peeled to the ground for any sign of implements. They spotted partially hidden in the mud what looked to be a very old stone tool.

Lee Yung-jo was then an archeology student at Yonsei University, and became familiar with Mohr and Sample. Today, Lee is a professor emeritus at Chungbuk National University in Cheongju in North Chungcheong province. Lee told me he recalled the Americans taking the sample to Seoul and having it tested at the Korean Atomic Energy Institute. What a discovery! The relic was 30,690 years old, the first-ever Stone Age tool uncovered in Korea. Prior to this, the oldest implements found in the country dated to the Neolithic period, to about 5,000 BC. Now here was proof that humans had inhabited the peninsula many millennia earlier. Archaeologically-speaking, the find was monumental for Korea.

Several months after the discovery, a Yonsei University archaeological team arrived in Gongju, and began excavating the newly-christened Seokjangri Paleolithic Prehistoric Site. For the next decade, Professor Lee spent every spring assisting on the dig. A total of about 10,000 stone implements — including pottery, bowls, knives and axes — were unearthed, many now housed at Seokjangri Museum.

We parked in front of the long, modern museum by the river, the area quiet and peaceful. Except for several guides at the front desk, the facility was devoid of people. Our guide was Jeong Seung-ah, a middle-aged, serious woman. (Was there any other kind in Korea?) Like other guides I'd been led by on the journey, Ms. Jeong relied on a memorized, well-rehearsed speech. She led us from exhibit to exhibit, explaining about some of the thousands of Stone-Age tools before us found in Gongju and in Europe. Knowing little about Korean archeology, I posed questions to her via Sung-jai.

When was the Stone Age? Were these tools at the museum the oldest found in Korea? Was there a difference between Stone Age tools found in Korea and Europe? When did humans first wander from the Asian continent to Korea? Had Peking Man — unearthed near Beijing, found to be up to about 770,000 years old — traipsed the relatively short distance east to Korea? Would I have made an exemplary caveman?

My interjections caused Ms. Jeong to lose her place in her memorized spiel, for its continuity and flow to be hampered. She took umbrage. I assumed too that she felt somewhat uncomfortable because she didn't know the answers to some of our questions. She eventually threw up her hands in exasperation.

Sung-jai was frustrated at our guide's perceived lack of cooperation. Out of her earshot, he whispered irritably to me, "She's not answering my questions!" By the time the three of us were back at the front desk, the guide and Sung-jai were suffering from frayed nerves.

In the parking lot, Sung-jai confided to me: "I said to Ms. Jeong, 'I don't mean to give you offence, but the information we're asking is very important. You really should know it.'"

I had to hand it to Sung-jai — he spoke his mind.

CHAPTER 12

Gyeongbu Expressway: Building the Impossible; Nogeunri: A Tunnel of Death

During a 1964 government visit to West Germany, South Korean President Park Chung-hee was so impressed with the famed autobahn as a lifeline for German industry, he determined his country must have an expressway too. A highway joining Seoul in the northwest to Busan in the southeast would be essential to ensuring the nation's industrialization and modernization, Park believed.

In 1964, there wasn't a single expressway in South Korea, and only 2,000 kilometers of paved roads existed, mostly around Seoul. A whopping 35,000 kilometers of earth foot paths and gravel walking tracks crisscrossed the peninsula, which Koreans had trod upon for millennia. The pathways weren't graded because horse-drawn carriages and four-wheeled wagons were never utilized in the country. About a third of the existing dirt roads were maintained by locals, using picks and shovels in a corvée system of unpaid labor. Only about 25,000 registered passenger vehicles — about half in Seoul, half of those taxis — plied the scant paved streets. Some roads and bridges that had suffered heavy damage during the Korean War still hadn't been repaired a decade later.

In Patricia M. Bartz's superb 1972 book, *South Korea*, she described in great detail the country's geology and geography. "By Western standards most roads were unfit for passenger vehicles and justly notorious," she wrote.

To construct a pan-Korea highway would require a massive financial infusion but the national legislature had little money. South Korea's GNP in 1964 was U.S. $142 and the average monthly wage just forty dollars. Between 1954 and 1970, the government received about $4 billion in aid from the U.S. Japan provided $1 billion in grants, loans and economic assistance over ten years. In a detailed study of the proposed expressway, the World Bank warned it was economically and technologically unfeasible. The South Korean national legislature agreed.

Lack of funds was but one challenge; the other was the rugged, inhospitable terrain. South Korea's physical topography has been likened to a million dinosaur humps. An expressway would need to be plowed through three mountain ranges: the Charyeongs in the north, Sobaeks along the spine and Taebaeks in the southeast.

Bartz categorized the Korean landmass as one of the world's oldest with some rock formations belonging to the Crystalline Schist system. Its genesis was in the Pre-Cambrian era, dating to between 550 million and 4.6 billion years ago when Earth was formed. The country's prevalent bedrock is the Granite-Gneiss system, older than 900 million years. Beginning in late Cretaceous – 140 million to 66 million years ago – the land mass of today's Korea underwent its last mountain-building period, with upheaval, violent thrusting, folding and faulting and an intrusion of "new" or "young" granite lasting possibly 100 million years. The emergence of this granite formed today's major mountain ranges: the Taebaeks, Sobaeks, Charyeongs and Noryeongs. Only about ten million years ago did the Korean land surface begin to assume its present-day shape, noted Bartz. For about the last 70 million years it's been undergoing erosion, producing large areas of exposed, worn mountain granite of generally low elevation. Seventy percent of the land surface is mostly steep mountains, only five percent taller than 1,000 meters. Bartz likened Korea to "a confused picture of mountain ridges running in all directions," and "a sea frozen during a tempest."

Through this taxing terrain, President Park wanted to build a major highway. The former school teacher and erstwhile major general in the ROK army — previously an officer in the Japanese army in Manchuria, even adopting the Japanese name, Tagaki Masao — led a military coup in 1961. Bernard Krisher, a reporter for the *New York World-Telegram* and *The Sun*, after interviewing Park at Columbia University in 1961, wrote, "He was an unlikely looking coup leader. He was short, barely audible and uncomfortable in a Western setting."

The President didn't give a hoot what the experts thought, and with his iron will and disdain for the democratic process, he used strong-armed tactics to get what he wanted. He desired an expressway and he got it.

Groundbreaking for Gyeongbu Expressway ("*Gyeong*" translates to Seoul, "*bu*" short for Busan) began in February 1968. Park chose Hyundai's young chairman, Chung Ju-yung — the driving force behind the then-nascent, global Hyundai automobile, ship-building and construction company — to oversee construction. Up to this point Hyundai's total road construction experience was limited to building a ninety-three-kilometer highway linking Pattani to Narathiwat in southern Thailand in 1964. The project didn't fare well, with Hyundai's shoddy equipment constantly breaking down, pavement laid in monsoon season buckling, and Thai workers, paid less than their Korean counterparts, staging violent strikes. But the Park government – working with Korea's family-run conglomerates, or *chaebol* – granted low-interest, government-backed loans plus credit for any reasonable export project.

Korean engineers favored a straight-line route joining Seoul and Busan, tunneling through the Sobaek Mountains' backbone. Chung favored a path that basically followed the existing rail line: Seoul south to Daejeon, south-east through a pass in the Sobaeks to Daegu, south to Busan. Chung won out. Hyundai led a consortium of seventeen construction firms, with Chung overseeing more than 200 kilometers of the most challenging terrain, including just east of Daejeon, through a notoriously difficult run of steep mountains.

Chung hired numerous crews to labor around the clock. Workers got only two days off a month. The boss ate and slept at worksites in a bid to motivate the men. But old machinery frequently broke down on steep, unforgiving slopes, forcing construction at times to grind a halt. Tons of earth were needed to fill in low areas between successive hills and to build up roadbeds. Short of quality equipment, Chung ordered 1,900 new units of heavy machinery.

Road-building through the mountains was dangerous work, wrote Richard Steers, in *Made in Korea: Chung Ju Yung and the Rise of Hyundai*, noting "several workers died in landslides and cave-ins." Accidents were frequent – "thirteen serious cave-ins occurring during the drilling of Tangjae Tunnel alone east of Daejeon."

A project engineer recalled President Park constantly flying in a helicopter over the route. "Up and down he would go, this time with a team of geologists to figure out what had gone wrong with some mountainside that had crumbled on our tunnel-makers, the next time with a couple of United Nations hydrologists to figure out how our surveyors had got some water table wrong. If he didn't know the answer on Tuesday, Mr. Park was back with it on Thursday."

After two and a half years of back-breaking labor, Gyeongbu Expressway's final, most difficult section east of Daejeon was completed on July 7, 1970. A total of 416 kilometers of black, smooth pavement and scores of tunnels and bridges connected the length of the country. An engineering feat.

I'd driven Gyeongbu Expressway's length from Seoul to Busan and return. The road toll fee is about $20 for a one-way trip. With little traffic, you can sweep along in about four and a half hours start to finish. Much of the immediate scenery is broad, low green mountains. On national holidays, when seemingly every one of the nation's twenty million-plus vehicles is simultaneously on the roads, Gyeongbu can morph into a giant parking lot. One Thanksgiving, Heju and I departed Seoul by bus at midnight – the expressway one continuous traffic jam. Thirteen hours and 400 southbound kilometers later, we rolled into our destination in Gwangju in South Jeolla province at 1:00 p.m.

Steers mentioned thirteen cave-ins occurring in Dangjae Tunnel east of Daejeon, workers dying in the collapses; Dangjae Tunnel warranted an investigation. The day after Sung-jai and my visit to Seokjangri Museum in Gongju, we were heading east of Daejeon to the tunnel on a tight, narrow winding road paralleling the impossibly serpentine, seemingly inaccessible but lovely Geum River. Its dark green waters here flow alongside remote wilderness in razor-thin valleys enclosed by steep-walled blankets of green.

A stone's throw west of Dangjae Tunnel in Okcheon County, we halted at the river in a tight valley at Geumgang Resort, next to the hamlet of Joryeong. A steep wall of woods rises on each side. The word "resort" is a stretch – more like a glorified rest stop with a motel, a few restaurants, a parking lot and a shallow section of river to wade in. Just up the road is a tall road bridge on which Gyeongbu Expressway crosses over the Geum River.

We drove behind the resort to the bottom of a steep low mountain to Joryeong village — all of a few dwellings. In the diminutive square we sat outside at a table at a restaurant devoid of customers. Sung-jai inquired of the testy, middle-aged proprietor — adorned in globs of glittering eye shadow — the cost of finger-length river fish swimming in a large aquarium in front of the restaurant. Informed the price was about $10 for several fish, he said it was too expensive and declined to order. We asked a villager ambling by if he knew of someone locally who'd witnessed Gyeongbu Expressway being plowed through the area decades ago. The man gave us a phone number of a local, Mr. Park, whom we phoned. Mr. Park said he'd witnessed the highway's construction. "I saw a worker fall off a bridge," he recounted. He offered to lead us to Dangjae Tunnel tomorrow. We accepted.

Nearby is a memorial site dedicated to workers who'd died laboring on the expressway, and we motored a short way up an obscure, narrow concrete lane running behind the village and stopped at a flight of steep stone steps at the side of the lane. At the top of the stairs is a clearing set in flagstone rock, in the center a thin, vertical slab of dark marble. Etched in the marble are rows of engravings — the names of seventy-seven men who'd perished.

I was gobsmacked. Steers had written that only "several" workers died, but seventy-seven was a whole lot more than several. That was one death every twelve days on average over two and a half years. A fact conveniently omitted by Steers, who'd been commissioned by Hyundai to pen a sycophantic book. President Park demanded construction catapult at breakneck speed. Chung pushed workers hard. Worker safety was obviously an afterthought.

Now late afternoon, we were on our way to a bridge where during the Korean War, local villagers were massacred by U.S. troops. The tragedy came to international attention in 1999, when three

Associated Press reporters published a series of articles revealing the slaughter occurred between July 26 and 29, 1950 at Nogeunri Bridge. U.S. planes dropped bombs and strafed villagers, and American troops machine-gunned men, women and kids, killing between 300 and 400. AP reporters Choe Sang-hun, Charles J. Hanley and Martha Mendoza co-authored *The Bridge at No Gun Ri: A Hidden Nightmare from the Korean War*. The trio won the 2000 Pulitzer for investigative reporting.

No Gun Ri (spelled Nogeunri today) is about twenty-five kilometers east of Joryeong village. Sung-jai and I headed there from Geumgang Resort, driving a short way along a country road paralleling the river, then entering Gyeongbu Expressway, moving east through a series of tunnels blasted through mountains looming vertically like great camel humps. Farther ahead we exited the expressway in the general vicinity of Nogeunri but got thoroughly lost in the surrounding quiet, isolated countryside. An hour later at sunset we came upon humanity in a pretty little hamlet. We stopped to ask directions and ended up sitting on a store-front porch sipping beer and talking with half a dozen locals.

I made the mistake of asking one of the men — a spry, eighty year old — if he'd seen action in the Korean War. Fifty minutes later he finished describing his battle exploits. He said he'd almost lost his life accompanying U.S. soldiers caught in a Chinese ambush in North Korea in the winter of 1950.

"Look at my right ankle," he said proudly, rolling up his trouser leg and slipping down his sock, revealing a large nasty gash. "That's where the bullet hit."

After ninety minutes of chatting, dusk upon us, we returned to the car and drove off. At a nearby hill in a picturesque dell was a lonely motel — the only structure for miles around — where we stayed the night. We were told the bridge was nearby.

In the morning we found Nogeunri Bridge in a secluded, narrow pass between hills, but without persistence and luck we wouldn't have located it. Not a dwelling or person was around, just still, quiet dry farmland and hills. It was 8:30, a scorcher of a morning, hot and humid. We had a nine o'clock appointment to meet a local, Nam Jong-hyeon, the father of a university student I knew in Seoul. Mr. Nam had volunteered to show us around.

Narrow, concrete Nogeunri Bridge doubles as a tunnel. A dual rail line runs over the viaduct-like structure joining Daejeon to the west and Daegu to the east. Underneath are two, side-by-side tall arched tunnels, a concrete lane passing through one, a tiny creek flowing through the other. We ambled into the tunnel. Pockmarks were in the concrete, some circled in blue, indicating where U.S. bullets struck. At 8:46 a speeding eastbound passenger train flew over the short trestle and disappeared behind dry hills. Seven minutes later, a slow-moving westbound freight train rolled over.

Mr. Nam arrived in his car. We followed him in our car for about five miles west. The narrow country road passes by strips of parched farmland. At Jugok village — all of a few agricultural plots and a couple of small farmsteads — we turned onto a narrow lane that soon dead-ended at a small farm back-dropped by a steep hill. We were in Imgye village — a mere hamlet. Our guide introduced us to the farm's owner, Yang Hae-chan, a handsome, lean man with a quiet, dignified no-nonsense air and intelligent sad eyes. "I'm busy doing chores so I can only talk a few minutes," Mr. Yang said gruffly. In 1950, the then ten-year-old spent four harrowing days trapped in Nogeunri's tunnel of death.

To evade the sun, the four of us retreated to a small canopied shelter where feed and fertilizer were stored. I sat on a yellow plastic milk crate, listening to Mr. Yang, Sung-jai translating. Mr. Yang said he'd been interviewed for the book written by the AP reporters about the massacre.

When North Korea attacked South Korea on June 25, 1950 it was a blitzkrieg, hundreds of thousands of enemy troops equipped with Russian-made T-34 tanks, pouring south over the 38 parallel. South Korea had only 95,000 poorly-trained, inadequately-equipped troops and no air force. Seoul was quickly overrun. Within days 34,000 ROK soldiers were either dead, captured or missing. The KPA (North Korean People's Army) quickly pushed south, citizens in Seoul and surrounding areas fleeing to safety in Busan. The road we'd just driven along from Nogeunri was then the main route connecting Seoul to Busan — single-lane, rutted, potholed dusty dirt.

"I was in the third grade at Hwagok Elementary School," recounted Mr. Yang. "After the North attacked, my teacher told us not to come to school anymore."

United Nations troops comprising mostly U.S. soldiers stationed in Japan, soon arrived on the peninsula. On July 22, a little more than three weeks after the war began, a battalion of about 600 U.S. soldiers entered Jugok — the hamlet off the main road near Mr. Yang's residence. North Korean troops were a few miles west. Near the enemy was another American battalion. On July 25, U.S. soldiers ordered all residents in and around Jugok to be ready to evacuate.

"There were about 600 or 700 villagers, mostly extended families of men, women and children," said Mr. Yang. "We moved onto the road at around midnight. Many people slept outside that evening." The next morning, the U.S. troops were gone. Village elders decided the mass should head on the dirt road toward Busan. "We had just our clothes, food and blankets on our backs," said Mr. Yang. His mother, father, grandmother, two aunts, two brothers and a sister brought up the rear.

We'd been listening to Mr. Yang for about fifteen minutes, when he grew agitated and grumbled, "It's planting season ... I have lots of work to do." We agreed to reconvene tonight at Nogeunri Bridge.

Still only mid-morning, Sung-jai and I headed west on a country road back to Geumgang Resort to rendezvous with Mr. Park for our afternoon tour of Dangjae Tunnel.

In isolated Yeongdong County, on the side of the road, we came upon a former school converted to Chateau Mani winery. We stopped to have a look. Chateau Mani's manager, Jong Dong-whan, kindly guided us through the property, showing us vineyards, a basement full of oak caskets, and a warehouse with a number of huge wine tanks. In the chateau's spacious second floor ballroom, a wine tour was underway, guests comprising a large group of retirees who'd ridden the train from Seoul. Seated at large round white-clothed tables, the folks were tasting wine, enjoying meals and listening to a talk on wine-drinking protocol from a woman. Mr. Jong invited Sung-jai and me to stay for lunch, the buffet table full of dishes of mouth-watering beef, pork and rice and delectable deserts. After many weeks on the road sustained mostly by sliced ham and processed cheese sandwiches, I was in smorgasbord heaven. I had second, third and fourth helpings – God have mercy on my soul. I observed that at a table near ours, two ladies wearing baseball caps were furiously working over big wads of gum in their mouths, the gentleman seated next to them contentedly dozing.

We arrived at Joryeong village and met Mr. Park, who had us follow his car up a nearby and permanently closed ramp leading to a former section of Gyeongbu Expressway. Mr. Park maneuvered around the ramp barrier, and we did likewise, then we drove slowly on the long-abandoned road. On our right was a long, steep wooded cliff descending far below to the Geum River. With the road's slight, tight curves, it wasn't difficult to fathom a speeding driver losing control of a car and plummeting into the river ravine.

We soon dead-ended at an abrupt, shrub-heavy, earthen mountain rising vertically above sealed Dangjae Tunnel. Hollowing through the mountain to create the tunnel decades ago, some laborers had been buried under tons of dirt and rock in cave-ins. Mr. Park explained that this section of the expressway was too tight and winding. "There used to be lots of accidents along here. In 1981 or 1982, a bus went over the cliff."

The government closed the road and tunnel in 2003. A new route was constructed just east through newly-built Okcheon Tunnels 1, 2 and 3.

"Is there anything behind the tunnel's door?" I asked.

"A food company stores kimchi there," Mr. Park said. Kimchi's spiced, salted vegetables ferment well when stored in large, breathable clay jars in dark, cool places.

***

At 7:00 p.m., Sung-jai and I were back at Nogeunri Bridge sitting at a picnic table, listening intently to Mr. Yang chronicle his story. The mass of 700 or so locals trundled slowly east from the village along the road that morning. Just before reaching Nogeunri Bridge, they were met by a U.S. military truck and troops blocking their way. Soldiers ordered the villagers onto the train tracks, and surrounded them and searched each person.

"I was wearing my school uniform of long black Japanese-style pants and white shirt and rubber shoes," said Mr. Yang. "It was hot. Soldiers were giving orders in Japanese because they'd been stationed in Japan, and some Koreans who spent time under the Japanese spoke it."

The soldiers abruptly disappeared. A short while later a small U.S. plane appeared low overhead, then flew off. Suddenly, three U.S. planes approached low to the ground. The pilots released bombs onto the assemblage of people and strafed them with machine-gun fire. Soldiers in surrounding hills and foxholes machine gunned the mass as well.

The AP reporters described in *The Bridge at No Gun Ri: A Hidden Nightmare from the Korean War*, bombs landing directly on some, instantly obliterating them, shrapnel tearing into bodies, slicing off arms, legs and heads. An estimated one hundred women – some pregnant – men and kids lay dead, dying or injured. The bombs had struck with such force that the nearby rail track was mangled, thrust vertically up in the air. Bedlam ensued, panicked villagers screaming and crying, some frozen to the spot. Others ran wildly. Some dove into ditches. Those who initially survived the bombing now had to escape gunfire blazing from hills and foxholes.

"People were running everywhere. Some just dropped ... they were too scared to run," said Mr. Yang. "I don't know how long it lasted – I was too scared to know. I think my grandmother was struck directly by a bomb and died instantly. My two brothers were killed too. My father ran into the hills."

Mr. Yang's thirteen-year-old sister, Hae-sook, was struck in the left eye by a bomb's fireball, her eyeball dangling by a sinewy thread from her eye socket. The book describes how Hae-sook "grabbed it in her own fist. She yanked it, broke it off herself ... then threw her eye away."

U.S. soldiers reappeared and checked dead bodies, prodding them with bayonets. Survivors, estimated at about 400, were herded into Nogeunri's duel tunnels, each thirteen meters tall, twenty-five meters long, seven meters wide. A minuscule creek flowed through one. Villagers huddled in the dry tunnel. The nightmare was far from over.

Later that first night, with hundreds in the tunnel wounded, bleeding, hungry and thirsty, U.S. troops, surrounding the tunnel, began an hour-long barrage of mortars, tracers and bullets. Machine guns spit out 500 rounds per minute. Babies, children, mothers, grandmothers and men were picked off and killed. The wounded lost blood and died.

"Dead bodies piled up," Mr. Yang recalled. "Some people hid behind bodies, others dug themselves into the ground. My mother, and sister and I lay together motionless. We didn't dare whisper a word or you'd get a bullet. One move got you killed — it was horror. I didn't even go to the bathroom, I was so scared. Maybe I fell asleep, but I have no memory of sleeping. I never even saw the soldiers."

As Sung-jai and I listened to Mr. Yang, darkness encroached. The diffused faint light from a nearby lone yellow street lamp was insufficient to illuminate my notebook, so I withdrew a small flashlight from my waist pack, shone it onto the pages and continued scribbling. The sound of chirping crickets permeated the still, quiet country air.

Mr. Yang continued: "If someone tried to crawl out of the tunnel to the creek to drink water they were shot. If someone tried to escape they were shot." The following day brought another barrage of gunfire and more death. At one point, U.S. soldiers and medics entered the tunnel to check on the villagers, but no assistance was given.

Why had the U.S. bombed and shot innocent civilians? A U.S. general had erroneously believed that North Korean soldiers had infiltrated the group, and the enemy needed to be eliminated. (North Korean soldiers sometimes donned civilian clothing, mingling with groups of refugees to avoid detection.) The order was given not to permit the mass past Nogeunri Bridge. If they tried, it was shoot to kill.

Mr. Yang scoffed at the idea the enemy had penetrated his assemblage. "Everyone knew everyone else — it was impossible for North Koreans to be among us."

On the morning of the fourth day of horror — July 29 — North

Koreans approached the tunnel. U.S. soldiers had disappeared. The "enemy" announced to the villagers that they were free. Mr. Yang's father appeared from the hills and carried his wounded wife home. Survivors returned to the tracks and tunnel searching for family and relatives. Corpses were strewn about decomposing in the searing summer heat. Some survivors found family members, others didn't. The bodies of Mr. Yang's two brothers and grandmother were never found. In total, ten of his family members were killed, including his uncle, two aunts and four cousins. No definitive count of the death toll was ascertained. Best estimates were about one hundred died in the initial bombing, 200 to 300 in the tunnel.

Now nine o'clock, Mr. Yang appeared haggard, his eyes sad, his spirit downcast. He had grown up without his brothers. "I missed them dearly," he said. I felt an enormous pang of empathy for him. When Mr. Yang's family members died, a part of his childhood and soul perished too. What he experienced at Nogeunri wasn't like hell, it was hell, a living hell. Horror seared into memories sure to haunt him and surviving villagers to their deathbeds.

CHAPTER 13

Gyeryong Mountain:
A Formidable Buddhist Nun

Among the more than 3,000 Buddhist temples in South Korea, Donghak Temple was designated for nuns only. In my years in the country, having wandered into a handful of temples, I'd noted the grounds usually occupied with a preponderance of monks. I was sure the nuns at Donghak Temple would have stories to tell. The day after our probe at Nogeunri Bridge, Sung-jai and I were on our way to get the lowdown from nuns.

Donghak Temple is in Gyeryong National Mountain Park between Daejeon and Gongju. The park encompasses sixty-five square kilometers and twenty-one granite peaks on a spur of the Charyeong Mountains in South Chungcheong province. The tallest peak is Gyeryong Mountain rising 845 meters from the surrounding plain.

The final kilometer to the park's entrance is on gently ascending, tree-lined Donghak Temple Road. A handful of restaurants, cafés, souvenir shops, convenience stores and a *minbak* (family home with rooms for rent) or two face the road. Everything is dwarfed by the parallel, looming, steep wooded rising slopes. On weekends and holidays, and when cherry blossoms bloom in spring and leaves turn vivid reds, oranges and yellows in autumn, national mountain parks can resemble fairgrounds with upward of 10,000 visitors daily. One Sunday fall afternoon, my friend Moonie invited me to hike a national mountain park south of Seoul. Parked cars and throngs of hikers there were so numerous, it was like attending a BTS boy band concert.

Today was a weekday near the end of May, and only a smattering of cars and a few hikers were evident. It was late afternoon, and most trekkers had completed their climbs.

At the park entrance, a sign at the ticket hut read: "Donghak Temple — 1.6 kilometers ahead." From the hut we strolled the wide path, ascending gradually through woods, bountiful leafy branches above forming a solid green canopy blocking the sun, resulting in welcome shade and a comfortable eighteen degrees Celsius. Not a twig rustled. The only sounds were the shrill tweets of songbirds and a gurgle from a crystal clear mountain brook. A couple of hikers passed us on the way down.

We arrived at Donghak Temple, built off the side of the path. In the compact grounds are a modest temple hall, a tall stone pagoda and several minor structures. In front is a small wood office, which we entered to find several nuns, one of whom appeared to be in her sixties. She had bushy eyebrows and a gold front tooth. She warmly greeted us.

Sung-jai told the nun that I was writing a travel book on South Korea and would like to include Donghak's nuns. I handed the nun my name card.

She sternly surveyed it, nodded, and slowly read my name aloud: "Dake Mark ... Dake Mark."

I politely corrected her: "Mark Dake," I said, which sent her into a merry fit of laughter.

"Now isn't a good time to talk," she said. "We're having a meeting soon. Go up the mountain and come back down, then we can talk."

"Good idea. I need the exercise," I joked, and she laughed heartily at this too.

We hadn't planned on hiking, and it would take several hours to go up and come back down. It was already 4:30 p.m., but why not. The view from the summit would be impressive, and it would do us good to stretch our legs. Sitting behind the wheel of the car every day, I noted that my chest was beginning to fuse to my stomach. If I wasn't careful, I'd soon appear like one of those elderly Florida retirees who strolls in public with his pants held up by suspenders, hiked up to his chest. We agreed to meet the nun back at the temple office at eight o'clock, giving us three and a half hours to ascend and descend the eminence.

Up ahead on the path, a trail map indicated three separate trails led to various peaks. We opted to trek the one summiting at Gwaneum Peak. Sung-jai, who was quicker, nimbler and lighter than I, went on ahead. I began striding the earthen trail. At first the incline was easy, which suited me fine. Soon it veered sharply upward. Generously strewn with an annoying and uneven layer of stones and small jagged rocks, it felt like a shallow, pebbly creek on which I was walking barefoot. After an hour of such pounding, I was unabashedly and loudly cursing park management.

Emerging from the gloomy shadows at the peak at about six thirty, Sung-jai was waiting for me at a wood gazebo on the wide, exposed jagged granite ridge. A sign announced: 816 meters – Gyeryongsan, Gwaneumbong. We'd made it, 8,000 meters shy of Mount Everest's summit. Still, a small matter of pride to reach the top. Koreans – particularly middle-aged and older – proliferate on mountain trails. The draw of alpine hiking is the thrill of summiting, of nature and fresh air, of broad views from crests, of comradeship, of the satisfying feeling of tight thigh and calf muscles after a vigorous climb. A while back, ambling on the low crest of Acha Mountain in Seoul, I heard long, loud bellows emanating from an unseen male hiker releasing pent-up energy. I understand — in an opaque sort of way — why the national pastime of mountain trekking in a country brimming with humps, hills, mountains, crests and peaks, is appealing. I, however, am content to view these numerous profusions and pinnacles from the bottom up.

The panoramic view from our perch was captivating, particularly under an arresting gray-purple dusk sky. Looking north and west is to a line of low rocky outcrops jutting starkly up from the surrounding flat plain. The view southwest is of vast, flat Geum River Basin divided into tens of thousands of small, rectangular yellow-brown rice paddies. Looking southeast far in the distance, is Daejeon and its innumerable blocks of white apartment buildings appearing like miniature models in a showroom. Directly below, but far off, is Donghak Temple at a V in the sweeping wooded slope.

"The temple's farther away than I thought," I said to Sung-jai. It was past seven o'clock, nightfall fast approaching. "We should start heading down." We began descending. Stepping on those pieces of sharp rock made the experience as enjoyable as undergoing a colonoscopy.

At 8:30 p.m., we puffed into the temple office. A lone nun gave us disappointing news. "No one's available to talk now, everyone's at a meeting. Come back tomorrow," she said.

We'd do just that. Sung-jai and I headed down the path. At the park entrance we encountered a park ranger, Park No-san, a thoroughly decent, loquacious chap who'd been employed with the Korean National Park Service for more than three decades. The three of us sat on a bench and chatted. Mr. Park said the biggest change he'd observed in more than thirty years at the park was in visitors' attitudes toward the environment.

"People used to throw garbage on the trail," he recalled. "They'd be drunk. We'd say to them, 'Please pick up your garbage.' They'd reply, 'You're the park officials, it's your job to pick it up, that's what you get paid for.' It's taken a lot of time to change. It's been a very gradual process."

He recalled a few deaths on climbs, several hikers succumbing to heart attacks. One woman began trekking in high-heel shoes but was relegated to removing them and traipsing in bare feet. About that annoying layer of sharp rocks Sung-jai and I experienced? "We've gotten complaints from other hikers too and are considering removing them," Mr. Park said.

Approaching ten o'clock, we began strolling down Donghak Temple Road, past brightly-lit but empty restaurants.

"Come join me for dinner," Mr. Park requested.

"Thanks, but we're sweaty and grubby and need showers," I replied.

"You can have a shower in my room," Mr. Park offered brightly, pointing to a small room where he stayed next to a restaurant.

I harbored a rather alarming vision of sharing a shower stall with a buck-naked park ranger beckoning to scrub my back under a jet of hot water. "Thanks again but we really should go," I said. Sung-jai and I trundled down the road to find a *minbak*. Later, I regretted not having accompanied Mr. Park for a bite to eat. He was perhaps a tad lonely stationed in this isolated area and simply wanted company.

Down the road a few hundred meters we rented a room at Gyeryong Minbak and took welcome long, hot showers. We soaped up our day's garments and stomped on and rinsed them in the shower stall, then threw the wet clothes on the line outside on the front porch. In the room, we unrolled thick comfortable mats on the floor. I fell asleep almost instantly. There must have been something in the mountain air.

**

We awoke to a cool, gray, still damp morning. We made our way up to Donghak Temple to hopefully speak with nuns. At the temple entrance I looked across the path and noticed standing on a modest knoll the outline of several robed nuns. We clambered up the knoll to find three nuns in loose, gray smocks tending a small vegetable garden. Two of them appeared to be in their early thirties. They wore oversized straw hats for protection against the hot sun, and were squatting on their haunches silently hoeing earth. The third nun was much older and obviously in a position of power. When we introduced ourselves only she spoke.

Her name was Ryo Myoung but I nicknamed her Attila the Nun, due to her hefty girth and aggressive disposition. Attila, whose head was shaved as Buddhist custom dictates, also wore a wide-brimmed straw hat.

"I've been a nun at Donghak Temple for fifty-two years," Attila boasted, "but I'm not the oldest here. One nun's ninety-five."

Since she'd initiated the topic of age, I asked hers.

"Why do you want to know?" she retorted brusquely. "Age is important to you?"

"No, but..."

She cut me off. "I'm sixty-nine."

Attila said new recruits are permitted to reside at Donghak on a two-year trial basis to acclimatize themselves to the Buddhist lifestyle and to ascertain if it is a calling they desire. An average of fifteen rookie nuns arrive annually. About 150 nuns currently resided at Donghak.

"Is the Buddhist lifestyle of early-to-bed, early-to-rise difficult?" I ventured.

"A stupid question!" she chastised. "Life's always a repetition. Today exists because there was yesterday. Tomorrow exists because there's today."

Even I knew that.

So not to stoke her wrath again, I opted for a more conciliatory approach. "Do you miss the outside world?"

"Another stupid question!" she declared. "Those who practice aesthetics don't think about the outside world!" I was beginning to wonder if Attila had voluntarily joined the nunhood or been mandated into it by court order.

Now fully cognizant that any query I uttered would get me labeled a dotard, I attempted to appeal to her latent emotional side and squeaked, "I know very little about Buddhism. If you could tell me a bit about it, I'd be very appreciative."

"Ah, ask more question!" she offered cheerfully.

Of course. "But how do I know what's a good, and what's a bad question?" I asked.

"There are no bad questions!" she replied testily.

Of course not.

"What's the most important aspect about being a Buddhist?" I put forth.

"To recognize the truth. To be like Buddha. All animals have the ability to live and survive, but only humans can do better than animals and attain a higher plane."

Attila believed in reincarnation. "I think I was a nun in my former life," she said thoughtfully. God help the nunhood.

"It must be wonderful to live here in the mountains," I continued.

"Yes, we're close to Buddha and enjoy fresh air, but it's cold in winter." She pointed across the knoll to the path in front of the temple where a hiker was taking a photo. She complained, "I don't like that. Before Gyeryong became a national park in 1968, people rarely visited here."

"But visitors are more environmentally-friendly now," I added optimistically, recalling what ranger Park told us last night.

"No they're not ... they still leave garbage!" she snapped.

Attila sat on a small wood stool, opened her lunch bag, and extricated a rice cake, melon slices and a small thermos of orange juice, and quietly began nibbling and sipping. Despite her outward gruff manner, a schoolgirl innocence shone through.

She suddenly announced: "Mark, why don't you become a monk!"

Oh my, the same offer the Venerable Jae-An at Jogye Temple in Seoul — who'd almost kidnapped me into the monkhood — proposed six weeks earlier. The thought of tucking into bed at 9:00 p.m., waking at 3:00 a.m., and living a highly regimented, disciplined lifestyle was totally out of sync with my free-spirited, occasional whimsical existence. Left to my own nocturnal rhythms, I'm not usually putting down a book or finishing reading internet news until two or three in the morning — the same time nuns and monks wake to begin their days.

"If I became a monk, I'd miss playing sports," I told Attila.

"The 108 bows monks do every day is a good substitute for exercise," she assured me.

The monks I'd observed at temples seemed more often than not, portly and stout under their billowy robes. "I need to move and swim and cycle and play tennis," I responded.

She pointed to my stomach — something of a habit, it seemed, for monks and nuns across the peninsula sizing up fellows with nascent bellies — and declared, "If you do 108 bows every day, you'll reduce its size!"

This was ironic. Attila's girth and weight made her an ideal candidate to crack the Korean Women's Olympic weightlifting team. Those 108 daily bows she'd apparently undertaken for the past fifty-two years (I suspected she purposely evaded them) hadn't seemed to have had much effect on her overall body mass.

After our nearly hour-long chat, ready to take our leave, we thanked Ryo Myoung and bade goodbye.

Not so fast – another *faux pas*. "It's not 'goodbye' Mark," she abruptly corrected me, and demonstrated the formal, Buddhist-style goodbye, placing her hands together in front of her, as if in prayer, and offering a slight bow. I did likewise. Satisfied, Attila granted us her divine permission to depart.

Sung-jai and I strolled back down the path to the park entrance and on to the *minbak*. Our clothes on the line were still damp, but we threw them in the car anyway. We needed to be on the road again. At the side of the *minbak*, we noted a small, mangy dog tied to the wall by a two-feet-long chain, no slack for the animal to move. Its water bowl was empty so I filled it up from my water bottle, then went to the car and grabbed a handful of strawberries I'd bought yesterday and fed them to the dog. Two elderly women sitting on chairs on the *minbak's* veranda were looking out.

"Excuse me, we're wondering if the dog's yours?" called Sung-jai.

"Yes," one replied.

"Does it get off the chain?"

"No."

In the countryside, I'd long observed that in the front of many small farms and homes were doghouses, a dog or two or several chained to them. In conversation with the home owners, I learned it wasn't uncommon for the animals never to be let off their chains for a walk or exercise in the dog's lifetime.

"Do you think sometimes you might let it off the chain? It might like exercise," Sung-jai suggested.

"No, if we do, it tries to bite people," a woman argued defiantly, as if the tiny mutt could injure someone.

"It's not healthy for a dog not to get exercise," Sung-jai pressed.

The ladies were unmoved: "Why should we let it off the chain? It's not sick."

I harbored an evil though thoroughly satisfying thought of tying the two women to the side of the *minbak* by two-feet-long chains.

Today was June 1, marking about seven weeks on the road for the Scoupe, thus far rolling over about 4,000 kilometers of blacktop — equal to driving the length of the country eight times. The big-hearted auto needed to hold together for another month or so, and eat up another 4,000 clicks.

We had a relatively long distance to motor on our next leg to the south coast to Sorok Island in South Jeolla province. We'd spend tonight in the city of Gwangju, 170 kilometers south, to rendezvous with a young woman named Miki, arriving from Seoul at 9:00 p.m. on the high-speed KTX train.

In Seoul, two weeks earlier, seeking a translator after Heju went missing in action, Miki had answered my online ad. She was a tour guide based in Seoul and led Korean tour groups in Japan. She spoke fluent Japanese, Korean and English. When I mentioned I'd be visiting Sorokdo — with its unusual history — she expressed enthusiasm to see it. We arranged that Miki would accompany Sung-jai and me to Sorokdo this weekend.

We drove south through remote back-country, paralleling the western edge of the Sobaek Mountains, then into the Noryeong Mountains — splintering west from the Sobaeks. It is lonely wilderness — big, steep, imposing wooded slopes engulfing us. About fifty kilometers northeast of Gwangju, we stopped for a rest break in Gangjin County, at the tiny mountain village of Imsil, a mere blip on the map. There is one gas station here, belonging to the national

SK chain. I asked the woman behind the counter if I could use the washroom, and she pointed me out back.

"It's dirty," she warned.

No it wasn't, it was filthy. The concrete and tile facility stood alone outside, off to the side. I entered and a stench hit my nose like a freight train. The urinals appeared not to have been cleaned since 1967, the odor overpowering. I dashed outside, drew a huge breath, held it, darted inside, used the urinal — my face bright red from lack of oxygen — raced outside, exhaled and quickly gulped in long deep breaths of fresh air.

"Was that a washroom?" I asked Sung-jai, incredulously.

He gave a knowing smile. "That's how public washrooms used to be in Korea before the government started a program for cleaner ones," he confessed.

In the 1990s, the national government began a campaign to engender pan-peninsula sparkling public toilets. These days, when one enters a public washroom, at say, the foot of a national mountain trail or at a highway rest stop, you'll almost always find clean, modern facilities of such high caliber, it can be like sitting on a five-star hotel toilet. You might even find a plaque reading, for example, "Best Toilet 2009" or "Best Toilet 2015."

When Heju and I hiked Acha Mountain in Seoul in March, at its base we entered a public washroom, a sign in front stating: "Seoul Best Toilet — August, 2002 — 1st Prize from Mayor of Seoul."

The owner of this Imsil SK gas station obviously hadn't gotten the official memo from her government to upgrade her commode. Two other SK gas stations we'd go on to stop at in the southwest Jeolla provinces also had washrooms beyond horrendously dirty.

***

In mid-evening we rolled into Gwangju, its 1.8 million marvelous citizens passionately following our epic journey, all of them on the roads in their vehicles warmly welcoming us. The Scoupe was on a main street, boxed by innumerable cars, taxis, Bongo trucks, SUVs and buses. Frustrated drivers even leaned on their car horns as an added complimentary personal salutation to us. It took more than an hour, crawling in a stop-and-go, bumper-to-bumper parade, to travel the short distance to the Gwangju Train Station, where we met Miki. A third would be along for the next leg of the odyssey.

SOUTHWEST

CHAPTER 14

Sorok Island: Hidden Lepers

Sung-jai, Miki and I cruised leisurely southeast from Gwangju toward Sorok Island through narrow agricultural coastal plains interspersed with low mountains rising like stalwart monoliths from the surrounding flatness. In mid-afternoon we arrived at the southern tip of Goheung peninsula at the attractive little port village of Doyang. Goheung is a large, prominent, irregularly-shaped arm jutting south off the mainland replete with numerous inlets, bays and offshore islands. Sorokdo is separated from Goheung and Doyang by a mere 300-meter-wide channel.

Sorokdo is a few kilometers long, and woodsy, with a couple of low mountains. A small ferry shuttles foot passengers back and forth between the island and Doyang. We parked at the port, boarded the ferry and a few minutes later were strolling the island, inland under a canopy of lovely old trees. We soon arrived at a large muddy bay. Directly across the channel, Doyang Port was visible. At the head of the bay is compact, white Sorokdo National Hospital, which we entered to inquire if guided tours of Sorokdo were available. An administrator asked us to return Monday morning, when a guide would meet us. Today was Saturday. Sung-jai, Miki and I would need to hang around Doyang for an extra day.

"I'll show you around Goheung tomorrow," I suggested, of our free day. They were up for that.

At six o'clock, we caught the last ferry back to Doyang then strolled along the harbor past a modest fleet of fishing vessels docked at the concrete waterfront. A bustling fish market is on the water's edge with scores of fish sellers equipped with innumerable large buckets of sea water, containing everything from live mini octopus and oysters to sea worms and myriad fish. Past the market at the far edge we climbed a grassy knoll. At the top was a plaque honoring two Korean naval seamen: Lee Dae-won, killed in 1587 by Japanese pirates based on the Japanese island of Tsushima fifty kilometers south of Busan; and Jeong Un, dying in Japan's assault of Korea in the 1592-1598 Imjin War.

Standing on the crest, Miki out of the blue suddenly griped, "Sorokdo's boring ... I want to go to Boseong." Sung-jai nodded in consensus.

I was taken aback. We'd only been on Sorokdo for a grand total of ninety minutes and hadn't toured it yet. Besides, several hours earlier just northwest of Goheung, we'd passed through the small rural town of Boseong, renowned for its tea leaves growing in long rows on picturesque lush green mountain slopes. I'd stopped the car there and asked my companions if they'd like to tour the tea plantations. No, they'd answered.

"Miki," I replied measuredly, "we were just in Boseong. You said you didn't want to see it when we stopped."

She contemplated this a few moments, then announced, "Well, let's go to Yeosu then!"

I gritted my teeth. Yeosu peninsula is immediately east of Goheung, but to reach it requires navigating north out of Goheung, then east, then south to Yeosu city, a couple hours' drive.

The purpose of our excursion was to explore Sorokdo, not Yeosu or Boseong. "Miki, you said in Seoul you wanted to see Sorokdo. We're here now so let's see it," I stated crisply. I could tell she and Sung-jai wanted to press their points, but declined.

We walked back to town passing the harbor and found a well-used *yeogwan*, where I rented a large, spacious room. We plunked down our stuff and unrolled mats and bedding. Sung-jai and Miki went out for dinner while I stayed in and rested. Over the past two days I'd driven a number of kilometers and was weary.

***

Sunday was perfect weather-wise — a balmy twenty-seven degrees, low humidity, bright sunshine, a fresh sea breeze and hazy blue sky. The three of us spent most of the day touring Goheung, which measures about thirty-five kilometers wide and forty kilometers north-south. The interior is generously sprinkled with clusters of low, steep wooded mountains and two large agricultural plains. The three coastlines vary with sections of muddy bays, rocky rough surf, plunging slopes and even small sandy beaches. In some areas are muddy bays within muddy bays within muddy bays. Tides recede and rise about four meters, exposing at low ebb shallow morasses of deep muddy goo.

I was familiar with Goheung. The previous year on an extended Thanksgiving holiday, Heju and I had rented a car for ten days and covered more than 600 kilometers on Goheung's every paved, gravel and dirt road to every nook and cranny. On a seaside lane in Dohwa County we puttered alongside clear turquoise water next to large smooth granite boulders.

The lane dead-ended at Balpo village's several dwellings at the bottom of a wooded hill. We walked on a dirt path up the hill through pine trees. On the other side of the hill at the bottom was a clearing with a pretty little grassy meadow. Meadows are rare in Korea. A handful of cows contentedly grazed on the grass. Immediately in front of the meadow was a large bay and half-moon sandy Balpo Beach. Not a soul was around, our own private Shangri-La.

I drove Sung-jai and Miki to Balpo Beach. The only ones there, we relaxed on the sand. Sung-jai and I even took a dip in the twenty-two-degree water. We traveled all over Goheung for the day. On the south coast we were high up on the road overlooking numerous small offshore, uninhabited islands dotting the green water. On the east shore we enjoyed a clear view across the bay in the distance to the wooded mountain ridge on Yeosu peninsula. At the end of a long, pleasurable day we returned to Doyang in early evening. Sung-jai asked to be dropped back at the *yeogwan*, while Miki — having recently begun taking golf lessons in Seoul — was keen to head north to Goheung City's golf driving range. No matter which town or city you're in this country, a driving range is almost always in close proximity.

We headed on Goheung's modern, almost empty parkway to just outside Goheung City — a small, concentrated, busy town built on a razor-thin slice of land sandwiched between low steep mountains. The driving range is just outside town, nestled alone by woods. It was 8:30 p.m.; we were the only customers. We rented irons (left-handed for me) and began swatting golf balls into the long, narrow fairway encompassed by high netting on the floodlit range. The facility's young golf instructor kindly offered me free pointers, and I concentrated on his every word.

I'd never had a golf lesson. In middle school in Toronto, my school mates and I played a fair bit of golf, but our swings were rough and homemade, none of us very good players. When we did connect solidly and squarely though, and the ball sailed long and hard in a glorious arc down the middle of the fairway, there was no more exhilarating feeling in the world. For a fleeting moment, at least, we experienced what our golf heroes of the day — Jack Nicklaus, Lee Trevino and Johnny Miller — did every stroke. Those several springs and summers on a foursome on the course with Richard Earl, Mike Day, Cliff Flint, Shane Bury, Stuart Nicol, Dennis Hisey, Rick Thorsteinson, Mark Richardson and Bruce McCann are cherished boyhood memories.

"Keep your posture straight when you address the ball," the coach advised; I was bending too far forward from the waist. "Your clubhead needs to move through the ball more," he added; I needed more clubhead speed. I followed his advice, and for the next thirty minutes, I was exhilarated, balls consistently rocketing strong, hard and fast off my clubface. Maddeningly, when I'm out on an actual golf course, such magic rarely occurs.

Miki was having a rough go of it, her swing so stiff and rigor mortis-like, her body was mimicking a corpse, golf balls weakly sliding off her clubface and skidding along the grass, decimating the entire population of poor, alarmed worms within thirty meters of the tee.

"Maybe try relaxing a bit," I suggested.

Miki replied defiantly, "No, my golf coach told me to focus only on the correct swing technique, not to worry where the ball goes." At least she had the latter part of his advice down pat.

Back in Doyang, at a booth at a mom-and-pop fried chicken restaurant, Miki and I shared a plate of chicken for dinner. Miki was in her early thirties, single and said she was seeking a partner in life.

"My mommy wants me to join a dating agency," she said.

"How does the agency work?" I asked.

"You pay two million, four million or eight million won."

"What does two million won get you?"

"A lower class of man," she said.

"Four million?"

"Middle class."

"Eight million?"

"Top class."

"What do you mean by 'class?'" I asked. I was unaware that the salary one earned automatically resulted in a corresponding rise in class.

The "lowest-class," two-million-won men, Miki said, included low-paid office workers with a bachelor's degree. Four-million-won fellows had a university degree and higher-paying jobs. Premium earners were top-gun, eight-million-won, blue-blood doctors, lawyers, industrialists and businessmen. Men without university degrees couldn't join the agency. Aspiring members were required to show proof of employment and income. True love had little to do with this dating site. To join it seemed little different than applying for membership at a university fraternity house.

"What if you met a taxi driver who didn't have a degree but whom you loved?" I hypothesized.

Miki dispassionately replied, "I wouldn't love him ... I couldn't. Taxi drivers don't think and most have bad character."

Well, I'd driven a taxi for six months in Toronto after high school and was somehow able to occasionally cobble together a mildly intelligent phrase. And depending on who you spoke to, my character wasn't that deplorable.

"What if a taxi driver had a bachelor's degree?" I tried, attempting to detect a weakness in Miki's wall of indifference.

"Then he wouldn't be a taxi driver ... he'd work a different job."

This admittedly made sense.

"But what if a banker lost his job and became a taxi driver?" I continued. During the 1997 Asian financial crisis, hundreds of bank branches in South Korea were permanently shuttered and thousands of bank staff, through no fault of their own, lost their jobs.

Miki remained unmoved. "No one would lose his job at a bank unless he was a failure. I wouldn't want him."

"What would happen if you married a taxi driver?" I asked out of curiosity.

"My friends and family wouldn't talk to me anymore."

"So then they're not real friends — they're phonies," I said, irritated by her sense of entitlement and maddening logic.

"No, it's how the Korean system works. We have to marry the same class of person."

What Miki was conveniently overlooking was, if she applied the same rigorous standards to herself as she did to potential male marriage partners, then she wouldn't make the cut with those eight-million-won doctors, industrialists, Samsung executives and sugar daddies. This logic escaped her, of course.

The next morning, Monday, Miki asked me to drive her to the Doyang Bus Station to head back to Seoul. She said she wasn't interested in touring Sorokdo anymore. I believe she preferred high-end travel. We said goodbye. I had no way of alerting Seoul's wealthy and elite bachelors to be on the lookout for a social climber. That is, if a taxi driver didn't bump off Miki first. There was always hope.

I returned to the *yeogwan* to pick up Sung-jai. We drove to the harbor, then boarded the ferry for Sorokdo. The morning was gorgeous: bright and fresh with a green, glassy smooth sea. A few kilometers south, formidable and mountainous Geogeum Island was enveloped in a blue haze.

We arrived at Sorokdo National Hospital at 9:00 a.m. to meet our guide, a Doyang Ministry of Health and Welfare official, Kim Gwang-moon. Mr. Kim led us behind the hospital into large, shaded Sorok Island Central Park. Off to the side is a modest row of handsome, small red-brick buildings, each about the size of a cabin. In a small private community not far from the park are about 200 similar buildings built many decades ago by island residents afflicted with leprosy. "The Japanese forced the lepers to construct the units. If the lepers resisted, they were sometimes punished by prison," said Mr. Kim, pointing to a nearby building that was once the island jail.

This is Sorokdo's sad, painful legacy: a depot for sufferers of leprosy or Hansen's disease. In 1916, the Japanese designated Sorokdo a national leprosy colony, rounded up afflicted citizens from around the country, and sent them to the island to be sequestered from the rest of society. Lepers were social outcasts, rejected by the public and forced to beg on streets. Japanese motives were far from altruistic. Life on the secluded island was often harsher than what the lepers had experienced on the mainland. When Korea gained independence after Japan's defeat in 1945, lepers continued to be involuntarily sent to Sorokdo.

Mr. Kim led us into a nearby, small red-brick unit known as the autopsy room or Building No. 1. Austere and bare, there is a permanent operating table on the concrete floor in the middle of the room. "When a leper died, Japanese doctors sometimes surgically experimented on the body to dissect organs," he explained. On the wall behind the operating table were several empty shelves. "Until 1996, glass jars of formaldehyde holding the organs of former patients were on the shelves."

To locate families of the deceased to repatriate the organs, the government tried to contact the next of kin. But because the Japanese destroyed records, no one knew how many autopsies had been performed and who the families of patients were. Fast forward to 1996 when public announcements were made to try to locate families. "They traveled to Sorokdo to claim body parts, but matching the organs to the correct family was almost impossible," our guide said.

Near the autopsy room, behind a low brick wall, is the former tiny prison. We entered the small cells built of fine wood and thick beams. Opposite the prison was a former five-room schoolhouse built in 1918. Near it are the long-abandoned, scant remnants of patchy grass and crumbling stone bleachers of a former baseball field. We entered a brick unit containing island memorabilia, including photographs on the wall. One photo was of Sorokdo's four Japanese governors, another of lepers laboring.

Mr. Kim led us back into the park, landscaped many decades ago under the Japanese using leper labor. Originally the park was a formidable, steep low mountain. "The Japanese forced lepers to excavate the mountain, to make a gradual slope. It took four years to complete," he said. We strolled up the path, passing several elderly patients, one with a disfigured face, another without legs, navigating a motorized wheelchair. A Sorokdo hospital nurse later explained lepers on the island often need limbs amputated due to infection.

We came to a plaque commemorating Pope John Paul II's visit to Sorokdo on May 4, 1984. Another plaque honored a Japanese military doctor, Hanai Jenkichi, a compassionate, caring man to the lepers during his 1921-1929 tenure on the island.

After two hours, the tour over, we thanked Mr. Kim and said goodbye. Sung-jai and I entered the deathly quiet, morgue-like hospital, with no sign of staff, doctors or patients. On the fourth floor we met a nurse, Park Seong-hui, who was glad to talk with us. She said to call her "Elizabeth."

We sat in Elizabeth's small austere office. The nurse was calm and down to earth, with a wise but tired visage, as if she had seen everything life had to offer, which she probably had considering she'd been caring for patients with leprosy on Sorokdo for twenty-seven years. It was immediately clear Elizabeth wasn't one to sugarcoat reality. Her displeasure with the families of patients was plainly evident.

More than 600 mostly aged men and women afflicted with leprosy live in their own private community not far from the hospital. "Most were brought here as children by their families. Sorokdo is the only home they've ever known," she said. "No patients came voluntarily." After parents dropped off a son or daughter, they usually never set foot on the island again. Of the 600 or so patients, only thirty-two have ever received any sort of visitation. The eldest resident is 103, the youngest, forty-five. Of the youngest, Elizabeth noted, "He was sent here by his family in 1997. They send him things but never visit. They're ashamed of him."

Some families purposely cut off ties with their diseased kin. "Sometimes they moved to another town and wouldn't leave a forwarding address. Other times they reported to the local government that their family member with the disease had died."

Most patients are religious. Marriages occur. "But the concept of marriage isn't in the traditional sense. If one is blind and the other deaf, they can be each other's eyes and ears," Elizabeth said.

Patients sometimes need infected tissue removed, resulting in disfigurement to the body and face, requiring plastic surgery. "We put ads directed at plastic surgeons in Seoul to volunteer some of their time to do surgery on patients' faces here, but not one doctor answered. I guess they were too busy making money," Elizabeth added sarcastically. The affluent, upscale district of Gangnam in Seoul is renowned for its legions of plastic surgery clinics.

Between 1962 and 1966, three Austrian nuns: Margaret Pissar, Marianne Stoeger and Maria Dittrick, arrived on Sorokdo and devoted themselves to the welfare of the lepers. The trio was instrumental in raising money in their home nation during a period when South Korea had scant funds. Donations were used to build a tuberculosis ward and a dormitory for the blind on the island.

In 2005, after about forty years on Sorokdo, Pissar and Stoeger returned to Austria; Dittrick had left earlier. "They were old – that's why they left," said Elizabeth. "They also felt South Korea was developed enough that they didn't need to serve here any more. And they didn't want the bridge coming over." Sorokdo Bridge was completed in 2009, connecting Doyang to Sorokdo, on to Geogeumdo. The bridge is an unnecessary, incongruous massive steel monstrosity intruding on Sorokdo's former vehicle-free solitude. Fortunately, there is no vehicle access to the patients' private residential community.

A campaign in South Korea began in 2017 to recommend Pissar and Stoeger for a Nobel Peace Prize for their four decades of service. More than one million signatures were garnered.

After two hours with Elizabeth, we bade goodbye. I then wandered alone through the hospital's fourth-floor hallways, peeking into open doors into several rooms. In one room was an aged man in bed lying on his back, his skin so pale and translucent, he appeared like an apparition. In another room an elderly, frail blind man lay on his back in bed and repeatedly raised and lowered his arms in an effort to exercise. What a fighter. Enough to break your heart.

Sung-jai and I stepped out into the mid-afternoon oppressive heat and strode up the path through the deserted, shaded park. At the top of the hill were several benches under trees. A man in a cowboy hat was holding a Polaroid camera. "Would you like your photo taken?" he called buoyantly.

"Thanks, not at the moment," I replied.

He seemed disappointed. I think he'd intended to charge a small fee for taking our photo. "Business isn't good these days," he lamented. "Everyone has a digital camera."

His name was Choi Yong-gap and he looked to be in his sixties. Mr. Choi had such an enthusiastic, outgoing way about him that in spirit he could have passed for being in his thirties. I wasn't sure if he was afflicted with leprosy. Other than a slightly tight appearance about his face he seemed to have no notable impediments. But when we shook hands, I felt his stiff, gnarled fingers and realized he had leprosy. Had I run into him walking on a street in public I wouldn't have given him a second glance.

We sat on a bench and conversed. Mr. Choi was born in 1943 in Mokpo in South Jeolla province on the southwest coast. "When I was six, I got leprosy," he said. "My mother brought me to Sorokdo. Since then she's visited just once in 1956," when he was thirteen. "My father, three brothers and sister have never visited."

At age twenty-four, he moved to Mokpo in an effort to connect with his family. "I tried to touch my nieces' and nephews' hands, but they walked away. Passengers wouldn't sit next to me on the bus. Restaurant customers didn't want to eat next to me. I wasn't invited to family birthdays." Six months after arriving, Mr. Choi returned to Sorokdo. Six years later, in 1973, he again moved to Mokpo and was similarly rejected. "I kept telling my family that I was safe, that they wouldn't get leprosy from me, but it did no good. Even today they won't accept me — they won't give me their phone number. I've given up ever seeing them again." Mr. Choi hasn't been back to Mokpo since.

As I was prone to do, I spoke before thinking, absent-mindedly spouting, "How does it feel to have been abandoned?"

Sung-jai translated the question into Korean. Mr. Choi remained silent a few moments, then burst into anguished, gut-wrenching sobs. He cried out in despair, "Even if I conquer the world it would mean nothing ... I just want to see my family once!"

Had a big hole opened up in the ground before me, I'd have gladly crawled into it. A few moments later, he regained his composure. I tried making amends. "Sung-jai and I'll be heading to Mokpo tomorrow — we could try to contact your family for you."

Mr. Choi shook his head. "My family moved. They don't want me to visit. I tried to find them with a friend's help but it didn't work out."

I persevered, "The police might be able to track them down. I could contact the police in Mokpo for you." I'd have been glad to do so, even just to observe the faces of a family bereft of empathy.

"No," he insisted resignedly, "I gave up a long time ago." I let the matter rest.

Mr. Choi's optimistic nature quickly rejuvenated, and he suggested he lead us on a tour through the park. We readily accepted. Our guide took us down the path, explaining that a brick-making facility here was once the source of bricks destined for construction of Seodaemun Prison in Seoul. He told us that the fourth Japanese governor of Sorokdo – a vainglorious man named Suho, ruling from 1933 to 1942 – had ordered a statue made of himself and had it erected in the park.

"Suho paid for the statue by stealing money from lepers," he said. "When lepers passed him, he forced them to bow." Lee Chun-sang, a leper, stabbed Suho to death. A month later Lee was executed by hanging at Seodaemun Prison. The Japanese melted down Suho's statue in 1943, to make ammunition for the war effort.

A group of nine middle-aged women friends touring the park suddenly wandered up to us. One of them cheekily approached me and touched the mini digital recorder hanging around my neck. Mr. Choi turned his attention to the ladies and began filling them in on Sorokdo's history. Sung-jai and I called goodbye and waved, but he didn't hear or see us. Mr. Choi was in his element happily tutoring new pupils.

Now four o'clock, we'd been on the island for seven hours and were hot, hungry and wilting. We headed to the ferry dock, but on the way diverted off the path for a respite at a nearby secluded sandy beach on the east shore. We looked over the water to large, green mountainous Geogeum Island several kilometers south. I used tissues to dry a picnic table's wet linoleum top and seats. The same nine ladies we'd encountered thirty minutes earlier, wandered up. Without saying a word they brazenly sat at my picnic table and began chatting among themselves. I was too surprised to think of anything to say. Sung-jai and I strolled the path back to the ferry, passing a Shinto Shrine – the sun god erected by Governor Suho in 1935.

Back in Doyang, on the edge of town, we checked into the modern, large but empty four-story Pada Spaland Jjimjilbang. On the deserted, gymnasium-like second-floor sleeping area all the windows were shut, the air sultry and stifling. I threw open a window, and a welcome breeze wafted in. Sung-jai and I were the only customers. I decided to take a much-needed siesta on a mat while Sung-jai engaged in his favorite past time – showering.

Later that evening, contentedly laying on our mats enjoying the entire floor to ourselves, we watched U.S.-produced *Greatest Police Chases* on the big-screen TV. (American television infiltrates the world's airwaves; even on remote little Sorokdo, Mr. Choi said his favorite TV program was American wrestling.)

After the program, as we prepared for bed, seven retirement-aged women wearing identical, *jjimjilbang*-issued orange shorts and T-shirts appeared on the floor. They silently and assiduously placed their sleeping mats side-by-side in a neat straight row near us, then lay down and went to sleep. They reminded me of the seven dwarfs in *Snow White*. When I woke at seven-thirty in the morning, the mats and the dwarfs were gone.

After the journey's conclusion, Heju and I visited one of many government-run residences on the mainland designated for leprosy patients, and spoke to a handful of elderly patients. Some were blind from the disease's ravages. A common theme underpinned a collective, sad narrative: patients deserted and abandoned long ago by families who'd never visited.

CHAPTER 15

Mokpo: Korean Maritime History; Dognapping

Despite the Korean peninsula being surrounded by seas on three sides, there hadn't seemed to be much of a collective desire on the part of the nation's citizens to explore beyond their own maritime doorway over the country's long history. While Europeans, from Marco Polo in the thirteenth century to James Cook in the eighteenth, boldly sailed to other lands, Koreans largely remained glued to their own corner of the world. During Joseon, the ultra-conservative, anti-foreign kingdom even fined its own fishermen for straying too far from shore. The lone prominent mariner was a merchant and quasi-naval commander named Jang Bo-go, who in the ninth century was said to control Yellow Sea trade between Korea and China. On Wando — an island tucked on the western edge of the south coast — Clear Sea Garrison (Cheonghaejin) was established in AD 828 and Jang commanded a small fleet there. Remnants of the garrison can still be seen on an islet off Wando's south coast. Jang's maritime exploits are so highly regarded that a 1965 Korean film,

Admiral Jang, was made about his life and the ROK Navy named its Class 209 submarines, *Admiral Jang Bogo*. Jang died at age 59, assassinated by a jealous faction of the king's court.

The sea's primary function for Koreans was as a supply of food and for transport. Domestically, rice harvested in the southwest agricultural plains was shipped by vessel up the coast to Seoul and Pyongyang, then on rivers by *hanseon*. *Hanseon* were the wood pack mules of the waterways, equipped with huge square sails and long poles for manual propulsion in shallow water. *Hanseon* measured about five meters long and two meters wide. I'd seen photos taken in the late 1800s of them plying the Han River in Seoul, some packed so high with crates and supplies the equivalent of several stories, they were seemingly just a breath away from capsizing. Isabella Bird Bishop described embarking on a trip from Seoul up the Han River to the interior on a sampan, though actually it was a *hanseon*.

The west coast was the primary route for domestic and Chinese maritime trade. More than a few ships sank off that flank in tempests. Beginning in the 1960s, the government embarked on a project to salvage ancient vessels. It wasn't easy to raise downed ships firmly embedded in thick mud on the shallow Yellow Sea floor. Several of the salvaged ships are on display at the National Maritime Museum in Mokpo. Sung-jai and I were heading there now.

We departed Goheung in the morning, cruising west across South Jeolla province's airy coastal plains dominated by infinite numbers of orderly agricultural fields and pockets of low mountains. The big sky was hazy and white. Life is slow and indolent on the coastal plains. We entered Mokpo from the east, the city highly energized and hustling, roads churning with vehicles. We passed many blocks of tall, white apartment buildings. Mokpo was once one of the country's more populated and important cities, a major commercial hub during colonization. Minerals, rice and lumber plundered from across Korea were shipped from Mokpo to Japan. With industrialization starting in the 1960s, waves of young men and women from rural villages, towns and cities began to migrate to Seoul and Gyeonggi province to labor in newly-opened factories. By the 1970s, Mokpo had lost a number of its residents and some of its significance.

Near the coast we crossed north on Yeongsan Dyke over the mile-wide mouth of the Yeongsan River, where it meets the sea. Mokpo is built mainly north of the Yeongsan River, its source about 130 kilometers northeast. On the inland side of the dyke is fresh water; on the opposite side, salt water. A satellite photo I'd seen showed sea water west of the dyke as deep blue-green, on the river side, pale greenish-gray. The long south bank of the river is concrete and industrial. The north shore is commercial and residential with apartments, shops and businesses, including the National Maritime Museum.

We found the modern, white large three-story museum on the concrete shoreline. We strolled onto its wide, stone square in front. The mid-afternoon sunshine was reflecting so brightly off the light-colored stone that I was forced to shield my eyes from the harsh glare. Docked in the water against the square was the strangest, most ungainly vessel I'd ever seen. We went over for a closer look. It was a veritable Noah's Ark, large and boxy, made of long, thick wood planks. If pairs of donkeys, goats and giraffes had started trotting out from its hold, I wouldn't have been surprised.

The vessel weighed thirteen tons and was an unwieldy forty-seven-feet long and twenty-feet wide. Perpendicular sixty-feet-long wood arms reached out from its port and starboard sides. From these appendages, giant nets would have been lowered into shallow waters to ensnare shrimp being swept along in the powerful currents and rushing tides between myriad islands off Mokpo. Between the coast and islands, and the islands themselves, channels act as narrow funnels, increasing current speeds to the point that rapids sometimes form.

An amazing 320 islands are off Mokpo, 258 inhabited — part of a 130-kilometer-long archipelago in the southwest. Many islands are close to the mainland though a handful are more than forty kilometers out. The farthest offshore — 60 kilometers away — is Gageo Island, part of an undersea ridge extending to China separating the Yellow Sea from the East China Sea. In 1816, British captain Basil Hall, sailing south off Korea's west coast on a voyage of exploration, was astounded by the hundreds of islands he passed, grouped in immense clusters, spreading in all directions. Hall thought to count and chart them but, realizing the extraordinary number, gave up. About 1,700 islands are off South Jeolla's coast.

In his published logbook *Voyage of Discovery to the West Coast of Corea and the Great Loo-Choo Island*, Hall described the islands: "They vary in size, from a few hundred yards in length to five or six miles, and are of all shapes. From the mast-head, other groups were perceived lying one behind the other to the east and south as far as the eye could reach. Frequently about a hundred islands were in sight from deck at one moment." The Korean land block tilts slightly down, northeast to southwest, and many nearby coastal islands in the southwest are basically the tops of submerged hills.

The vessel before us was named *meongteongguribae*, translating aptly to "fool's boat." Befitting its name, it had no locomotion, no engine, no sails, no oars. For hundreds of years, fool's boats were common sights on the west coast. They would be towed by other vessels from the mainland or from islands to the sea and anchored.

These factory ships remained at sea for up to six months, a crew living aboard. To replenish food and water and to relieve the hold of catch, smaller vessels would sail or motor out to fool's boats. During foul weather, smaller craft couldn't get out to assist them, and *meongteongguribae* were involved in some maritime disasters.

From late summer to early fall is typhoon season in East Asia. The genesis for many such tempests is the equatorial western North Pacific. On July 9, 1987, Typhoon Thelma spawned in the Philippines Sea and swept north. Korean meteorologists predicted the storm would bypass the peninsula, but it suddenly veered toward the south coast and roared inland, winds recording 150 kilometers per hour, causing widespread damage and death. A number of fool's boats were anchored off the coast during Thelma, and twelve capsized and fifty-three men drowned.

About 150 fool's boats had been plying southwest waters at the time. As a result of the tragedy, the government permanently banned the vessels from active duty. Shrimp fishing would now be undertaken by motorized craft. Fool's boats were destroyed. By 2000, reportedly only one remained. The *meongteongguribae* before us had been towed from Nakwoldo, a small island sixty kilometers northwest of Mokpo, to the museum, and staff told us it was the last fool's boat in existence in the county.

In the middle of the square was the ship's giant, medieval-looking catapult-like wood anchor weighing an astonishing three tons. Its vertical beam is eight meters long, its crossbeam nearly six meters wide.

Entering the air-conditioned museum, we gratefully escaped the humid, searing heat. At the front desk we met Kwok Yu-seok, director of the museum's Maritime Heritage research division. Mr. Kwok kindly volunteered to accompany us through the airy premises. Only a handful of visitors were present. We came before a Korean vessel that had sunk in about AD 900 in the Goryeo Kingdom period. Brought to the surface off the southwest coast in 1983, its hull had been embedded in deep thick mud. Visibility for divers in such murky, muddy waters is near zero. The hull was just nine meters long and three meters wide, yet its cargo was a mind-boggling 30,645 celadon ceramic pieces plus quantities of bronze and iron. I'm no seafarer – and certainly no mathematician – but even I could deduce that loading 30,645 of anything onto a modest-size vessel seemed foolhardy.

"Do you think it sank because it was overloaded?" I asked Mr. Kwok.

"No, carrying 30,000 pieces of pottery wasn't unusual for the time," he replied.

Sung-jai quipped, "You know how some trucks overturn in Korea because they're loaded too high – it was the same with *hanseon* … they were overloaded too." I thought the joke adroit; Mr. Kwok didn't see the humor.

We came to a Chinese ship salvaged from waters south off Mokpo in 1967. It was elegant with three masts – a trim, sleek, 200-ton, fourteenth-century Yuan Dynasty ship restored to its full grandeur. Its cargo was 28,000 tons of ceramic pieces and eight million copper coins, the latter a major Chinese export to Japan.

"The Korean salvager must have gotten rich from the eight million copper coins," I noted to Mr. Kwok.

"Actually no, the coins had more academic than monetary value," he said.

We continued on, viewing glass display cases holding artifacts like ceramic vases recovered from sunken ships. The museum contains many interesting pieces.

***

In early evening at a nearby restaurant we enjoyed bowls of delicious bibimbap – rice, fried egg, bean sprouts, mushrooms, seasoned spinach and diced carrots with sesame oil and *gochujang* (red chilli paste). Bibimbap is healthy and reasonably priced. After dinner we checked into the nearby multi-floor Yeongbingwan Boseok Sauna, or *jjimjilbang*, in a commercial building. Sung-jai immediately sought out the showers while I embarked on a two-hour stroll on the walking path along the waterfront promenade and across Yeongsan Dyke. The evening was pleasant and balmy. The promenade parallels modern restaurants and cafés wreathed in bright neon lights — the path busy with families and power-walkers.

Back at the *jjimjilbang* at 10:00 p.m., Sung-jai was freshly scrubbed. Despite searching high and low for a mat to sleep on, to my consternation I couldn't find a single one. It wasn't that the *jjimjilbang* had temporarily run out or that customers were using them all — the place simply didn't carry mats. Imagine — customers expected to sleep on a hardwood floor! This would never do, of course. I asked Sung-jai to accompany me to the front office where I intended to put up a spirited argument about our sacrosanct right to sleep on something quasi-soft.

"Excuse me," I said to the female manager sitting in a small booth on the first floor, "but where are your mats?"

"We don't have any," she replied impassively.

"How are we supposed to sleep without mats?" I added incredulously.

"It's our policy."

"Your policy?"

"Yes," she said, unconcerned.

"But we need to sleep on mats. We can't stay here if there aren't mats."

Which was fine with the woman, who refunded us half our fee. It was ten thirty, but I figured the best option was to seek nearby accommodation with mats. We packed, got in the car and drove around the general area seeking a *jjimjilbang*. We stopped at two, though curiously neither had mats. Mokpo *jjimjilbang* owners are either tight with money or Mokponians have the world's strongest backs. We expanded our search from the original *jjimjilbang* but couldn't find another one.

I checked the road atlas: the next nearest town was Muan, twenty-five kilometers north. We headed to Muan, now past midnight. Cruising Muan's streets we couldn't find a single *jjimjilbang* in the small town. I scanned the atlas again. The next nearest town of any consequence was Naju, twenty-five kilometers east.

"Let's try Naju," I said to a resigned Sung-jai. On a more positive note, we were viewing places not on our list of sights to see. In the darkness though, it was difficult to savor any local flavor.

In Naju we stopped at Korea Jjimjil Sauna and asked the receptionist if they had mats.

"No," she said.

"How can we sleep without mats?"

She shrugged glumly.

We pulled up to a second *jjimjilbang*. Hallelujah — mats! I paid the entrance fee, and Sung-jai and I crept into the crowded, dark fourth-floor sleeping area. We immediately retreated though due to a symphony of outrageously loud snoring. The quieter, second-floor sleeping area was packed with slumbering parents and kids, but we managed to secure a sliver of open space by the window, which I cracked open to allow a shaft of cool night air to seep into the stifling enclosure. Koreans prefer indoor temperatures equivalent to those of the Sahara Desert. Exhausted, we lay on our golden mats.

But in the middle of the large room, a lone fellow was laying supine on a mat, his head propped on his elbow, watching the big-screen wall TV, volume notable. It was 2:40 a.m. Everyone was sleeping, or at least, trying to. I hadn't crisscrossed three cities taking three hours to have my slumber interrupted by a renegade.

I tiptoed over to the man and whispered in Korean, "Excuse me sir, the TV's loud. Could you please turn it down."

He grudgingly turned his head and shot me a quick, uninterested glance, then defiantly replied "no," and turned his back to me and continuing watching his program.

I'd rather expected such a response; after all, he was a Korean male in his forties. "Sir, people are sleeping," I said more resolutely this time.

He waved me off again. I was contemplating how best to get rid of his body without alerting authorities, when to my immense relief an anonymous male patron — among the crowd of recumbent bodies — suddenly came to the rescue.

"Yes, turn off the TV!" commanded the loud, commanding voice.

I picked up the remote, pressed the off button and the TV screen went dark. The perpetrator said nothing, quashed by the will of this great democracy called South Korea!

I contend the national government should enact The Jjimjilbang Television Law: TV sets off by midnight, except when events of national importance — World Cup Korean soccer, presidential elections and the final episode of a highly-rated soap opera series, air. On this night, I slept well in a hard-mat sort of way.

***

Naju isn't far south of Gwangju, the latter in the general ballpark of our next destination, Sinchon, a remote hamlet north of Gwangju in the Noryeong Mountains. I became cognizant of Sinchon after reading an *International Herald Tribune* article describing it as home to the country's most upstanding citizens. The good people of Sinchon had collectively decided that since there weren't enough townsfolk in the village to support a local shop, they'd establish a non-staffed co-op store with payments made on the honor system. A little box was placed on the shop's counter for cash to be deposited into when a customer bought items.

Need *ramyun* noodles, cigarettes, soda or a chocolate bar? No worries, simply drop the requisite coins into the box and exit with the goods. The idea was a success and nothing apparently got stolen. A local priest notified the press about the unique place and the story went national. Korea's largest steelmaker, POSCO — sensing a feel-good scoop — ran full-page newspaper ads featuring a photo of the appealing, snug cottage-like shop, with about a dozen smiling residents in front. The ad's headline announced: "This Store Doesn't Have a Keeper. It Has a Village of Trust."

To view this history-making establishment and to mingle with its reputable citizens, Sung-jai and I were on our way to Sinchon. We drove into the remote, fetching Noryeong Mountains north of Gwangju, through picturesque, narrow dells dotted with pretty, neat orderly little farms, and by low wooded mountains tight against the road hemming us in on each side. In this backcountry were no road signs indicating where Sinchon was. In rural, isolated Jangseong County we pulled off the road onto a short, quiet lane we hoped might house the store. We puttered a short way, passing a few dwellings, not a soul around.

"You think this is the right place?" I asked Sung-jai, skeptically.

"I'm not sure," he said.

On our right we drew parallel to a small, well-worn wood unit, its big front window somewhat resembling a storefront, and stopped in front.

"Is this it?" I asked in disbelief.

"I guess so," said Sung-jai.

The door was open so we stepped inside to find a few old shelves with several paltry sundry items on them, on the counter a box for coins.

"This is it!" I exclaimed. How underwhelming. The photo in the POSCO ad depicted an attractive, homely little cottage. This austere place resembled the tuck shop at Gert and Ernie's Cut-Rate Kids' Camp, where your parents dump you off as a kid for the summer.

I'd envisioned television cameras whirring, visitors jostling for the novelty of procuring a Hostess Twinkies cupcake. "What a thrill to have driven 300 kilometers through a typhoon in the middle of the night to experience this. Nothing like it back home. Come on kids, time to head back to Seoul."

We wondered what to do next. The naughty notion of swiping a candy bar and not depositing the required coins in the box danced in my head. But with my karma, there'd be a security camera hidden behind the can of peas on the shelf and I'd be arrested and deported. I glanced out the front window and froze: directly across the lane, three elderly men were pulling on a rope looped over a stout, low tree branch, the other end of the rope tied around a big yellow-white dog's neck. The animal was dangling in mid-air. If you haven't witnessed a dog being hanged, and I hadn't, it's a surreal sight.

"They're hanging the dog!" I yelled to Sung-jai. I immediately flew out of the shop to try to save it. I grabbed the rope from the men. They wouldn't let go. I wrestled them for possession. They continued to haul away. My adrenalin jacked, I began hurling invectives at them. After perhaps thirty seconds – both sides still tugging mightily – I managed to lower the dog to the ground. The men backed away, all three staring at me with expressions resembling how you might look if you opened your parent's bedroom door and found Brad Pitt in bed with your mother. I supposed at the moment I presented the image of a madman: bulging eyes, foaming at the mouth. A handful of villagers had gathered and were gawking.

"Call the police!" I shouted to Sung-jai.

He dialed 112 on his cell phone. "The police will be here soon," he called.

I noted the dog still curiously gasping for breath as one of the men approached it.

"Stay away!" I threatened him, thinking he'd grab the dog.

The man said something to Sung-jai, who advised me, "Relax Mark, he just wants to untie the cord around its neck."

The fellow put his hands around the animal's throat and removed an unseen cord tied so tightly it wasn't visible. The dog breathed normally again. I saw one of the men clandestinely retreat to the corner of a nearby dwelling to hide a blow torch attached to a small canister of gas used to sear the fur off the dog before it's cooked and eaten.

About ten minutes later a squad car pulled up. Two officers exited and conferred with the three men and Sung-jai. I was told I could press charges against the animal's owner – a powerful rather unkempt fellow (one of the trio of dog-hangers) – and he'd be fined.

I agreed. Not because I particularly wanted the owner to have to pay a fine, though the prospect was enticing. Mainly I was curious what the legal ramifications were for hanging a dog. I thought I might get an answer at the police station. The officers asked that we follow their car to the station in the nearby town of Bukha. The dog's owner slid into the backseat of the police car while the dog happily hopped into my back seat, bounced about and excitedly wagged its tail, shedding copious amount of fur all over the car seat. We followed the police car for about ten minutes into Bukha, then entered the police station, where several officers were behind the front desk. One of them informed Mr. Jung, seventy-eight, that he would be fined 200,000 won for "hanging a dog in a public place."

Hanging a dog in Korea for its meat is legal, I knew. I wondered aloud why Mr. Jung was being fined. An officer got on the phone and dialed a local government official – possibly the director of the "Bukha

Department of Opaque Dog Hanging Rules and Regulations," and handed the phone to Sung-jai. Several minutes later, after speaking to the official, Sung-jai announced the verdict: Hanging a dog in public on a public lane, as Mr. Jung had attempted, is illegal. Hanging it on one's property is legal. Mr. Jung had tried to kill the dog on a public lane; a public-versus-privacy issue.

Eating dog meat is a sensitive subject in the country. Many citizens oppose the practice and many people have pet dogs, though most are those annoying yappy poodles wrapped in cotton sweaters in winter, the animals too little to be considered real dogs; more like glorified rats with fur — just cuter. A group of hardcore mainly conservative old-timers condone eating dogs, and politicians are loath to introduce new laws to ban the sale of dog meat. Brigitte Bardot, the former exotic French movie star and current animals rights activist, decided during the 2002 World Cup competition in Japan and Korea to publicly call out Koreans for eating dog meat. Ms. Bardot likened Koreans to a species lower than apes. Big mistake. She failed to take into account national pride. South Korea is also arguably the world's most comprehensively-wired and internet-savvy country, and her website was inundated with millions of furious and crude messages. Ms. Bardot responded she'd never before received such vile tidings. Her website crashed.

Suddenly realizing it was permissible to kill a dog in one's own yard, Mr. Jung morphed into an angry bear and began wildly gesturing and shouting, and tried to get at me. Several bemused officers physically restrained him.

An officer informed me I had to return the dog to Mr. Jung. If I did, I knew it would be dog stew tonight. I believe Korean law should stipulate that dogs can't be hanged twice, let alone once. Double jeopardy and all that.

"I'll buy the dog from Mr. Jung," I said, but he demanded 300,000 won — highway robbery. I rescinded my offer.

I quickly formulated a diabolical plan and announced, "I'll return the dog, but first it needs to go to a vet. Its vocal cords were injured by the rope." I knew this wasn't true, but the officers bought it. Sung-jai, the dog and I loaded into the Scoupe, and we followed the police car on the street toward the vet's office in Bukha. Farther ahead we stopped at a traffic light, where the road split in two: left heading into woodsy countryside, right into town.

When the traffic light turned green, the squad car motored right. I darted left onto the country road and sped away. In a mere instant I'd transformed from mild-mannered Canadian buttercup to a fugitive on the run from the feds.

Sung-jai's mouth dropped, and he yelped in panicked alarm, "What are you doing?"

"I'm taking the dog," I replied calmly, belying a pounding heart. At any moment I expected to hear a police car siren approaching from behind, officers ready to pepper spray and taser me. For the first time in my life I was committing a (relatively grievous) crime.

"I can't be part of this!" Sung-jai blurted in distress. "I can't get caught. I have convictions for drinking and driving and for violence."

I understood the drinking and driving part, not so much the "violence" aspect. "What kind of violence?" I asked.

"For fighting," he said. In Western parlance I think he meant assault. Was I traveling with a convicted felon?

The late afternoon sun was directly behind us so we were heading east. I glanced at the atlas and noted the nearest town east was Damyang, about twenty-five kilometers away. We'd stop in Damyang.

Sung-jai, unnerved, declared, "I can't take a chance getting caught — I'm taking the bus back to Seoul!"

I tried to calm him. "It's my responsibility, nothing will happen to you," I said, but he remained tense.

In Damyang I stopped at a little grass park in the small town's pleasant downtown. We got out of the car. Sung-jai, livid, shouted angrily: "This trip's so much work! I have to read maps, I have to give directions, I have to make phone calls!" His protestations were curiously similar to Heju's on Ganghwa Island.

He forgot to mention we also had long days. Anyway, was checking a few maps, making a few phone calls and being ferried around in a car hard labor? I suppose so, if one hadn't ever worked before, which I was coming to believe was Sung-jai's case.

Sung-jai wasn't finished. He heatedly declared, "And you! All you do is talk, talk, talk!" I had tried to engage him in dialogue on the trip, but he'd mostly sat silently in the passenger seat.

Hot under the collar, I retorted, "It's called conversation ... try it sometime!"

Sung-jai reached into the car's back seat, grabbed his little suitcase on wheels and strode onto the sidewalk, pulling his luggage behind him in search of the Damyang Bus Station.

I hollered: "Momma's boy!" and immediately regretted it. Actually, he was a momma's boy. But he'd patiently undertaken a lot of translating for me in our fourteen days together, and I appreciated his effort.

"Shut up!" he yelled back.

At the moment, the more pressing issue was the dog. I couldn't keep it and certainly couldn't drop it off at the police station, which I noted with a jolt of trepidation was directly across the street. I figured the animal — probably confined to a leash or cage by Mr. Jung — would appreciate a walk so I went to the car and opened the door and let it out. It happily skittered about the park. Being highly intelligent — its memory fresh with the image of almost dying at the hands of traitorous humans — it wisely skipped to the rear corner and disappeared from view. I rushed over and peered down the street but not a trace of it. It was the last I saw of the mellow, good-natured dog. At least it was free now. Thankfully, the provincial Mr. Jung was deprived of chowing down on dog stew. For this I was grateful.

I was in a heap of doggy-doo though. I'd committed an offense and for the second time in three weeks, my translator had gone AWOL. I sat on the park bench trying to figure what to do next. I decided to do what I usually did when stressed and blue — which is to eat heartily. Parked across the street was food truck selling barbecued chicken from a rotisserie. I purchased a tinfoil-wrapped whole chicken and sat on the park bench and happily devoured the delicious bird. Then I walked on the sidewalk paralleling the attractive main street and entered a bakery and bought two pastries, two donuts and a creamy strawberry milkshake and contentedly consumed them too. Fully satiated — a surfeit of cholesterol surging through my blood — I returned to the park, sat on the bench and had an internal discussion on how best to proceed.

My days on the road were long and tiring. I wasn't sleeping well on *jjimjilbang* mats. I was fatigued and cranky ... well, more cranky than usual. My patience was thin, my feng shui out of whack, my karma beleaguered. I wasn't relishing the endeavor, or translators, or men who hanged dogs, or Korea or Koreans. The latter were the most hidebound, intransigent people I'd ever encountered; I fit right in. I'd been behind the Scoupe's wheel for eight weeks since April 7, yet still hadn't emerged from the country's western half. I still had the south, east and north regions to explore. I contemplated ending to trip on the spot but resolved I'd come too far to give up.

It suddenly occurred to me, with Heju returning in eight days from her month-long vacation in Thailand, she might want to rejoin me. What better transition after a relaxing, peaceful sunny beach holiday, than to reunite with the stress and misery she was accustomed to. I entered a nearby PC room and emailed her my proposal. Her reply was soon forthcoming: Yes, she'd continue on Part Deux – Mark's Marine Boot Camp. My feng shui was back.

I next phoned my friend, Moonie, in Seoul, and asked if he'd contact the police station in Bukha to try to iron out the situation with the dog. Moonie did so and relayed to me: "The police want you to pay Mr. Jung 180,000 won for the dog, and they want to know your location." To pick me up and haul me to jail, I was sure. I wasn't about to give them my whereabouts due to my aversion to prison food. The next day, I deposited 100,000 won – an amount I thought fair – into Mr. Jung's bank account at an ATM bank machine. Over the next couple of weeks though I was the recipient of daily phone calls from tenacious Bukha police, who wanted to know my location. I didn't reveal it – a public-versus-privacy issue.

I determined that a brief respite was in order and that I'd return to Seoul for the upcoming weekend for a change of scenery. I'd resume the journey in a few days. That night I stayed at a *jjimjilbang* in Damyang and in the morning was on the road to Seoul.

Later, reviewing my trip's newspaper clippings, I came across the full-page POSCO photo ad featuring smiling Sinchon villagers standing in front of the store. I recognized a grinning Mr. Jung.

CHAPTER 16

Jeonju: A Wannabe King;
Gurye Centenarians

Just south of the Han River in Seoul is Jamsil-dong, a busy, hectic upscale hub dominated by landmark Lotte Tower, the country's tallest structure at 125 floors and 555-meters. The tower dwarfs innumerable surrounding blocks of high-rise apartment buildings. On the same block is the affluent Lotte Department Store, Lotte Hotel and the outdoor Lotte World Amusement Park. Underground is Jamsil Subway Station and a busy shopping arcade. A few blocks east is Olympic Park, site of the 1988 Summer Olympics. Gangnam, the country's most renowned, toniest district – where purchasing an apartment unit can set you back at least $2 million – is home to Korea's prolific cosmetic surgery industry.

Up until the 1970s, Jamsil or "Raising Silkworm Place" (a form of sericulture practiced during Joseon) and the surrounding area south of the Han River was farmland and fields. North of the Han, where Seoul was developed in the 1400s, many roads are curving and meandering in a hodge-podge of directions, rather like London.

In contrast, Jamsil and south of the river had primarily adapted a modern road grid system.

The day after arriving from Damyang I was out in my Scoupe on a Saturday evening driving through Jamsil, a few miles west of my neighborhood, Myeongil-dong. I was stuck in bumper-to-bumper traffic near Lotte Department Store. The wide sidewalks were jammed with throngs of young people enjoying a balmy, sultry June evening. The energy, crowds and bright lights could have passed for New York's Times Square.

At a busy major intersection I turned right. Glancing out my rolled-down window, I saw a surreal scene. In the middle of four lanes of traffic a man was lying face-down on the road, motorists slowly and prudently maneuvering around him, gaping at the prone figure through open car windows. I noted the man's head move so I knew he was alive. I didn't know how long he'd been lying there. Not a car had stopped to assist him.

I pulled over to the curb, exited the car and dashed back to the intersection, where a gaggle of pedestrians was looking at the prostrate figure. I lassoed a couple of university-age fellows and we waded into traffic, picked the man up by his legs and arms and hauled him back to the sidewalk, placing him on the ground. He immediately jumped up and darted back into the lanes and lay face-down again. Again we ventured out and lugged him back, this time though I leaned my weight on him as he was on his back on the sidewalk so he couldn't get up. He was slight, maybe 150 pounds soaking wet, about forty-five-years old.

"Did anyone call 112?" I called to the small crowd.

"No," replied a voice among the surrounding onlookers.

"Phone it please," I said.

The man was distraught. He shouted in English: "Family! ... Die!"

After a few moments he relaxed a bit and whispered to me, "Where are you from?"

"Canada," I said.

He told me something in Korean that I couldn't understand. The young man next to me translated. "He's saying, 'If it wasn't for you, he'd have died on the road.'"

I was surprised that no motorists had stopped to help. But in my experience, Koreans were loath to get involved in others' affairs if it didn't personally affect them. The man motioned that I bring my face close to his and I did. He presented an angelic smile and murmured, "Friend," and shook my hand in a strong grip. He seemed like a good guy. I'm sure he hadn't wanted to perish, but Koreans can be very emotional, particularly after having downed a couple of bottles of *soju*, which I guessed he'd done. He'd likely lain down in traffic as a plea for help. The police soon arrived and put him in the patrol car and hopefully took him to a hospital.

✳✳✳

That weekend I got a phone call from a man named Yi Seok, whom I'd been trying to contact for months. Yi Seok was the royal prince to the abolished Joseon throne. In 1907, the Joseon Dynasty was severely weakened when Japan forced Korea's King Gojong – who'd reigned since 1863 – to abdicate. The Japanese also stripped Gojong's son, crown prince Sunjong, of power. And they sent another of Gojong's sons - Yi Un, a ten-year-old future crown prince, to live in Japan. In 1910, the Japanese effectively abolished the Korean Empire, ending 519 years of the Joseon Dynasty.

The Joseon Dynasty's genesis in 1392 was engendered by General Yi Seong-gye (Yi being the Joseon-era spelling of Lee). Yi hailed from Jeonju in North Jeolla province and had led the overthrow of the erstwhile Goryeo Kingdom. When Jeonju's ruling clan elevated Yi to king he henceforth became known as King Taejo, the first of twenty-seven Joseon Yi monarchs. Yi Seok is a descendant of King Taejo, and grandson of King Gojong, and tenth son of Gojong's fifth son, Prince Yi Kang, who died in 1955 at age 78. Yi Kang obviously had too much time on his hands, producing nine daughters and twelve sons, including Yi Seok, with thirteen concubines. Through the arcane, convoluted genealogy of Yi royal ascension, Yi Seok is the last remaining heir to the Joseon Dynasty throne living in Korea. He would be His Royal Highness today if Korean royalty had prevailed.

After the fall of Joseon in 1910, the extended royal family and its numerous descendants didn't exactly faded quietly into the night. Many held on for decades, believing to have been ordained for life. Peter Bartholomew recounted an amusing story about leading a tour group through Seoul palaces. His group was standing before a Joseon palace, when an elderly female royal descendant, residing in a front room, appeared on the porch and waited for the amassed tourists to bow to her.

I became aware of Yi Seok after reading an *International Herald Tribune* feature describing his topsy-turvy life. Just as Lee Byeong-hee, imprisoned at Seodaemun Prison, had been a window to the Japanese occupation, I thought Yi would be an excellent conduit to royal family history. The article noted Yi was a part-time lecturer on Joseon history at Jeonju University. I contacted the university and left a message on Yi's office phone but hadn't heard back from him until this weekend. Yi Seok surprisingly conversed in excellent English with me. We agreed to meet Monday at his Jeonju residence. A mere commoner like me did not keep a hoped-to-be king waiting. I'd be in the presence of His Highness on Monday.

Jeonju is on the peninsula's west wing at about its midpoint, on the long Honam Plain. Cruising south from Seoul on Monday morning through the plain, I felt like I was in Canada's central prairies. Farther south in the distance at the end of the flat horizon, the hazy outline of Jeonju became clearer and larger as I neared it.

Like other medium-sized cities, Jeonju bustles with cars and people and hums with activity. Jeonju University is on the city's outskirts. I pulled up to its front gate to rendezvous with a student who'd volunteered to translate for me at the meeting with Yi Seok. I'd contacted the Jeonju Tourism Agency by phone, and its staff had kindly communicated with Jeonju University to find a student in their English program. (During my pan-Korea circumnavigation, I stopped across the country at city halls and government tourism offices, and employees were always uniformly hospitable and eager to assist.)

The middle-aged guard at the university front gate inquired why I was here.

"To meet Yi Seok," I said in Korean, certain he'd instantly recognize the famous name.

"Who?" the guard asked.

"Yi Seok," I repeated.

"I don't know Yi Seok," he said.

I reached into my file folder on the passenger seat, picked up the *International Herald Tribune* article with Yi's photo, and handed it to the guard. "The king of Korea. He teaches history at this university," I explained.

The man studied the photo but not a hint of recognition crossed his face. He wasn't going to grant me access until he ascertained who this Yi chap was. I phoned the translator in the university and handed the phone to the guard. After a brief conversation with the student, the guard waved me through. Such is the sad state of royal affairs in Korea that even an employee at the institution where His Majesty teaches at was blissfully unaware of his presence.

The student was a personable, intelligent twenty-one-year-old who spoke excellent English. "Call me John," he said, so I did. We drove across the flat, rather featureless city to the concentrated, attractive hub of Pungnam-dong, where Joseon's Gyeonggijeon Palace was built in 1392. Handsome, cobblestone Taejo Road runs in front of the palace. Jeongdong Cathedral — an impressive, tall, faded red-gray stone church constructed between 1908 and 1914 — is across the road. Jeonju Hanok Village contains a network of quiet lanes replete with about 800 traditional *hanok*. Nearby, hulking Pungnam Gate was built in the 1700s. There is a lot of history here.

Yi Seok resided in Jeonju Hanok Village. We crept along in the car on quiet lanes passing rows of wood and clay-walled *hanok* with heavy, black-tiled curved roofs. We stopped at the front gate of a *hanok* and rang the buzzer. An attractive, regal-looking woman exited the home and walked across the small front yard to the gate.

"Excuse me, is this where Yi Seok lives?" we asked her.

"Yes," she said.

We introduced ourselves, and she opened the gate and led us across the yard into the handsome *hanok,* into a plain, unencumbered living room, a long, low wood table in the middle, the wall lined with bookshelves. A large window provided a view of the front yard. John and I sat on the floor at the table and waited. Ten minutes later, His Eminence made his grand entrance wearing traditional Joseon royal garb of a long, dark silk robe. Yi Seok walked slowly, carrying himself proudly in a dignified and reserved manner. Possessed of a sense of gravity, he appeared aloof and distant. He was fit and handsome with a healthy mane of thick, gray-black hair and vaguely resembled Hong Kong action movie star Jackie Chan.

The woman who'd answered the gate was his personal assistant provided by Jeonju City, he said, but I suspected the two had more than a professional relationship. Yi sat cross-legged across from us at the table. He understandably chose to communicate in Korean. After introductions I asked about his childhood growing up in Seoul.

He said he was born in Seoul in 1942 and enjoyed privileged times as a boy. "We had a Cadillac and a Ford," he recalled of a period when car ownership was unheard of. "We lived in a palace and had fifty servants. Servants walked me to school every day and delivered my lunch for me." Since royalty wasn't permitted to do physical activity, Yi's school principal had to run for him during gym class, he said.

Yi was a lonely child, competing with twenty-one siblings for his parent's attention. "I had no opportunity to speak with my father or mother," he said wistfully. His father was sixty-four when he was born.

A cloak of forlornness permeated Yi. I guessed he hadn't received the affection children needed from parents. When the Korean War broke out in 1950, eight-year-old Seok and the extended royal family, fled to the safe zone in Busan with millions of other citizens evading North Korean troops. After eighteen months in Busan the family was back in Seoul in 1952. The next decade was a trying one for royal descendants. Right wing, dictatorial President Rhee Syngman, who assumed power in 1948 and ruled until 1960, blamed the royal family for having allowed the Japanese to colonize the nation.

"President Rhee despised the royal family," said Yi. In 1960, Rhee ordered royal property confiscated and the family stripped of its assets. (In 1961, President Park Chung-hee permitted the royal family to return to the palaces.)

In the 1960s, Yi, now in his twenties, won first prize in a singing contest at the YMCA in Seoul, and became a college disc jockey and sang at U.S. Army officers' clubs on military bases. His royal brothers, sisters, aunts, uncles and cousins believed work undignified, beneath the vaulted airs of aristocracy. Yi thought differently. In 1965, he joined the ROK military and fought in the Vietnam War.

"Did you witness Korean troops participating in atrocities against

Viet Cong villagers?" I asked, as had been reported, conjuring a dark part of the Vietnam War.

Yi Seok paused, winced, and answered yes, but didn't elaborate. "I couldn't do it," he said, referring to extra judicial killings he said he witnessed.

Back in Seoul after his tour of duty, he settled into a routine of singing at night clubs. In the 1970s he even hosted a Friday night live television variety show. A first marriage lasted one year, a second five years. The year 1979 was another challenging period for the extended Joseon family. President Park was assassinated, and Major General Chun Doo-hwan inserted himself as president less than a year later. Chun's soldiers ordered the royal family at gunpoint to depart a Seoul palace. The clan dispersed, some moving to America, including Yi Seok's brother. When the brother died in San Diego in 1980, Yi flew to the U.S. on a three-month tourist visa.

"At first, I thought America was wonderful," he said. "I visited the Pentagon, San Francisco, Los Angeles and Korean communities. They recognized me as a prince. I even sang in Kodiak, Alaska."

But with funds running low he was forced to work. He cleaned swimming pools and gardened in Beverly Hills. In a rundown area of Los Angeles he was the manager of Eddy's Liquor Store. "I was held up at gunpoint at the store more than a dozen times. I pretended to be Mexican and grew a mustache and beard and spoke Spanish. It was safer that way."

In Los Angeles, Yi forgot about being a prince. To continue living in the U.S., he wed an American woman in a marriage of convenience. In 1992 — after twelve years in America — when a family member died in Seoul, Yi returned home, the marriage to his American wife ending. Yi resumed singing at nightclubs in Seoul but after a night of drinking he was hit by a car and in a coma for twelve days. The prince's life spiraled downward. For several years he was unemployed, broke and homeless, his go-to beds — *jjimjilbang* mats. He visited a Buddhist temple to become a monk but was rejected. In 2005, now sixty-three, he contemplated suicide. He wrote a will that somehow ended up on an office desk of a Seoul magazine. When his sad story went public, Jeonju officials reached out to help, providing him with a *hanok* and a fashion makeover, including ten new teeth, among other perks.

These days, Yi presides over civic functions and does public speaking engagements across the country. At Jeonju University he lectures students on Korean royal history but laments his pupils' lack of awareness on the subject. "Thailand, Spain and England have monarchies, and Korea once did, but the students I teach know nothing about the Joseon Dynasty," he said. He confessed to occasionally pining for his former life in America, but said Jeonju suited him well. (On October 6, 2018, in Beverly Hills, California, Yi Seok named American Andrew Lee, 34, as his successor and new crown prince of the Korean Empire.)

After we departed I took John to dinner at a restaurant in Pungnam-dong where he complained about his university professors of English being sub-par, and Jeonju University being mid-tier. He envied students who attended top-tier Korean Ivy League institutions, or "SKY" — Seoul National University, Korea University and Yonsei University. To gain acceptance to SKY requires near perfect scores on the annual national university entrance exam. I suppose John's misgivings were similar to an American student not gaining admission to an Ivy League institution such as Yale, Harvard or Princeton. I told John the important thing was getting the education, not the name or status of the university, but this didn't appease him. He was still despondent when we departed. After I drove John back to his dormitory, I returned to the city's center and found a *jjimjilbang*. Close to midnight and exhausted, I quickly fell asleep on a mat.

Back in Pungnam-dong, the morning hot and bright, I ambled to Pungnam Gate, which is in the middle of a traffic circle. I marveled at the structure's size and grand magnitude, and at its meter-thick, cut granite boulders. I drove the short way to Gyeonggijeon Palace, originally constructed in 1392, and strolled the grounds' sandy earth by a small number of handsome, low modest wood buildings spaced well apart. In the main courtyard off to the side was a series of paintings on easels depicting Joseon's twenty-seven kings: severe, somber-looking men, not the type you'd want coaching your son's little-league baseball team. Noting a small group of foreigners following an English-speaking Korean tour guide, I quietly tagged along at the rear. The guide was a retirement-age, regal-looking woman in a long, dark silk *hanbok* – the formal attire of Joseon's upper-class. At the front of the open courtyard our group approached a set of two, stand-alone, side-by-side wood door frames.

"Exit the door on the right," the guide announced, though I absent-mindedly went through the one on the left. Immediately I received a severe reprimand: "I told you to go through the right door!" she angrily rebuked me. "It's tradition to go through the right door. It shows respect to the king!"

"But the king's dead," I sputtered.

"It doesn't matter. You're disrespecting Korea. You're in Korea now. You must obey customs here!"

Oh my, she obviously wasn't aware only minutes before, an elderly Korean gentleman standing near me viewing the kings' portraits had loudly passed gas. Which sin was greater – slipping through an inconsequential doorway or farting before royalty? Off with his head, I say. I was now a pariah in the guide's eyes, rejected and ignored, my only option to slink away in ignominy.

I headed across the road to the dominating Jeongdong Cathedral where I hoped men of cloth would be less judgmental, more accepting of sinners like me. Construction on the church began in 1908 under the stewardship of Father Xavier Baudenet, a French Catholic priest. A plaque in the square stated: "Many Catholics were executed at this place, including the first martyrs, Yun Ji-chung (Paul) in 1791 and Yu Hang-geom (Augustine) in 1801. Yu Hang-geom's head was hung on this corner stone." A welcome sight, I'm sure, for children playing in the area at the time.

The main church is long and narrow and rises twenty-three meters – forty-five meters total with the clock tower, steeple and three bell towers included. I entered the church through heavy, thick wood front doors, into a grand interior and invigorating coolness, a much appreciated reprieve from the afternoon's oppressive heat and humidity, conditions I don't do well in. Except for the wood pews the interior is entirely stone. The nave is tall and narrow. Running lengthwise on each side are a row of eight stone columns reaching floor-to-ceiling. The walls are white stone lined with arched stained-glass windows framed in intricate brickwork.

. I sat in a pew. Several rows behind me four people were praying. I don't pray but considered making an exception for salvation of the palace guide's soul. I decided against it – she was beyond redemption. Visitors were opening the church's front doors and poking their heads in and snapping photos. I sat contentedly entrenched in the pew and would have stayed all day, maybe even a week, it was so blissfully peaceful and cool. But I had to keep rolling and thirty minutes later, reluctantly dragged myself out to the car.

My next destination was the small town of Gurye about a hundred kilometers southeast, on the southwest edge of the Sobaek Mountain range massif and Jirisan National Park.

An interesting newspaper feature I'd read profiled three distinct mountainous regions in the country where sociologists discovered locals live longer on average than the national average life span of eighty-eight years for women and eighty for men (Easy on the *soju* and cigarettes, guys). Living past the age of one hundred isn't unusual in these areas. Gurye is one of the three. Mere mortals like me aren't getting any younger so I expediently hastened to Shangri-La.

From Jeonju, it is one continuous drive southeast through mountains: first into the short Noryeong range, then into the western edge of the massively thick Sobaeks — the peninsula's rocky spine. The pleasurable, lonely trip is on a smooth, winding road carved tightly between enveloping, picturesque narrow walls of green rising steeply on each side. I emerged from this shadowy corridor of gloomy lushness in late afternoon at a lovely, secluded green plain in the Seomjin River valley in Gurye. The Seomjin River is the country's most isolated waterway, its source about one hundred kilometers north, where it drains the south slopes of the Jiri Mountain massif. The 212-kilometer waterway empties just east of Yeosu at the south coast. Gurye seems cut off from the rest of the peninsula.

I drove to Gurye City Hall and immediately noted the building was too grand for such a modest town. I poked my head into the large main office and discovered a significant number of government employees wearing white shirts and black pants, sitting in front of computers, doing what civil servants in black pants and white shirts do worldwide — playing online poker. I jest.

I announced to the staff I hoped to meet a Gurye centenarian. To assist me the kind folks jumped to life and bustled about, busily checking files and leafing through notepads, trying to locate a list of Gurye's one-hundred-year-old-plus club. I was honored by the collective response. A list of sorts was finally produced, though apparently it hadn't been recently updated. As officials perused it, they conferred among themselves and began crossing out names of people on the list no longer on this Earth.

They finally announced that a woman named Go Yeom-nok was potentially not dead. After a couple of phone calls to track Ms. Go's whereabouts, it was learned she was indeed alive and 106 and living in Gurye. (Excellent detective work, Gurye officials.) I was soon being driven to Ms. Go's residence by an English-speaking official, Kim Hong-geun. What service!

We stopped just outside town at a bend on the road by a wooded hill. The beckoning and lonesome Seomjin River flowed off to the side. Looking over the greenery of wooded hills and the river, Mr. Kim remarked candidly, "When I was a boy there were no trees here. Now, everything's tree-covered."

This isolated area seemed unusual for a house, particularly for a someone aged 106 to live in. We crossed the asphalt and strode up the hill on a dirt path through trees, emerging at a small clearing by a solitary, modest traditional dwelling. Waiting outside the home was Ms. Go's social worker who checked in on her daily. I knocked on the door, and a tiny, white-haired woman wearing a loose yellow silk shirt and baggy purple pants, answered. It was Ms. Go! Amazingly, she lived alone.

Ms. Go looked closer to eighty-six than 106 and was the picture of serenity with an enchanting smile and a soul of innocence. I sat on the living room floor opposite her and prepared to chat, but alas, Ms. Go had little to say. She was content to remain silent, happily and absent-mindedly staring into space for spells, probably lost in her own private reveries from decades past. After more than a century on this planet, she was entitled to daydream.

Several times she murmured softly, "I want to die. Why can't I die?"

After twenty minutes, Ms. Go had only mumbled a few words so I regretfully bade her farewell.

"Why can't I die?" she whispered again, to no one in particular.

Back in the car, Mr. Kim opined on why Gurye townsfolk tend to reach the century mark: they don't stress about material possessions or money, the mountain air is clean, they eat fresh produce, and they are active. Back at City Hall, the supervisor generously presented me with a gift of a thick, soft-cover book authored by a professor. I leafed through its pages, detailing why residents in the three regions live lengthy lives. Written in Korean, I couldn't understand it, but having had the pleasure of sharing a slip of time with Ms. Go, I suspect that besides breathing mountain air, eating vegetables and walking, loving everyone and peace of mind were also reasons for her long life, qualities she radiated.

The following year, Ms. Go was granted her wish and passed away.

CHAPTER 17

Yeosu: Great White Sharks!

One winter evening several months before beginning the trip, I was relaxing in my flat in Seoul, when Heju phoned me from Deajeon.

"Quick, go to your computer!" she excitedly announced. "A great white shark was caught off Yeon Island. There's a photo of it hanging from a crane. It's huge!"

My immediate reaction was disbelief. "That's impossible ... there are no great whites in Korea."

"There are!" she insisted.

I went to the website she gave me, and lo and behold there was the photo of a walloping great white dangling from a harbor crane on Yeon Island thirty-five kilometers south of Yeosu. The Megalodon-type beast weighed 2.5 tons and was 4.6 meters long, the kind that snacked on meaty fellows like me. It had gotten tangled in a trawler's nets and been hauled aboard.

Here's the thing: a while back I'd spent an entire July residing on Ando just a kilometer north of Yeondo — where the shark was caught — and had swum in sandy, idyllic Ando Beach's warm, shallow waters. As I innocently splashed about, this particular great white or any of its buddies gliding past, could have easily taken a chunk out of me. Had I even an inkling great whites patrolled Korean waters, or even briefly passed the peninsula on their way to hunting swimmers and surfers off South African and Australian coasts, it would be with a high degree of caution and circumspection that I'd enter waters at local beaches. It would be with eyes wide open, scanning the surface for any object remotely resembling a shark's fin.

Here's the other thing: except for this obscure website that Heju happened upon, posting the shark's capture, no other medium — newspaper, TV or internet I was aware of, carried the story or mentioned a single word about it. In fact, in all my years in Korea, I'd never read or heard a single word in the media about great whites popping their snouts up off one of the three coasts. I suspect the government suppressed such information. If the mainstream media reported it, would swimmers frolic off seashores in summer? Or would panic set in and beaches morph into a collective Amity Island as in the movie *Jaws*, with Korea's versions of Roy Scheider and Richard Dreyfuss hunting the man-eaters?

I don't have much confidence in the autonomy and independence of the Korean media. In 1997 and 1998 I was employed as a copy editor at *The Korea Herald*, and then at the national news-gathering service *Yonhap News*' English-translation office. I consider *The Korea Herald* a government mouthpiece that does no real reporting. *Yonhap's* Korean English translators were nationalistic.

To acquaint myself with the oceans' most feared creature, I bought a large soft-cover book — *Great White Shark*, written by shark-diving experts Richard Ellis and John E. McCosker. On its map titled "Known Great White Shark Distribution," oceans and seas were light blue, while dark blue shading delineated great white shark presence. As expected the temperate waters off the coasts of Australia and North America were dark blue, as were South Africa's south shore and South America's west coast. Surprisingly, the Mediterranean Sea was dark blue too. Here was the shocker: the three seas surrounding Korea were dark blue! I shuddered.

Heju contacted the Yeondo government office to track down the fisherman who'd hauled in the brute and phoned the man, Cho Sun-hyun. He said he'd be glad to meet us when we were in Yeosu.

I was departing Gurye City Hall after my short visit with Ms. Go, now on my way to Yeosu, and phoned Mr. Cho to arrange a meeting. We agreed to rendezvous tomorrow on Yeon Island. I'd take the ferry to the island from Yeosu Port.

From Gurye I piloted south between lonely coastal mountains onto the long, narrow arm of Yeosu peninsula, surrounded by pockets of mountains and expansive green seaside plains. At the south tip of the peninsula, I arrived at Yeosu City in late evening, checked into the massive Yeosu Naek Ok Sauna several miles west of the port, and sent a thank you text to Mr. Kim in Gurye for having driven me to Ms. Go's home.

His text reply came soon: "My pressure."

I awoke to British-type weather of a thick blanket of ominous gray clouds, light drizzle, blustery winds and cool temperatures. Now 10:50 a.m., I was scheduled to board the noon ferry bound for Yeondo to meet Mr. Cho. About to drive to the ferry terminal, I thought it prudent to confirm our meeting.

To my surprise, when Mr. Cho answered his phone, he said he was in a bank at Yeosu Port.

"What time will you return to Yeondo?" I asked, hoping to catch him in the port rather than on the island.

"On the noon ferry," he said.

"Can we meet at the bank?" I asked.

"Yes, but hurry!" he barked.

I had only seventy minutes until he departed on his ferry. I immediately phoned my friend, Kate, an English-speaking Korean tour guide employed at a small tourism office at the foot of a short, narrow jetty linking Yeosu to little Odong Island just offshore.

"Can you do me a favor and translate, Kate!" I asked, filling her in on the details as I rushed in my car to her office near the port. She agreed, and I picked her up and we zipped to the bank, entering it at 11:25. Mr. Cho was standing at a table, jotting figures into a notebook.

"I can only talk for fifteen minutes," said the buoyant, self-assured man, who appeared older than his forty-nine years. I expeditiously posed questions.

Mr. Cho was born on Dolsan, the eastern arm of the two, long, narrow, mountain-strewn fingers running south from Yeosu Port, encompassing ten-kilometer-wide Gamack Bay. Dolsan is east of Gamack Bay, Hwayang west. On Dolsan, a long dominating tall ridge line parallels the shore.

Mr. Cho is the captain of a twenty-five-ton fishing boat with a crew of eight. "I've been fishing in Yeosu waters for thirty-five years," he said. "The day I caught the great white we were east off Yeondo using nets."

"How big are the nets?" I asked.

"Two-hundred-and-sixty meters long and forty-five meters wide," he said.

"How deep is the water?"

"Forty-five meters."

"How did you catch the shark?"

"We check the nets twice a day. When we winched the net up the great white was thrashing in it. It took thirty minutes using the crane to haul it on board."

"Was it alive?"

"Oh yeah. It was tough and fighting. It had three rows of teeth and was trying to bite us."

"Were you scared?"

"Oh yeah."

"Was this the first great white you've seen?"

"No."

I paused for elucidation. Mr. Cho continued, "In past springs, we've seen great whites here before but they didn't get reported. The government doesn't want to scare off tourists. My shark was the first one reported."

When word of Mr. Cho's shark catch was made public, the news spread rapidly through Yeosu's community of *haenyeo* ("women of the sea"). *Haenyeo* are mainly middle-years-and-up ladies who earn their livings on the three coasts and off many islands, free-diving in wet suits, fins and masks, bringing conch, abalone, sea urchins and sea squirts to the surface to be sold at local markets. "*Haenyeo* divers in Yeosu were scared after hearing about the shark," Mr. Cho recalled. "They stopped diving. It wasn't until a month later they got back in the water."

After fifteen minutes, the Yeosu native hurried off to board the ferry back to Yeondo. Kate departed to meet colleagues for lunch at a nearby restaurant. I decided that for old time's sake, I'd ride the ferry after all, the day's last one departing the port at 2:00 p.m. for Yeondo and return. With a couple of hours to spare until sailing, I opted to visit the Yeosu Maritime Science Museum on Dolsan. I drove onto the nearby tall, imposing Dolsan Bridge, crossing high over the deep, swirling channel waters below in front of Yeosu Port. On the bridge I looked north over the busy port. It is a pretty scene of fishing vessels, small freighters and ferries docked at the harbor — the old, congested, hustling downtown core with myriad flat-top low buildings, and farther behind, on a low, steep mountain, concrete, bungalow-type residential dwellings of white, pale blue and soft green hues.

I entered the museum, the only person walking through its well-appointed, large dark rooms containing numerous brightly-lit aquariums brimming with fascinating species of fish and sea life. I was dismayed to observe some sea creatures in tanks clearly too small for them. In a one-meter-long narrow tank was a one-meter-long type shark, no room for it to swim or turn around. I wondered if the museum's curator and staff didn't realize living marine animals needed space to move.

I slowly wandered through in peaceful silence, happily detached from the outside hectic world. An hour later, hearing the unmistakable sounds of elementary school students arriving on a field trip, and loud chatter, I made a beeline for the door, so not to get trampled.

I headed back up Dolsan to Yeosu Port and parked the car at the ferry terminal next to a long lane paralleling the water. On the lane are dozens of old shops overflowing with a wide array of fishing and marine merchandise, including nets, anchors, chains, rope, tarpaulins, fishing gear and lures. A little before two o'clock, I boarded the large, roll-on/roll-off passenger-vehicle ferry. Most passengers were mid-aged and elderly women returning to the islands where they live, having stocked up on food and supplies purchased on the mainland.

I stood on the ferry's second-level outer deck, rain sprinkling, and attempted to shelter in a large passenger room with yellow linoleum floor. Not an inch of floor space remained. The place was crammed with perhaps one hundred supine, chattering women islanders sitting and lying shoulder-to-shoulder. We sailed out of port under Dolsan Bridge, then south into Gamack Bay, passing large Daegyeong Island and smaller islands with agricultural plots. Sea gulls floated above, shrill squawks piercing the air. Fishing trawlers low in the water with their catches motored north into port. A fresh sea breeze was blowing. It was an unhurried scene. Looking west far across the bay to Hwayang's shoreline, rows of white, high-rise apartment buildings were dwarfed by a low, straight long mountain ridge rising steeply behind.

Once south of Gamack Bay, we passed a chain of small islands reaching west to Goheung, open sea to our east. We continued south, paralleling the long eastern shore of Geumo Island, its steep wooded mountains plunging abruptly into shallow, green-blue water. Near Geumodo's south end we entered a large, well-protected harbor and stopped at its pier. Elderly women disembarked, trundling gingerly across the bow deck – some hunchbacked from decades of working in fields – weighed down by bags, tubs and buckets full of goods. We sailed out of the harbor to the island's south tip where a 200-meter-wide channel separates Geumodo from Ando's north flank.

I'll diverge here a moment to recount an instance illustrating how perilous the local tides and currents can be. Living on Ando that July, I had a nerve-racking experience in this same narrow channel. That spring, I'd purchased a used outrigger sailing vessel from Indonesia and had it shipped to Ando. The boat's massively thick, hollowed-out narrow hardwood hull was balanced by a long bamboo outrigger on each side. A tall bamboo mast tethered a giant billowy sail. Unfortunately, I was rarely able to get the heavy, temperamental craft to sail in a straight line, so I converted it to a motorized putt-putt by removing the sail and attaching an old, three-horsepower Mercury outboard engine to the stern.

One weekend that July, a Korean teacher friend of mine from Seoul, accompanied by a group of her young adult friends, visited Heju and me on Ando. I took three of them out in the outrigger, from Ando Beach on the island's east shore, motoring around the island's front into the channel between Ando and Geumodo. The Merc engine was prone to suddenly sputtering and dying and chose to do so now. The tide was rushing, forming frothy white rapids in the middle of the channel. I yanked and yanked on the engine cord but silence. We drifted toward the channel's bubbling vortex. With four adults on board weighing down the craft, the top of the hull was a mere four inches above the water line, my three passengers oblivious to the danger.

After a couple of minutes of pulling the cord the engine finally coughed to life. I steered to safety away from channel's middle and back to Ando Beach. Had the motor not started we may have been pulled into the churning cascade and swamped. The three wouldn't have stood a chance in the water – none could swim well. I'm a strong swimmer, but I wouldn't have liked my chances. Local fishermen had warned me about the tempestuous tides and currents, but I hadn't seriously heeded their cautions. I'd learned my lesson.

The ferry pulled up to Ando's north shore pier at the channel. Behind the pier is a tiny village – hidden off to the side, a long, narrow, well-protected harbor where fishing vessels were moored. A single, narrow concrete lane bordered by two low concrete walls sneaks back through the village of maybe a couple hundred residents. A handful of concrete homes are behind the walls. Among the structures are a post office, bank, two small old general stores and a utilitarian austere restaurant, the latter with a concrete floor and several small tables. Off to the side on the island's shore is Ando Minbak, where I'd resided that July. Past the *minbak* rises a slight gradual hill, steeply descending on the far side at hidden, beguiling Ando Beach, protected by a long, narrow bay with rocky shorelines. At Ando's high south end are tall cliffs far above greenish-blue water and an angry white surf crashing against rocks.

The ferry reversed from the pier and rounded the island's treed west shore where scores of magnificent white herons floated in the air and rested high up on the branches of tall, dark green coniferous trees. We crossed the kilometer-wide strait separating Ando from Yeondo. Even on a vessel as heavy and stalwart as this I could feel the hull shudder underneath from the immense stress caused by powerful currents. We reached narrow Yeondo's long, desolate rocky west coastline and paralleled it south, docking at the large, well-sheltered harbor, where the fisherman Mr. Cho moored his vessel. A Korea Post mini-truck raced onto the pier, the driver unloading outgoing mail onto the ferry and picking up incoming mail. After docking for just five minutes the ferry began the thirty-five-kilometer return voyage north to Yeosu. It was four o'clock.

As the ship hugged Geumodo's long, steep eastern shore, my memory was jogged to a previous excursion on the outrigger at the same location. Heju and I had departed Ando that July so I could begin my English teaching job at a *hagwon* in Yeosu. The outrigger was heavily loaded with my belongings. We were motoring parallel to Geumodo's shore, the morning bright, sunny and fresh. A stiff westerly breeze was blowing in off the open sea, forming robust, formidable tall rolling whitecaps buffeting the hard-wood hull. The wood creaked and groaned under the stress of nature's triad forces: wind, waves and current. In a battle between the sea's immense strength and the august, time-tested seaworthiness of the outrigger, the latter easily prevailed.

At about six o'clock the ferry docked at Yeosu Port. I navigated the car north out of the busy, hustling downtown core on the main thoroughfare, passing old worn shops, automobile repair garages, flat-roof dwellings, apartment blocks and Mediterranean-style concrete homes all hemmed in on each side by a long row of low, steep mountains. Not far ahead the old, worn Yeosu Bus Station was off the side of the road. I wondered if the station's soap hoarder was still gainfully employed there. During my year as a teacher in Yeosu, I sometimes took bus trips, and in the station's men's washroom there was never any soap. I suspected the soap hoarder was the reason.

Prior to boarding a bus one afternoon, I purchased a bar of soap at the station store, entered the washroom, placed the bar on the sink and entered a toilet stall. Five minutes later I went to the sink to wash my hands, but the soap was gone. Standing alone in the washroom corner was the cleaner — a tiny, hunched, elderly woman — facing me, glaring, clutching my new bar.

"It's mine. Give it back!" I called.

The woman remained glued to the spot, her fierce eyes locked on mine. I approached her, removed the soap from her hands, returned to the sink, washed my hands, and put the soap back on the counter. "Leave it there," I told her.

Her angry gaze never left me — it was unnerving. I exited the washroom and sat in the station waiting area. Ten minutes later, curious as to how my soap was doing, I returned to the washroom; both the woman and the soap were nowhere to be seen.

I decided now wasn't the time to revisit the soap hoarder/man hater, and instead I turned the Scoupe off the main road and drove the short distance toward Hwayang — the long narrow peninsula paralleling Gamack Bay's west shore. In nearby Singi-dong, at the bay's headlands, in a bright, modern entertainment district packed with night clubs and motels, I had dinner with Kate and her husband. Later in the evening, I cruised south a short way past the pretty harbor on Hwayang's coastal Soho Road, passing parallel rows of tall white apartment buildings and the Soho Yacht Club, where my outrigger was stored on dry-dock. On Soho Road, just past the yacht club, is Pattaga Pensions, where I'd resided while teaching in Yeosu. Pattaga is a half-dozen trailer-type metal boxes available for rent, perched on a low rocky shoreline.

That fall in Yeosu I'd moved into a Pattaga unit and to save on costs, I decided to do without gas heating for the winter. (I'm of Dutch-Scotch blood, after all.) As well, Yeosu locals had blithely insisted Yeosu winters were mild. In an *International Herald Tribune* feature, writer Ingrid K. Williams described Yeosu as having a "temperate climate."

Now, I'm guessing Ms. Williams had never spent a winter in Yeosu. Had she, I doubted she'd bandy the term "temperate" about, evoking a pleasant moderate climate, similar, say, to a Spanish winter. The particular winter I braved in Yeosu was so frigid it would have frozen the gonads off a polar bear. Every night after finishing teaching at my *hagwon* at 10:00 p.m., I'd stroll the seven kilometers south on Soho Road to my Pattaga metal ice box. I'd immediately jump into the shower – the small bathroom steaming up from hot water meeting the room's Siberia-like cold air – then sprint to my bed. Once under the covers I'd flick on the little portable electric space heater next to the bed and wouldn't leave its warmth until early the next afternoon when it was time to return to work. Many nights that winter the temperature in my uninsulated refrigerator hovered at a chilly seven degrees Celsius (45 degrees Fahrenheit). For comparison, fridges are recommended set at about four degrees Celsius (39 degrees Fahrenheit).

Out the pension's large front window, I enjoyed a dazzling array of vistas over Gamack Bay of myriad, malleable editions of the sea: rolling, sparkling whitecaps on fair days; light mist or thick white blankets of fog; gray, angry swells on stormy days; an inky, placid black mirror on moonless nights. At the crack of dawn, a huge, bright orange sun would peak above Dolsan's mountain ridge ten kilometers east across the bay, sunshine flooding my room in a stark, jarring brightness that always woke me up.

From the pension it took mere minutes to be hiking a nearby ridge, or paddling my sea kayak, or cycling up and down Hwayang's steep, winding interior roads, or trekking a coastal plain. One weekend spring afternoon, the rock face under my pension rumbled and shook — my first earthquake. (Korea, on the far fringes of the western Pacific Ocean's volcanic "Ring of Fire," occasionally gets jolted by minor to moderate earthquakes.) The temblor lasted a mere fifteen seconds, but what a sensation to feel the earth's bowels momentarily shifting.

One Saturday afternoon that spring I hiked up the earthen path on an easy ascent to the grassy top of the low mountain ridge behind Soho Yacht Club. From the crest is an arresting panoramic view far over Gamack Bay's green islands protruding in the shallow, sparkling blue-green water. Everything so bold and fresh, it is as if you can reach out and touch it. Looking west in the opposite direction far below is a wide agricultural plain reaching to Hwayang's west shore, a wide bay separating it from Goheung to the west.

I lay on my back on the grassy ground to absorb the afternoon's weak spring sun, to thaw out, having been rendered a popsicle that winter. Suddenly, a curious hawk appeared about five meters directly above me. Hawks commonly soar high in Yeosu skies. Despite a stiff breeze bending tree branches, the bird remained stationary, eyeballing me, fixed to a singular spot in the air, only the occasional minute flick of its wing tips keeping it frozen in place. For a remarkable five consecutive minutes it floated motionless, statue-like. I'd never seen anything like it. I'm guessing the U.S. Department of Defense — keen to develop new technology — would love to incorporate the hawk's remarkable innate navigational skills into its fighter jets. It was a rare human-hawk interaction — I was close enough to see the bird's eyes intently focusing on me. Finally deciding I was too big to enjoy as a snack, it tipped a wing, and was carried gracefully and majestically by the wind like a dive bomber, hundreds of meters across to the neighboring ridge.

Despite Yeosu's many outdoor advantages, I yearned for the familiarity of Myeongil-dong, my old neighborhood in Seoul. Yeosu just wasn't "home." After my one-year experiment living on the south coast, it was time to depart. When my one-year contract at the *hagwon* ended in July, I loaded my possessions into a large hockey bag and bussed myself back to Seoul.

***

It was past 11:00 p.m. when I departed Pattaga Pensions and cruised on Soho Road to the Soho Yacht Club. I parked in the quiet club's lot. Exhausted, I reclined the driver's seat all the way to the horizontal position, lay back and promptly fell asleep. It had been a long day.

SOUTHEAST

CHAPTER 18

Namhae and Tongyeong:
The Admiral and Turtle Ships

I woke in early morning and looked out from the car over silent, shimmering Gamack Bay, so glassy smooth, it was as if you could walk on it. No vessels were on the water, no cars on Soho Road, no one around. Everything was still, like a photograph. I checked my watch — just past 7:00 a.m. I'd slept like a log. I got out of the car to stretch my legs and strolled onto the yacht club's concrete square, inhaling deep breaths of fresh sea air. Then I got behind the wheel and headed out of Yeosu.

At the top of Yeosu peninsula I turned east, hugging the highly indented southern coastline, moving slowly on the winding road, passing small isolated bays — a tiny village here and there. The picturesque, placid, shallow sea is dotted with ubiquitous little offshore wooded islands. I had the quiet road almost exclusively to myself, contentedly rolling along like an elderly retiree navigating an RV.

The next major peninsula jutting south into the sea east of Yeosu is Namhae. Technically, Namhae is an island, separated from the mainland by a few hundred meters of water and linked by a bridge. At about 300 square kilometers, Namhae is the country's fifth-largest island. When my parents visited me in fall 2000, we rented a car and explored Namhae, and the big island of Geoje immediately east. On Namhae are occasional narrow belts of coastline with small seaside villages, but much of it is broad, rugged forested hills and mountains. Its charm and allure is that it's laid-back, unassuming and off the beaten path.

From the mainland I crossed the impressive, 660-meter-long Namhae Bridge, towering a dizzying eighty meters above Noryang Strait, a narrow strip of dark green water. I cruised south on a lovely winding, rolling country road though hills and farmland, reminding me of English countryside. In thirty minutes, about half way down-island, I arrived at Namhae City on the shore of expansive, muddy Jinju Bay. The tiny city appeared more like a small town – slow, quiet and unpretentious. I liked it.

In the 1960s, South Korea – struggling financially – agreed to send up to 10,000 nurses to Germany. As one might expect, some of those young Korean female nurses married German men. In the 1990s, some of these married unions created a typical German-style mountain village of chalets on Namhae, and Germantown was unofficially born.

A foreign enclave in homogeneous South Korea is unusual. Except for Incheon's Chinatown – comprising a mere few streets with Chinese restaurants – Germantown is the only other distinct foreign district on the peninsula I'm aware of.

I'd phoned ahead to Namhae City Hall to find a translator to accompany me to Germantown. At city hall I rendezvoused with a friendly, helpful guide, Cho Hye-yeon, and together we drove in the Scoupe east across the quiet island. On Namhae's north shore in Mulgeon village, in Samdong district, behind a modest, quiet sandy bay and beach lined with a row of trees, we spotted the chalets half way up a large hill. In total were perhaps forty two-story white chalets with orange-shale A-shape roofs. We puttered up the lane to the homes. It was deathly quiet, not a soul around. We began knocking on doors, but no one answered. After about fifteen minutes, about to give up, a door was finally opened by a retirement-aged Korean woman and an equally aged foreign male. The latter, I quickly surmised, was German – tall, heavy-set, stern and dominating, viewing me with great suspicion.

The guide, Ms. Cho, spoke to the pair in Korean, explaining I was writing a travel book on Korea, had heard about Germantown and hoped to speak to villagers. After several minutes of interrogation in which I had to divulge my nationality, employment, workplace and IQ – the couple kindly invited us in. The chalet's interior was lovely – compact yet airy with light-colored wood and a large front window offering an impressive view over the sea. Some chalet materials were imported from Europe, including the orange-tile roofs of shale.

"Can you speak German?" the man asked me.

"*Schlaagen sie den ball auf der ganzen linie* (hit the ball down the line)," I replied, one of a few German sentences I'd learned while teaching tennis in 1986 at a tennis club near Frankfurt.

The four of us sat in the living room. Communication began by me posing a question in English, Ms. Cho translating it to Korean, the woman transcribing it to German for her husband, he answering in German, translated by his wife to Korean, and Ms. Cho changing it to English for me. It was a ponderous, highly inefficient and unsustainable method. As I expected, the German man quickly grew impatient, cut out the superfluous intermediaries, and began to converse in English.

"I'd been employed as a streetcar operator in Germany," he said.

"When I was ill, I went to the hospital and met my future wife," the woman by his side. He said that German-Korean couples who owned chalets in Namhae divided their time between Germany and Namhae.

Ms. Cho and I departed after ninety minutes, disappointedly having not been offered a cold German Beck's or Lowenbrau brew. Germantown's unique design and architecture is a welcome breath of fresh air in a country where many resorts tend to be bland, cookie-cutter, white concrete condominiums.

We drove back to Namhae City, where I took Ms. Cho to a restaurant for a meal, to thank her for her assistance. Now late afternoon, I dropped her off at Namhae Bridge to rendezvous with a tour group she would lead. I glanced far below to Noryang Strait, spotting a most unusual-looking docked vessel. Curious as to what it was, I maneuvered the car down the steep side road to the water and discovered a stunning replica of *geobukseon* (turtle ship). Turtle ships were successfully used by Korean Admiral Yi Sun-sin during Japan's invasion of Korea in the 1592–1598 Imjin War. Two months prior to the 1592 assault, ordered by Japanese warlord Toyotomi Hideyoshi, Admiral Yi launched the first turtle ship.

The word "turtle" was derived from the vessel's enclosed, almost impenetrable shell of thick, bulwark wood planks. The ship before me was constructed by the Korean Navy in 1980, with assistance from Korean *geobukseon* experts. It measures thirty-four meters long and ten and a half meters wide, is flat-bottomed and keel-less. On the top deck are two twelve-meter masts. Short, sharp spear-like spikes protrude from the deck to have discouraged sword-wielding Japanese soldiers from boarding. On the port and starboard sides are rows of eight portholes for long oars and up to ten portholes for cannon. Openings on the prow and stern are for more cannon. On the bow is a mounted dragon's head, inside it four guns armed with gunpowder to send iron nails flying. The vessel reminded me of a

Roman warship. In it, I imagined Charlton Heston as the slave rower in a scene from the 1959 movie *Ben Hur*.

Korean history books sometimes state that *geobukseon* was the world's first ironclad ship. Samuel Hawley, author of the meticulously researched *The Imjin War: Japan's Sixteenth-Century Invasion of Korea and Attempt to Conquer China*, contends the ship was constructed solely of wood. Nevertheless, to build a single *geobukseon* required significant manpower and a large supply of timber. Historians believe no more than twenty in total were constructed. More common was its cousin *panokseon,* a smaller, open version of *geobukseon*.

I was the only person on the dock. I boarded the ship. The interior was magnificent — imported pale wood planks. (Korean forests are new growth, lumber too thin and narrow for such planks.) On the lower deck on each side are eight long rows of benches, each for eight oarsmen. I tried lifting an oar, but it was outrageously heavy. Above the lower deck is a mid deck for cannon. About 130 oarsmen and several dozen crew were needed to propel the vessel and fire cannon and wield other weapons. Up to 160 sweaty men were squeezed into this rectangular box. During sweltering summers, I imagined the interior was a sort of hell.

Tomorrow I'd learn more about Admiral Yi Sun-sin on a visit to Hansan Island, off the coastal city of Tongyeong in Goseong, the next peninsula east. Off Hansando, Admiral Yi had won a renowned 1592 naval battle against the Japanese.

After departing Namhae and back on the mainland, I headed northeast along the indented coastline to Sacheon, an industrial port on a large bay. I drove into Sacheon — it had an old, dowdy feel to it. Early evening depressing gray clouds didn't help. I strolled the fringes of its weary downtown, its streets differing little from those in other small cities. My mobile phone hadn't been picking up signals well for the last day or two, so I entered a major Korean electronic company's after-service center to have it repaired. In the store's large showroom – replete with appliances and big screen televisions – I sat in a soft office chair and watched a movie on one of the TVs on the wall. Unable to keep my eyes open, I soon fell into a deep slumber, and awoke forty-five minutes later when my name was called to pick up my now-functioning phone.

Having spent the previous night in Yeosu sleeping in the car, I decided I'd splurge tonight and upgrade to a motel. Near downtown, I found the modest Songnam Motel. In its austere empty lobby was a tiny office with a small window, its blinds pulled half way down. I lowered my head to see if anyone was behind the window and received a fright – only inches from my face, behind the window, appeared the weathered, shriveled bird-like visage of an aged woman glaring at me.

I retreated a few paces, then asked Birdwoman, "Excuse me, how much is a room?"

"Thirty thousand won," she chirped menacingly.

"Do you have rooms for 25,000 won?"

"No, rooms are 30,000 won on weekends," she said. Today was Friday – a weekend.

"Thanks anyway," I said, and began to walk away. As I suspected she drew me back.

"Are you alone?" she called.

"Yes."

"Twenty-five thousand won then," she said. She eyed me suspiciously. "You sure you're alone?" Perhaps she thought another person might later join me in the room. I assured her I was traveling solo. She accepted the money.

After stomping on my day's used clothing in the shower, I slipped on a pair of shorts and T-shirt and skipped down to the lobby to borrow a few coat hangers to dry my wet clothes on. Birdwoman was nowhere to be seen. I stood in the lobby waiting for her, and soon began to hear muffled, guttural half-dog/half-bear growls emanating from the office. The frail old woman crept into the lobby, glaring at my feet. I believe her glowering and growling was her way to let me know bare feet in the lobby were unacceptable.

❖❖❖

I slept in until noon the following day to take advantage of every available second lying on a real mattress. Back in the car I was soon heading southeast to Goseong. The early afternoon was brilliantly bright, the mid-June day balmy, minus humidity. At the north end of Goseong I proceeded south on the highway to Tongyeong City, at the narrow peninsula's far tip.

Today being Saturday, Tongyeong's vibrant downtown core seemed to have all its 140,000 citizens cruising streets in cars or busily sauntering on sidewalks. The small, concentrated hub is built predominantly on a north-south axis, on narrow slices of lowland between clusters of low, steep rocky mountains. An amazing number of dwellings, apartments, buildings and shops are crammed into the tight slivers of real estate. The physical landscape is arresting.

I rolled slowly though downtown stuck in bumper-to-bumper traffic and finally reached busy, appealing Tongyeong Port. Looking south across the half-kilometer-wide bay is a long mountain ridge on Mireuk Island's north shore. Several freight cranes and freighters were on the far shore's long industrial concrete wharf.

On the Tongyeong Port side, numerous fishing trawlers and small merchant vessels were moored at its concrete shoreline. Inside the weathered, busy Tongyeong Ferry Terminal, a huge map of Tongyeong on the wall showed an amazing number of small offshore islands: 151 in total, forty-one inhabited. Seven kilometers southeast of Tongyeong is ten-kilometer-long Hansan Island, where between 1593 and 1597, Admiral Yi headquartered his navy. These days the island is a popular tourist draw for Koreans.

I purchased a ticket for the 4:00 p.m. sailing to Hansando on a small, compact passenger-only ferry. Packed with visitors, we cruised out of the bay into the beguiling green sea. In 1968, this arrestingly beautiful maritime area was designated as Hallyeohaesang National Park. We passed several small islands – their lower halves vertical rock, the upper reaches, tree-covered.

After forty-five minutes we docked at a small pretty cove on Hansando's north shore, the island all wooded hills and low mountains, not a shop, dwelling or structure to be seen. We disembarked, replaced by a small horde of day-trippers returning to Tongyeong. A walking path – Hansan Road – leads from the dock back around the wooded cove. I let my fellow passengers go ahead, then near the dock read a plaque titled *Song of Hansan Island*.

In the bright moonlight at Hansan-do Isle
I sit alone upon a lookout pavilion,
Wearing a long sword at my side.
Full of cares about the fatherland.

How poignant! I imagined a Korean soldier standing atop the island's tallest mountain on a moonlit night in 1592 peering over the surrounding water, on the lookout for enemy Japanese ships.

The path winds back around the cove, then gently ascends through woods culminating at a large square, where the Hansan Great Victory Monument honors Admiral Yi's victory in the Battle of Hansando on August 14, 1592. The square was packed with visitors. I joined a tour group of mostly men led by an earnest male guide. I turned on my mini recorder to record his words.

"Do you understand what he's saying?" asked a man in the group of professors from prestigious Korea University in Seoul, visiting Tongyeong for the weekend.

"No, but I'll translate it later," I replied.

The guide stopped us in front of a big whiteboard on which were drawn two separate groups of little short black dashes. One group represented Korean ships, the other a Japanese fleet in the Battle of Hansando. The ships commanded by Admiral Yi were positioned in a U or "crane-wing" formation signified by single-file black dashes enclosing dashes marking enemy ships.

In Samuel Hawley's book *Imjin War,* he wrote that in May 1592 "Japanese dictator Toyotomi Hideyoshi sent a 158,000-man army aboard a thousand ships from Kyushu to Busan." The invaders set up camp in Busan, then marched north and spread across the country, leaving in their wake a trail of death and destruction. About 100,000 Japanese troops were based in Pyongyang in today's North Korea. Hideyoshi's ultimate goal was to invade and subjugate China. Japan was in it for the long term but required reinforcements of men, supplies, food and weapons. To transport men and weapons 700 kilometers overland from Busan to Pyongyang was dangerous, time-consuming and physically taxing. Instead, the Japanese planned to resupply troops in the north by ship, sailing west along Korea's south coast, then up the western seaboard to Pyongyang.

That was the plan — but Admiral Yi had something to say about it. Yi's mission was to protect the sea lanes off Korea's south coast, to block Japan's attempts to convey supplies to troops over seven years of war, and to annihilate any enemy vessel his navy encountered. He proved superbly successful on all fronts. In numerous sea battles off the south coast, Yi ruthlessly won each. Not a single enemy ship made it north. Yi's bravery and cunning against huge odds almost certainly saved his country from defeat.

In the Battle of Hansando, Japanese Admiral Wakizaka led seventy-three ships — predominantly flimsy merchant and transport vessels converted for battle — crammed with warriors armed with swords, bows and arquebus guns. If the expert Japanese swordsmen — skilled in hand-to-hand combat — boarded a Korean ship, heads would roll. Wakizaka sailed west from Busan seeking Yi's navy and anchored just north of Hansando between Tongyeong and Geoje Island in the half-kilometer-wide Gyeonnaeryang Strait. Hidden off Hansando, Yi's fifty-six ships included several *geobukseon* and many smaller open *panokseon* loaded with cannon, multiple arrow missiles, archers and up to 120 rowers. As a decoy, Yi sent six ships north into Gyeonnaeryang Strait, trying to lure the Japanese south into the open. The impulsive, aggressive admiral fell for the ruse and ordered his fleet to chase the Korean ships.

Wakizaka sailed into the center of Yi's crane-wing formation — *geobukseon* in the center of the semi-circle, *panokseon* on each flank. Oarsmen kept the Korean ships turning in circles while cannon fire hammered the Japanese from all sides. Yi's priority was to keep his vessels far enough away from the enemy so as not to be boarded. He tightened the noose, hemming in the invader's ships so they were unable to maneuver. Japanese arrows and bullets weren't effective in penetrating *geobukseon* and *panokseon's* thick hulls. The bombardment continued unabated from mid-morning through late afternoon.

"Fireballs shot at our ships, which were burned and destroyed," wrote a source aboard a Japanese ship.

Wakizaka was hit by several arrows but survived in armor. Forty-seven Japanese ships sank, twelve were captured, fourteen escaped. About 9,000 invaders died. Many jumped overboard, swimming to nearby islands. One Japanese commander committed *hara-kiri*, disemboweling himself as his vessel sank. Yi lost 123 men but no ships. At the Hanson Great Victory Monument our guide paused in front of Yi's portrait and commanded solemnly: "Everyone bow your heads to honor the admiral." We did so, remaining silent for half a minute.

The tour now over, a professor invited me to ride back with his group on a powerful motor launch to Chungmu Resort, across the bay from Tongyeong. I gladly accepted. We were soon noisily cruising across the greenish water. The tour guide, Park Jeong-uk, who'd led the group on Hansando, was on board. I corralled a professor, who spoke English, to put several questions to Mr. Park.

"Why did Admiral Yi use the U-formation?" I shouted above the din of the engine. Despite standing immediately next to Mr. Park it was almost impossible to hear him.

He hollered, "Yi didn't want his ships to be in a straight line. He'd tried that tactic before. He wanted a U-formation, to encircle the enemy, to use his full range of cannon from the sides and front."

I asked about the admiral's propensity for decreeing heads be chopped off. I'd read the English version of Yi's log, *War Diary of Admiral Yi Sun-sin (Nanjung Ilgi)*, and it seemed Yi reveled in ordering heads to roll. For example, on February 1, 1593, Yi wrote: "Ordered execution of Ch'oe E, the garrison inspector of Palp'o, for violating Martial Law twice – punished him in accordance with law." Two days later, on February 3, Yi penned: "I ordered the arrest of the two runaways, Kim Ho-kol and Kim Su-nam, and had their heads cut off the same day." On April 29, 1596: "Took a hot bath in the evening. Ordered Minami Uyemon to cut off the head of Sago Youm, surrendered Japanese." One year later, April 28, 1597: "Late in the day, I punished two collaborators, Chong Un-bu and Kim Sin-ung's wife, who had led the Japanese to kill our people, and Kim Ae-nam, who had raped a virgin in a literati home, by cutting off their heads and hanging them as a warning." Seven months later, Yi described five "rascals" who had interfered with farmers bringing in the autumn grain. He had the leader decapitated.

"He had to order executions," answered Mr. Park. "He had to send a message to soldiers of what awaited if they tried to desert."

Desertion was a problem. More than a few "soldiers" — usually forcibly-recruited peasant farmers from the provinces — bolted naval camps. How terrifying to enter battle against sword-wielding Japanese warriors. Deserters who were caught usually lost their heads.

Yi Sun-sin met his fate on December 15, 1598 in the Battle of Noryang, west of the Noryang Strait off Namhae Island. Yi was on a ship when struck in the shoulder by a bullet from a Japanese ship. He was fifty-three years old. Yi is a national hero in Korea. Citizens consider him on a par with Britain's renowned naval commander, Horatio Nelson, who died age 47 from a bullet while commanding a ship in the 1805 Battle of Trafalgar. A huge statue of Yi — his powerful chest puffed out, sword in hand — stands prominently on Sejong Street, the broad avenue running up to Gyeongbok Palace in Seoul. Yeosu — where Yi built some turtle ships — honors the admiral with an annual parade. *Roaring Currents*, a 2014 film centered on Yi's famous 1597 Battle of Myeongnyang — the admiral leading a handful of Korean warships to victory over more than one hundred Japanese ships, was a blockbuster hit drawing a record fifteen million Korean cinema-goers. In 2022, the prequel to *Roaring Currents: Hansan: The Emergence of Dragons* — portraying Admiral Yi's 1592 historic sea battle over the Japanese off Hansan Island underpinned by his exceptional turtle ships — premiered.

Our vessel docked in front of Chungmu Resort at the wharf across the bay from Tongyeong. "Resort" is a stretch. It is more like a small group of condominiums, hotel and a small swimming area sandwiched on the industrial port. I entered the hotel's well-appointed lobby crowded with scores of well-heeled, formally-attired, middle-aged Koreans. I approached the front desk to pick up a business card and spoke a few words to the young female receptionist, who seemed indifferent to me.

A few moments later I glimpsed at myself in the full-length lobby mirror. Staring back, while not exactly a homeless person, was a scruffy looking fellow in a worn T-shirt, wrinkled shorts, sandals, backward-facing baseball hat and five-day crop of facial hair. Being on the road for weeks, one tended to forget about keeping up appearances.

I strolled back around the bay to the Tongyeong Ferry Terminal about five kilometers off, the early evening lovely and balmy. On the Tongyeong side, I enjoyed a delicious dinner of *jajangmyeon* (noodles in black bean sauce) at a cubbyhole takeout. Then I walked past the ferry terminal to the city's quaint, quiet harbor, where the lights from storefronts reflected in darkness off the mirror-like black water. Nearby was a huge, formidable 24-hour *jjimjilbang* where I stayed the night.

***

In mid-morning's marvelously bright sunshine, I crossed the big bridge from Tongyeong over Gyeonnaeryang Strait, then continued east across Geoje Island to Geoje City — a small but surprisingly energetic, bustling port town with numerous apartment buildings by a bay on the island's north shore. I toured the former Geoje Prisoner of War Camp on the edge of the city next to a low mountain. The camp, established by the Americans in the Korean War, had once held more than 100,000 North Korean and Chinese prisoners. Walking with other visitors through the downsized camp, I read how North Korean prisoners had divided themselves into two factions — hardcore supporters of North Korea versus those for South Korea.

The acrimony and hatred was so great that each side carried out secret executions against the opposition.

Later that day back across the bridge on Goseong, I slipped northeast up the coast to Masan – a small but surprisingly hectic city built on a narrow slice of land wedged between a big bay, and a ridge of low but steep mountains a kilometer inland. I stayed the night in a palatial *jjimjilbang* in downtown Masan, getting thoroughly lost and discombobulated among the facility's numerous hidden staircases, hallways and backrooms.

Late the next afternoon I moved east toward Busan to meet Heju, who would be arriving there the next day on the train from Daejeon. Approaching Busan from the west offers a tantalizing view of the north-south axis mountain ridge guarding the city like a rampart in a scene from a *Lord of the Rings* movie. Immediately west of this wall of eminences is the expansive green Nakdong River Delta – 200-square kilometers of thousands of fertile agricultural plots. As I cruised east across the delta, the size and mass of the mountains became evident. At their base, high-rise apartment buildings looked like miniature models.

Patricia Bartz wrote that after one hundred million years of mountain-building, the Korean land block has been in a pattern of erosion for about 70 million years. Sediment has been removed from much of the peninsula's north and west via the Han, Imjin, Geum and Yeongsan Rivers emptying on the west coast. But in the southeast Gyeongsang provinces, much of the former freshwater sea and lake deposits, including mudstone, sandstone and conglomerate, weren't removed. Today, these deposits exist at a thickness possibly greater than 20,000 feet. The southeast, including the Nakdong River Delta, Bartz explained, has probably the greatest freshwater deposit of sediment anywhere in the world.

Driving east in darkness through the mountains into Busan wasn't easy. The Scoupe was one of innumerable vehicles jammed on the road. In front were streams of oncoming white headlights and a line of rear red tail lights. The road goes through a series of long tunnels under the mountain mass, emerging in Busan's northwest on the east side of a broad slope. I needed to head east some distance through these tangled web of streets to get to the Busan Train Station. I immediately got disorientated and hopelessly lost. Little wonder, there is no rhyme or reason to the road layout; London's convoluted mass of city streets seem benign in comparison. Relying on my road atlas was useless to get my bearings and to find east. Instead I repeatedly stopped the car every few minutes on the side of the road to take compass readings. (The needle on my hand-held compass always points north while driving — something to do with the engine's ignition coil interfering with Earth's magnetic field, a car mechanic told me.) After an hour of stopping and starting, I finally entered a major north–south parkway, and flew south on it toward the port area to the Busan Train Station. It was now late evening.

Across the busy main street from the station, I drove into Choryang — an old, expansive, brightly-lit dodgy entertainment district — to find a *jjimjilbang* for the night. Choryang is replete with narrow, brightly-lit back lanes and numerous bars, karaoke clubs, restaurants and motels. Tall, blond Russian hostesses stood in front of some bars on lanes beckoning me to stop. I continued on. After half an hour of searching, about to concede that Choryang was devoid of a single *jjimjilbang*, I finally located a bright, large busy one. The female manager at the front desk adamantly refused me entry though. I was White, she explained, something I'd known for some years. I discovered that Russian ladies of the evening had apparently been using the *jjimjilbang* to entertain male customers, resulting in the establishment's blanket ban on Whites.

Again puttering though Choryang, I found a small motel I thought might offer reasonable rates. I entered its empty, dimly lit, eerie-looking lobby and was startled to observe standing stiffly in the shadows in the far corner, the rigid, silent figure of an aged woman staring at me.

"Excuse me," I called across the lobby to the apparition, "how much is a room?"

Not a peep. Not a muscle moved. I think she'd been dead for some time and embalmed – propped up like a Native American squaw wood mannequin you'd find at Bubba's Gun and Ammunition Store in Gatlinburg, Tennessee.

Now past 1:00 a.m., I headed east on the main road to a nearby gritty, industrial port district, where I spotted the doleful-looking Shinjang Yeogwan Inn, arguably the oldest inn in Korea. The lobby was a tiny, dark space where a little old woman was holed up in its closet-like office behind a window.

"May I see a room, please," I asked the woman.

"Yes," she kindly agreed.

I climbed the narrow staircase to the second floor and poked my head into a shadowy cubbyhole of a room. I tested the water faucet in the bathroom – no hot water. The yellow linoleum floor had cigarette burn marks on it. Exhausted, I just needed a bed to flop on.

The lady asked 20,000 won but accepted 15,000. I don't think the inn got many customers, for reasons I could completely understand.

I retired to my penthouse suite and lay on the bed. The dank pillow smelled as if Admiral Yi himself had slept on it more than 400 years ago. I extricated a fresh T-shirt from my backpack, removed the pillow slip and replaced it with the shirt. I immediately fell asleep and dreamed that tomorrow Heju would shower me with numerous edible goodies she'd purchased in Thailand.

CHAPTER 19

Busan: An Unnavigable City

On the second floor of the expansive, modern Busan Train Station, Heju burst through the turnstiles with a rush of passengers. The first thing I noted was she was relaxed and effervescent, in contrast to early May in Gunsan when she went AWOL on the trip. Now tanned after four weeks in Krabi in Thailand — absent an imperious slave driver — the vacation obviously had done her a world of good.

She filled me in with news of her trip, which included meditation, beach-side Thai massages, sunbathing and sampling delectable cuisine.

Then she surprised me: "I'm going to move to Krabi!" she exclaimed enthusiastically, something she'd repeat over the next few days. "I don't want to live in Korea anymore. I hate it here. I'm going to open a business in Krabi. I'll buy land with palm trees on it and sell palm oil."

Now, it's necessary to understand that the half of Heju's brain where neurons fire up her imagination, dreams and whims, far out-duels her hippocampus, where rational thought and problem-solving occur. I have no reason to boast of being in possession of common sense; the good lord was asleep at the wheel when it was my turn to be imbued with such traits, but even I realized Heju's plan had holes.

"Who'll buy the palm oil?" I wondered aloud.

She contemplated this for a moment, then said, "I'm going to export it."

"To which countries?"

She hesitated and was silent.

"Can you make money exporting palm oil?"

"I don't know," she said, a little less assuredly.

"How much does it cost to buy land in Thailand with palm trees on it?"

She said she wasn't sure.

"Heju, if you want to start a business, you need to learn a little about it," I suggested. "I'm not saying it isn't possible to export palm oil from Thailand. All I'm saying is you're probably not the first person to have the idea. I'm guessing people have been exporting palm oil from Thailand for some time."

Realizing her plan might not be as novel as she hoped, she brightly announced Plan B: "Then I'll take a massage course in Thailand and give massages there."

If she did, she wouldn't save money because the cost of getting a massage in Thailand is inexpensive.

She declared Plan C: "Then I'll move to Sweden and give massages there." Heju's Korean aunt had married a Swede, and the couple lived in Sweden.

To illustrate the difficulty in landing even a short-term, casual position in the European Union, I related to Hjeu an experience I faced in my twenties traveling through Europe. Hitchhiking through France one early fall — in need of pocket money — I stopped at a vineyard in Bordeaux to get a job picking grapes. Hundreds of young EU students were picking the fruit in the fields. The vineyard owner said he couldn't legally employ me due to prohibitive EU regulations that stipulated jobs must go to Europeans. Heju and I let the matter rest.

She eagerly presented me with a gift of a one-kilogram block of imported American cheddar cheese she'd purchased at a Daejeon department store. A lovely thought. In South Korea, cheese is imported and expensive. Over the next couple of days, we dined exclusively at breakfast, lunch and dinner on cheese and baguettes until the last sumptuous morsel was gone.

"Here's my gift for you," I buoyantly announced, presenting her with a bag containing four pairs of sports socks I'd carefully chosen the day before at a department store in Masan.

She viewed the socks skeptically. "They were on sale, weren't they," she said accusingly. How did she know? It must have been a woman thing. I feigned hurt. "How can you say that? Just because I occasionally buy a few things on sale doesn't mean everything I buy is on sale!"

She remained unmoved. "How much did they cost ... one thousand won each? Two thousand won?"

It was hard to fool Heju. The socks had been on sale, and I'd paid one thousand won each. I'd mistakenly believed that due to their snazzy design and color, they'd easily pass in the three-to-five-thousand-won range. Anyway, it was the thought that counted.

It was now time to get on with the show and reintroduce Heju to the pain and suffering she was accustomed to. Our first stop was high atop nearby Busan Tower. Heju was ambivalent about ascending the tower, saying it wasn't a popular landmark for Koreans.

Busan Tower isn't hard to miss, rising 120 meters — equivalent to a forty-story building — built on a rounded hill in Yongdusan Park, not far west of the train station. We drove to near the landmark and parked in a tightly-packed, old residential area, then walked to the tower base. It was immediately evident the structure's best years were behind it. Built in 1974, its tall faded, worn concrete stem was in need of new white paint.

We rode the elevator to the observation floor and on the outer deck were rewarded with a grand panorama of Busan's vast metropolis. The view east is over a never-ending panoply of concrete stretching forever dominated by a million flat roofs. Busanites are clearly expecting a mass landing of alien spacecraft on their roofs. The city is built largely along the sea, though long fingers of it snake from the sea north through narrow, V-shaped valleys between steep, low mountains. In this vast congregation of humanity stretching below I couldn't see one iota of green space.

The sea is close, abundant and sparkling blue. Busan is the world's fifth-largest port. Reaching many kilometers east is its industrial shoreline replete with uncountable numbers of wharfs, piers, cranes, warehouses and docked freighters plus tens of thousands of brightly colored shipping containers stacked high atop one and other. Tug boats were cruising the water. At the International Ferry Terminal, located between the tower and Busan Station, Pan Star, a large white passenger ship, was plowing out from the port on its regularly-scheduled voyage to Osaka.

Unlike Seoul, Busan was never a capital nor historically important. For most of its past it was a mere fishing hamlet and minor trading center for Japanese merchants. After the Imjin War ended in 1598, Japan and Korea signed a peace treaty permitting the former to maintain a permanent post on the coast. The Japanese chose Busan.

In 1876, Japan forced an unfair treaty on Korea mandating several ports be established for Japanese trade; more Japanese merchants arrived in Busan. As late as 1909, Japanese outnumbered Koreans in the small city. During the Japanese occupation, the colonizers constructed wharfs, piers and the main East Harbor in Busan. In 1914, it attained city status. At the end of World War II, Busan's population was still under 300,000. This abruptly changed with the onset of the Korean War in June 1950, when several million refugees streamed south into the city to escape advancing North Korean soldiers.

Shelter was suddenly urgently needed for the masses. Makeshift shantytowns of wood and tin sprang up, some temporary housing remaining in use to the 1970s. The dynamic population explosion resulted in a largely unplanned cavalcade of districts and streets, the reason, I believe, I didn't have the foggiest notion of where I was driving here. By 1971, two million people resided in the city. Today, 3.5 million make Busan their home — the nation's second largest urban center.

After ninety minutes we descended the tower and at ground level we entered an old, low, narrow concrete structure housing a public aquarium. On each side of the forlorn, dank basement, run two long rows of fish tanks. We were the only visitors, the lone staff member a friendly, university-age fellow.

"I just started working here so I don't know much about the fish," he confessed.

At the far end of the aquarium was a tank holding about a dozen finger-length piranhas. Hollywood movies feature unfortunate people falling into piranha-infested rivers and lakes, victims being viciously chewed to death, water turning bright red with blood.

"Would you like to see the piranhas feed?" the student asked.

"What do you feed them?" I wondered.

"Goldfish."

I'd assumed aquarium piranhas dined on flakes of fish food. I imagined a swirling, slashing feeding frenzy, the poor goldfish stripped to the bone. If I agreed to his proposal, I'd forever be responsible for the sad demise of an innocent goldfish.

"Okay," I replied, my morbid sense of curiosity winning out over my sense of humanity. The fellow proceeded to the big goldfish tank, netted a little fish, returned to the piranha tank, and dropped it in. The piranhas seemed momentarily stunned by their sudden good fortune. One approached the goldfish from behind then suddenly inhaled it in a nanosecond like a vacuum cleaner sucking up a piece of dust. Thank goodness the little victim hadn't suffered (much).

With heavy hearts, Heju and I exited the aquarium and sat in the large stone square by the tower under a warm sun. A group of high school girls in school uniform was shrieking in delight chasing pigeons, their collective shrill, piercing pitches just slightly lower in decibels than the whine of a super jumbo jet engine. Unable to bear their discomfiting screams any longer, we tootled in the car to nearby busy, popular and fashionable Nampo-dong overflowing with university students patronizing cafés, restaurants and shops. At a Nampo-dong bookstore I bought another road atlas since I'd accidentally left mine at the train station several hours earlier. After taking a break at a café, in early evening we took a long stroll through Nampo-dong, then drove back to near the Busan Train Station and stayed the night in a nearby *yeogwan*.

✻✻✻

Our plan for the morning was to breach Busan's west mountain rampart to explore the coast immediately west of the city and take in the small city of Jinhae — headquarters of the Korean Navy. At 8:00 a.m. we sat in the car outside the *yeogwan*, our road atlas open to Busan as I skeptically viewed thousands of mysterious green, yellow and red squiggly lines masquerading as roads. There didn't seem to be a clear route out of the city.

"I have no idea which road to take," I griped to Heju, exasperated.

"Let's go to the police station and get directions," she suggested, so we drove to a nearby police box and showed the officer our map of Busan. He chuckled and advised, "If you use the atlas you'll never get to where you're going — Busan's streets are too complicated. It's very easy to get lost."

We took the officer's advice and spent much of the morning lost. We attempted to maneuver out of this Byzantine quagmire, but missed turnoffs, back-tracked more than a few times, constantly checked the atlas and, not knowing north from south, engaged in fervent debates, some involving my grumbling that my official navigator wasn't having a stellar day.

"Heju, if we were supposed to turn left at the intersection we just passed, why didn't you tell me this before we got to the intersection?" I complained, moments after she'd announced we'd missed the turnoff at the intersection we just passed.

"How am I supposed to read the sign before the intersection if the sign's the size of a book?" she replied, pointing to a tiny sign on a traffic light pole at the intersection. Good point. (Note to the "Busan Department of Road Sign Planners" — make damned larger signs!) Eventually we made our way out of the maze of humanity, and I hereby nominate Busan's streets as the world's most confounding.

We spent most of the rest of the beautiful afternoon west of the mountains, enjoying arresting rural shoreline, including pretty coastal villages, and viewing tiny offshore islands. We even relaxed for a couple of hours at a little patch of beach. I was stymied how Heju had concocted the misconstrued notion that I was a merciless taskmaster.

***

A solid blanket of dark, low cloud cover and a steady downpour wiped out the entire following day, confining us to our *yeogwan*. The next day – the sky still overcast and light rain sprinkling – we made our way east into the heart of the city, to the United Nations Memorial Cemetery. Some foreign soldiers who'd fought under the UN umbrella on South Korea's side in the Korean War, were interred there. We paid a small fee at the front gate and entered an enormous, expansive sea of grass the collective size of many football fields. The bleak, lonely grounds are enclosed by a wall and a continuous row of tall evergreens. We were the sole people here. The grass is meticulously landscaped and manicured with neat, precise rows of shrubbery and low bushes interspersed by blocks of small granite headstones and white crosses. Between 1951 and 1954, about 11,000 foreign soldiers were buried here, thousands more the following year.

A total of 40,896 soldiers from sixteen nations under the UN umbrella were killed in the war. Aside from 1.8 million U.S. soldiers, other countries sent relatively small contingents: about 60,000 Brits, 26,000 Canadians, 17,000 Australians and 15,000 Turks. The U.S. lost 33,652 in action; U.K., 1,100; Turkey, 721; Canada, 516; Australia, 340 and France, 269. Belgium, Colombia, Ethiopia, Greece, Luxembourg, The Philippines, Thailand and the U.S. eventually transported their war dead home. About 2,300 soldiers remain in the cemetery, including thirty-six Americans.

We strolled alongside blocks of gravestones, halting before graves of fallen Turkish soldiers, then Canadians, and read inscriptions. The dates of the soldiers' deaths engraved in stone starkly highlighted their youth, most lads barely out of their teens, thrown into a lions' pit of bullets, bombs, shrapnel and bayonets. Had they survived, the men today would be in their late eighties and nineties.

Every June 6 in South Korea is national Memorial Day to

remember the sacrifice of those who died in the war. School pupils are taught UN soldiers were killed, but generally students are unaware of the number. Were it not for brave ROK, U.S. and foreign soldiers holding down the Busan Perimeter (the defensive boundary nearly broken) from attacking North Korean troops during the war's first few months, there might not be South Korea today.

The cemetery is a grim, depressing reminder of how we as humans seemed largely incapable of peacefully coexisting, of young lives snuffed out due to megalomaniac North Korean leader Kim Il-sung's desire to rule all Korea. War and killing have been constants in history. I was melancholy and introspective when we departed.

We drove east across the densely packed metropolis to the city's southeast tip, to Haeundae Beach, the country's most famed piece of sand. At 1.5 kilometers long and a hundred meters wide, Haeundae isn't the nation's largest beach but without a doubt is the most popular — the choice of the young and the hip, of those wanting to be seen, of families, of anyone seeking a reprieve from summer's basting temperatures. Every July and August, newspapers and TV news splash images of up to 100,000 bodies crammed shoulder-to-shoulder along the entire length and width of the sand, huddled under a colorful canopy of thousands of oversized beach umbrellas. About fifteen million people visit Busan beaches annually. If one can cope with neighbors resting beer cans on one's stomach, and elbows gouging ribs, Haeundae is the place to be. Heju and her mother, sisters, brother, nieces and nephews patronize it annually, staying at a beach-side, high-rise luxury hotel. I don't go near it.

We drove on Haeundae's beach road, lined with steel, glass and concrete high-end motels and condos, then strolled onto the sand, the mid-June late afternoon cool, cloudy and blustery. Only a handful of university-age students — warm in long pants and sweaters — were on the beach. The masses hadn't arrived yet.

I floated my thermometer in the water and recorded a chilly twenty degrees Celsius. Water off Busan and the east coast is typically three to four degrees cooler in summer than off the west and south coasts. The sea south of Busan is under the influence of the warm, north-flowing Kuroshio Current, its genesis the South China Sea. The local Tsushima Current — named after Japan's Tsushima Island, fifty kilometers south — draws its water from the East Sea/Sea of Japan, the latter's average depth almost 6,000 feet.

In 1929, the International Hydrographic Organization officially named the body of water between Korea and Japan as Sea of Japan. South Korea has been fighting for years to have it recognized as East Sea; Japan adamantly opposes the motion. Korea argues that prior to Japanese colonization, the water was referred to on maps as East Sea. In 1929, Korea had no legal standing to counter Japan. Today, Koreans zealously refer to it as East Sea as a matter of national pride and principle. Some international maps compromise, using "Sea of Japan [East Sea]." For the sake of brevity and Korean sensitivities, I'll henceforth refer to it as East Sea.

Tsushima Current's direction alternates twice daily — east at high tide, west at low tide, and flows rapidly in the Korea Strait between Korea and Japan. I can attest to the current's volatility. On a return voyage riding the high-speed ferry between Busan and Tsushima Island, the sleek, modern vessel swooshed along the surface on skis being rocked by enormous, rolling, scattershot waves. Moments after precariously balancing atop one monstrous surge, I squeaked to the purser, "Can this ferry tip?"

The good-natured man grinned and, with a reassuring smile reserved for daisies, calmly replied that it was both scientifically and physically impossible for this particular model of ferry to capsize. (Meanwhile, a loose suitcase was sliding back and forth in the aisle.) Hadn't the same thing been said about *Titanic*?

From Haeundae Beach, Heju and I walked across the road and entered a McDonald's for dinner. Heju was content, even giddy. It wasn't every day that we dined at a restaurant, enjoying the luxury of sitting on real chairs, at real tables using real plastic knives and forks, eating a warm meal. Munching on staples like sandwiches, baguettes and cheese in the car on the fly was more like it.

After dinner, now early evening, we began the first leg of the journey up the east coast. We were finally heading in the general direction of home; we could sense the finish line. It felt good. I'd been on the road for more than two months since early April. It was now mid-June. Heju had been along in the Scoupe for a total of six weeks. Our aim was to reach the border with North Korea, 500 kilometers north, in about two weeks.

CHAPTER 20

Sinri: Lucky Divers;
Gyeongju's Really Big Tombs

The peninsula's east half is profoundly different from the western side. The east has been traditionally cut off from the more prosperous, populated west by the north-south Sobaek and Taebaek Mountains. Through the country's center, the Sobaeks average about 1,000 meters high; the Taebaeks parallel almost the entire east coast, average 1,500 meters, and crest twenty kilometers inland.

It was historically challenging to travel west-east and vice versa. It wasn't until 1971 that an expressway marrying Incheon and Seoul in the west to Gangneung on the east coast was constructed. Until then, to move the 200 kilometers cross country from, say, Seoul to the coast meant riding the bus for eight hours on bumpy dirt roads or taking the train requiring three line transfers over eleven hours. (The government completed a high-speed railway for the 2018 PyeongChang Winter Olympics through a series of tunnels with a stop at PyeongChang for the mountain events, ending in Gangneung for ice sports.)

After I arrived in Korea, I recalled the surprised reaction from a tour agent when, in my naiveté, I mentioned my desire to ride the rails from Seoul to Gangneung. "It'll take you eleven hours and three transfers!" she warned. I took the bus instead.

Yeongdong ("east of the Taebaeks") Expressway No. 50 sweeps far south of Seoul, then east into Gangwon province through the Daegwallyeong Pass and the Taebaek Mountains. The most direct west-east path is actually on Seoul-Yangyang No. 60 Expressway, completed in 2017, running well north of No. 50.

I'd regularly traveled No. 50 by bus for a while between Seoul and Gangneung to visit a friend when I arrived in Korea. On the route's final stretch into Gangneung, the bus lurched on switchbacks down the Taebaek's steep, long eastern slope to sea level. The herky-jerky motion — resulting from the bus swinging around sharp turns and the grinding of gears — always made me nauseous.

Before modern highways came to fruition, road transportation was a challenge. A western missionary described in a book how in the 1960s he drove a pickup truck from Daejeon southeast to Busan. With no space in the front cab for a missionary couple, the latter rode in the open flatbed in the rear. About ten hours later — having been jostled over potholed, dusty red dirt roads — the shell-shocked couple arrived in Busan, faces unrecognizable, caked in thick red dirt. The duo departed Korea never to return.

Today, major highways join most of the country, except on the east coast. There, a seventy-kilometer segment links Yangyang to Donghae in Gangwon province; a sixty-kilometer section connects Busan to Ulsan. Riding the bus from, say, the popular northeast resort city of Sokcho south to Busan, will take a tortoise-like six to seven hours on slow coastal roads.

The northeast is sparsely populated. In a poster-size photo I have of Korea taken by satellite at night, bright lights emanate from major cities, except for near total darkness in the northeast quarter. The region's biggest city, Gangneung, has only 215,000 citizens.

Patricia Bartz described the east as a geographic anomaly. While the old interior mountains have been worn down due to erosion over the last 70 million years, a new era of uplift – the Taebaek Orogeny – emerged on the east coast in the Miocene era, from 22 to 5 millions years ago. The gentle mountain-building force was enough to nudge up the Taebaek Mountains and create a broad tilt of the Korean peninsula – up in the northeast, down in the southwest. The tilt's hinge line is an undersea fault escarpment paralleling the shore about ten miles out in the East Sea. Bartz believed the cause of the tilt is due to the collective weight of sediment deposited in the Yellow Sea by rivers in Korea and North China. The east coast is one of emergence, the Yellow Sea has been undergoing gradual downward settling for 70 million years.

The Taebaeks run so close to shore that water runoff is minimal. Only short streams find their way to the sea, forming sandbars, lagoons and scores of sandy beaches. Tides on the east coast are half a meter high compared to up to nine meters on the west. Off the west and south coasts are too many islands to count. Only two, both volcanic, are in the East Sea: Ulleungdo, formed 2.5 million years ago, 160 kilometers east of the mainland; and tiny, rocky windswept Dokdo, 4.6 million years old, seventy kilometers east of Ulleungdo.

I was largely unfamiliar with the peninsula's starboard, and was glad we wouldn't be traveling on expressways anyway. I avoided them at all costs. Instead, we'd slowly thread our way north via a series of lonely, quiet, picturesque coastal roads past numerous isolated fishing villages. Many east coast seaside dwellings are simple, single-story concrete structures with soft colors and bright tile roofs. In the interior we'd drive on lonely roads into the Taebaek wilderness.

It was dusk when we departed Busan, heading north on the

coastal road. Surprisingly, we were almost immediately out of the city's hub of humanity into rural quietness, our vista the haunting, primitive rugged East Sea. Not far along at a desolate stretch of sand we spotted two abandoned concrete pillboxes surrounded by weeds — once lookout posts for the ROK army on alert for North Korean spies. In the 1970s and 1980s, North Korean submarines covertly slipped up to beaches in Japan, spies kidnapping a total of at least thirteen Japanese citizens who were taken to North Korea. Simon Winchester's *Korea: A Walk Through the Land of Miracles*, describes his 1988 trek north up South Korea's east coast past military arc lights, barbed wire and pillboxes on beaches.

Back in the car, a few minutes farther ahead, we stopped on the shore at two more pillboxes by a small lighthouse and strolled onto a low, rocky windswept bluff. A strong tang of salt permeated the fresh sea breeze. Close in the water was clean, clear and light-green. A formidable, punishing white surf crashed against big boulders. You wouldn't want to swim here if you valued your life.

Continuing on, twenty kilometers north of Busan, we were in Wolnae, home of the Kori Nuclear Power Plant built in 1976, the nation's first nuclear power facility. Today, four nuclear power sites host twenty-four nuclear reactors filling about a third of the country's energy needs.

In Wolnae, we passed a large roadside sign announcing in translation: "If you report a spy, it's worth 150 million won. If you report a spy ship, it's worth 100 thousand won." What better incentive than big bucks for the public to keep a vigilant eye out for disorientated, waterlogged North Koreans in tall, Soviet-style army hats and boots.

In darkness we turned onto a lonely paved side road leading to the Kori Nuclear Power Plant at the coast and soon were stopped at a guard post.

"Is it possible to get a tour of the power plant?" I asked the guard. It was nine o'clock.

He looked at me as if I were bonkers and barked, "Absolutely not! There are no tours here. The public's not allowed in."

We turned around and headed back to the main road. At the nearby attractive little seaside village of Hwasan — fronted by lovely Jinha Beach — we stayed the night in a modern, inexpensive motel, rooms just 30,000 won.

***

I'd read an unusual story in the *Korea JoongAng Daily* about a nearby seaside fishing hamlet named Sinri, where some *haenyeo* (women of the sea) dove for a living. Due to warm-water discharge from the Kori nuclear facility affecting sea life, the local Ulju County government had decided to reimburse Sinri divers for potential lost wages of up to 150 million won each.

A total of about fifty women and one man were recognized as divers in Sinri, but when applications for payouts were received by the Ulju government, 232 of Sinri's 267 residents had listed themselves as "divers." Included were college students, office workers, sixty-six men, eight people over the age of seventy-five, two children and a disabled person. An Ulju official admitted that no official test or certificate was required to become a diver. "Practically anyone can register," he said.

Heju and I were keen to witness this mass flotilla of 200-plus, happy Sinri divers bobbing in local waters. In mid-morning, we departed the motel at Jinha Beach, cruised a few kilometers along the coast then turned onto a quiet, deserted lane leading to the sea and Sinri. At the end of the lane was Sinri's tiny town square, its faded old concrete and clay dwellings bleached white by the sun. We stopped the car in the square. Nothing stirred, no one was around. The brightness, austerity and deathly quiet reminded me of a scene from a Clint Eastwood spaghetti western, where Clint rides his horse down from parched, dry hills into a deserted, wind-swept dusty town. We waited in the car, and about ten minutes later, an elderly man came sauntering along the lane. Through the open window, Heju called, "Excuse me sir, are you a diver?"

A bit bewildered, he replied, "No."

We walked across the square and entered a concrete, bunker-like building doubling as a restaurant. "Excuse me," we asked the female owner, "are you a diver?"

"No," she answered.

Next door, in Sinri's drug store, we met the pharmacist — a handsome woman in her seventies with intelligent eyes. "Would you happen to be a diver?" we inquired.

She replied, baffled, "No, I've been working in this drug store for fifty years."

We walked on the dusty lane around the corner toward the water and poked our heads into an old mom-and-pop shop where three retirement-age citizens were shooting the breeze.

"Come in," invited the good-natured shop owner, Mr. Lee. We entered and sat down and began to chat.

The floor was concrete, the shelves appearing not to have been dusted or restocked in ages. On them was a meager, haphazard array of sundry items, including cans of food whose expiry dates had probably lapsed in 1900. The other old-timers were Ms. Ji and Mr. Ahn.

"Would you happen to be divers?" we asked the trio.

To my surprise, Ms. Ji said yes. And Mr. Ahn said he'd been the manager of a *haenyeo* team of divers.

Half in jest, I asked if they'd ever encountered great white sharks in local waters.

To my amazement, Mr. Ahn answered yes. "In 1995, I was the manager of a small crew of *haenyeo*. We were diving off the west coast, near Anmyeon Island (in South Chungcheong province). We were in about seven meters of water, and a diver was under the boat. Suddenly, a shark surfaced with her in its jaws. When it went under we never saw the woman again."

I gulped and asked, "You sure it was a great white?"

Mr. Ahn nodded solemnly. "Oh yeah ... they're the only ones that eat people."

Well, Tiger and Bull sharks, among others, have been known to take chunks out of people as well but I assumed Mr. Ahn knew the difference between those breeds and a great white. "Great whites have babies along the west coast too," he added – the first I'd heard of this. I'd swum off the west coast!

After an hour of chatting we rose to depart. I bought a couple of bottles of *soju* in the shop for the trio. I suspected Mr. Lee was already into the sauce. As we headed to the door, he reached into his breast pocket and proudly showed us his pacemaker. Things got stranger in front of the shop. A tiny elderly grandmother paused directly in front of me, looked me in the eye and with grim resolution demanded that I give her a piggyback ride. I'm not kidding.

I contemplated doing so but thought it somewhat undignified galloping around Sinri with a granny hooting and hollering on my back, smacking my backside with a horsewhip. I politely declined. The woman resumed walking along the path. Now Mr. Lee and his pacemaker wanted in on the action. "Jump on my back. I'll give you a piggyback ride," he ordered. He was serious too. He weighed all of about 150 pounds and I tipped the scales at 240.

"I think I might be a little heavy for you," I suggested, but this didn't discourage him in the slightest. He flexed his biceps and confidently insisted, "No problem, I can lift you!"

He would have tried too. There must have been something in the water. Sinriites were in the wrong business: stand-up comedy was their forte.

Heju and I strolled to the deserted waterfront, to a small pretty harbor with a concrete breakwall protecting a few moored fishing trawlers. The dark green water was glassy smooth — not a single diver's head breaking the placid surface.

"No divers here," I concluded.

"None," Heju concurred.

Behind us, at a row of low concrete dwellings, a quartet of townsfolk was squatting at a faucet, gutting, cleaning and rinsing a bucket of fresh fish. We went over and introduced ourselves.

A squat woman of perhaps sixty said her name was Mrs. Jang.

"Are you a diver?" we asked.

"Yes," she said.

Finally, a diver.

"I've been diving in Sinri for thirty-five years," Mrs. Jang boasted. "I'm famous here. I can dive down fourteen meters and hold my breath for three minutes." She motioned to the elderly woman sitting next to her. "This is my mother. She dove too. She's eighty-six."

We asked Mrs. Jang how many divers lived in Sinri.

"Thirty-five full-time and seventy part-time," she replied.

"How many are men?"

"Six."

We mentioned the nuclear power plant's warm water discharge and financial compensation.

"It doesn't bother me that some people who aren't divers will get money," Mrs. Jang said. "We're all neighbors, everyone knows each other. But I'm the most experienced diver here, so I'll get the most money — 150 million won."

We departed Sinri's soon-to-be-wealthy residents and headed north up the coast to Ulsan.

* * *

Ulsan was a mere fishing village when in 1962, President Park Chung-hee designated its future role as an industrial port. Manufacturing in South Korea began on a large scale in the 1960s. Gyeonggi province, Seoul, Busan, Pohang and Ulsan became industrial hubs. By the 1970s, a number of major factories were operating in Ulsan. Today the city's population is more than a million, and Ulsan is home to Hyundai Motor Company's massive factory (birthplace of the Scoupe); Hyundai Heavy Industries' enormous shipyards, and an oil refinery. Seventy kilometers north in the coastal industrial city of Pohang sprawls POSCO, one of the world's top-producing steel mills. Not bad for little Korea.

We entered Ulsan crossing a low bridge over the shallow, slow-moving Taehwa River, the only river of note in the east to flow to the sea. The afternoon had suddenly turned overcast, dark clouds shading the river a steely gray color. We headed along the river's north shore toward Ulsan Port, where blue-collar city streets rolled up and down, reminding me of the famous hilly streets in San Francisco. At the gritty industrial port, at the wide mouth of the Taehwa River, vessels and small freighters dotted the sea, entering and leaving port.

We strolled onto a tall concrete jetty and chatted with three young men fishing, enjoying a day off from their work attaching steel plates to form ship hulls at Hyundai Heavy Industries. "We can build a small ship in forty-five days," one boasted. "It's hard work but good pay."

In *Korea: A Walk Through the Land of Miracles*, Winchester described how in the 1970s, British shipbuilding was supplanted by the ruthless efficiency of Ulsan's shipyards, which helped put British yards out of business. Koreans could build huge ships for much cheaper and faster than the Brits, relying on regimented teamwork and long hours. In an ironic twist, Ulsan's yards today are competing against the Chinese, who can manufacture vessels cheaper than what South Korea can build them for.

Darkness upon us, a heavy downpour beginning, we dashed from the jetty back to the car and drove north though the city, paralleling the coast accompanied by hordes of traffic. We passed Ulsan's shipyards. Nearby, we took a room in a motel for the night.

**

Not far north of Ulsan and inland is a small, ancient city virtually unknown beyond Korea's borders. Once grand and august, "Gyeongju was certainly one of the world's great cities in the ninth century," Bartz wrote.

Gyeongju was the capital of the royal Silla Dynasty, ruling a series of walled town states in the country's east from 57 BC to AD 935. After Silla defeated Baekje to the west, and Goguryeo to the north in the 660s, it reigned over a vast area including today's South and North Korea and far beyond. Koreans consider Silla the first unified version of Korea.

Bartz estimated Silla Gyeongju's population between 600,000 and one million. The city was progressive and cosmopolitan, its economy producing paper, silk, hemp, cloth, lacquerware, pottery, bronze, silver and gold trinkets. Trade and cultural ties were established with China and Japan. Sciences and math were studied. Buddhism flourished. Temples became wealthy and monks powerful. But hubris, avarice and corruption prevailed among power-hungry kings who failed to appease angry lords and aristocrats and rebellion was a constant. A weakened Silla fell to a new dynasty, Goryeo, in the north in AD 935.

My South Korea guidebook listed a plethora of sites to visit in Gyeongju. Kingpins were "tumuli," earthen tombs honoring Silla's long line of fifty-six kings and queens. Aristocracy, generals, and government officials were sometimes awarded stately tombs too. More than 670 tumuli – some huge, some no larger than a few meters in diameter – dot Gyeongju. Another must-see was a Buddha granite carving named Seokguram (Stone Cave Hermitage), sculpted in the seventh century. I hadn't been to Gyeongju. I was looking forward to using a nine-iron to swat golf balls to the top of the tallest tumulus.

First we needed to pay a visit to the tomb of a Silla king, who more than 1,300 years ago, bucked the trend of spending eternity buried under a massive earthen Gyeongju mound. When King Munmu passed away in AD 681, he requested that his burial place be the sea, believing he could protect his people from a serpent terrorizing the East Sea, an idea not out of the ordinary for the time. Munmu's tomb is forty kilometers north of Ulsan, at Bonggil Beach in Yangbuk Township. In early afternoon, overcast and gray, we arrived at Bonggil Beach's large busy parking area, next to a wide stretch of sand and several shops and restaurants. We traipsed out onto the beach, people loitering on the sand. About two hundred meters offshore was a seagull-poop-splattered rocky shoal jutting just above the water line.

Pointing to the rocks, we asked a woman, "Is that where King Munmu is buried?"

"Yes," she said.

To our disappointment, there wasn't access to the rocks, to have a peek at the king's watery tomb, no small vessel to transport visitors to the outcrop. Yangbuk Township officials apparently didn't believe this to be a good idea.

We departed and cruised west toward Gyeongju, soon entering Gyeongju National Park. My goodness, what a lovely area – a sea of pristine broad rolling, green rounded ridges, not a man-made edifice, gas station, building or restaurant, just woods. The quiet, winding road climbed gradually into steeper eminences. Just east of Gyeongju we stopped at a parking lot near the top of broad, wooded Toham Mountain where a path led to Seokguram. Next to the path entrance was a shop containing Buddha paraphernalia, and food stalls. There were a number of visitors.

We bought tickets and walked through the front gate trekking a wide earthen path on the side of the wooded mountain, fellow walkers coming and going. After fifteen minutes we came to a simple, traditional wood structure — tucked against the rising slope — with a mammoth double-deck, black-tiled roof. We entered its narrow, shadowy hallway. A glass partition separated people from Seokguram Grotto, constructed in AD 776. Bathed in a soft yellow light, the inner walls are exquisite granite blocks arching smoothly and gracefully to about nine meters high. In the center stands the Buddha, carved from white granite. Buddha's visage is calm and wry, as if he's contemplating the meaning of life. The statue sits on a carved stone lotus, the combined height of the carving and lotus, 3.5 meters.

I guessed the statue and lotus weighed a few tons. The guide in the hallway said the actual weight was between forty and a hundred tons. I was amazed. The Buddha was carved from white granite not native to Toham Mountain, meaning the forty-to-one-hundred-ton slab was likely hauled to this location from somewhere else, she said. "How did it get here?" I asked.

"No one knows," she replied. "It's like the pyramids — no one knows how they were built. But we believe Europeans trekked the Silk Road to Korea and vice versa. Maybe Europeans had a hand in constructing the grotto."

At a Royal Asiatic Society lecture I'd attended in Seoul, the speaker, Sam Vermeersch — a professor of Buddhism at Seoul

National University — described how in the seventh century, thirteen Korean monks separately embarked on journeys from Korea to India, the origin of Buddhism. The monks traveled the Maritime Silk Road: by sea to today's Thailand or Malaysia, where they likely spent time at a local monastery, then west across today's Myanmar, probably with a group of merchants for protection. They'd have sailed across the Bay of Bengal to India, finally a trek overland 500 or so kilometers to Bodh Gaya village's Mahabodhi Temple, the holiest in the Buddha world, constructed in about 260 BC. Vermeersch said no one knows what happened to the thirteen monks after they arrived in India — there's no record of them ever returning to Korea.

From the grotto we walked back along the path in twilight, looking west over Gyeongju far below in the grand Gyeongsang Basin, the huge oval-shaped plain surrounded by hills and low mountain ridges. The city has a rustic ambiance and is tranquil, not a single high-rise apartment blighting the landscape, just simple dwellings and small agricultural plots in shades of brown and green. Gyeongju resembled a country town. How different from the towns and cities we were accustomed to seeing.

We descended to the plain in darkness and on the immediate outskirts of Gyeongju took a room in a motel.

***

In mid-morning we drove into Gyeongju proper on Taejong Road on alert for tumuli. Near the center of town off the side of the road, in a big lush grassy park seemingly stretching back forever, was a series of tumuli. But not just any tumuli. These earthen, grass-covered mounds are so tall, massive and broad, it was immediately clear aliens had deposited them as a pre-welcoming gift for earthlings.

In the foreground of grassy Daerungwon ("Big Tomb Park")

rears Hwangnamdaechong ("Hwangnam" being the district name; *daechong* meaning "Great Tomb"). The Great Tomb of Hwangnam-dong was erected in the fifth century — the tallest, baddest Big Daddy tomb in Gyeongju, rising the equivalent of seven-stories and more than a hundred meters wide. The International Ski Jumping Federation could use this hill for a ski jumping event, if snow ever fell in Gyeongju. Great Tomb is just one of twenty-three tumuli scattered in Big Tomb Park.

We stopped on the side of the main road across from the park and walked through a wrought-iron gate into the tree-lined grounds. A short way along the path was a tourist office where several Chinese and Japanese tour groups milled about in front. Off to the side was Cheonmachong ("Heavenly Horse Tomb"), rising forty feet. This tomb was unsealed in 1973, and discovered inside was a saddle with the painting of a galloping horse on it. Horsemanship was an important skill of Silla's military. The tomb's interior was converted to a museum and opened to the public, the only tumulus in Gyeongju available for tours.

Surprisingly, nearly all tumuli in Gyeongju remain sealed. The Mongols invaded Korea in the twelfth century but didn't touch the burial mounds. In the 1590s, Hideyoshi's Japanese troops spread out across Korea, and ransacked Gyeongju, destroying wooden structures and carting off myriad treasures but left the tombs intact. Perhaps the labor needed to remove the hundreds of tons of earth and stone to break into a tomb kept thieves at bay. In 1921, doing repair work on a home in Gyeongju, the Japanese unearthed a gold crown, and subsequently excavated several tombs, the unearthed artifacts on display at the National Museum of Korea in Seoul.

In 1926, future Swedish King Gustav VI Adolf, an archaeologist, assisted on a Gyeongju tomb dig. It wasn't until 1973 that a Korean team began excavating tombs, starting with Heavenly Horse Tomb.

About 12,000 artifacts, including gold crowns and jewelry, were discovered, many on display at Gyeongju National Museum.

The Great Tomb of Hwangnam-dong in the park's foreground was unearthed in 1973 — thousands of artifacts found inside. At a 2013-2014 New York Metropolitan Museum of Art exhibition titled: *Silla: Korea's Golden Kingdom*, some of the tomb's treasures were on display. On the museum's website was film footage of the tomb's construction process, revealed in the 1973 excavation. I viewed the film. The tomb is about the size of a football field, the burial chambers at its north and south ends for the king and queen.

First, the ground was covered with a layer of stones, wood beams placed vertically to form a frame around the chambers. To bolster the frame, rocks and small boulders were added as walls. Coffins were placed in the chambers, a layer of earth and stones thrown over the chambers to seal them. Finally, thousands of tons of earth were heaped on top, resulting in the The Great Tomb's seventy-five-feet mound. In 1975, the tomb was resealed.

Only five royal tombs have been positively identified in Gyeongju — belonging to Silla Kings Hyeondeok, Heungdeok, Muyeol and Wonseong and Queen Seongdeok. The vast majority of mounds remain unearthed and anonymous.

A tour guide led us through Heavenly Horse Tomb. Inside were two tour groups — Japanese adults being quietly led in hushed tones by a Japanese guide; young Chinese adults, loudly chattering, being ushered by a Chinese guide talking above their unfiltered discourse. The interior is cavernous, walls arching uniformly up to a rounded ceiling. Around the perimeter are glass cases containing replicas of artifacts discovered in the tomb, the originals in the Gyeongju museum. In one chamber are a sword, saddle, whip, stirrups, gold crown and a behemoth gold belt.

"Silla's ancestors originally came from Mongolia where horses were common," our guide said.

"Which Silla king was buried here?" I asked.

"We don't know," she replied. "No written records were found. When the king's coffin was opened, there were no bones or ashes. They probably disintegrated. Experts believe the king's body was buried in the fifth century and he was fat; his belt measured 125 centimeters (fifty inches)."

Outside, Heju and I wandered back through Big Tomb Park, surprisingly the only ones in the entire tranquil, quiet grounds. How pleasurable to stroll on acres of grass and feel the soft lushness underfoot. As we were admiring one particular massive tomb, I surreptitiously walked around the corner to pee. Moments later I was startled when Heju appeared at the tomb corner. "What are you doing!" she hollered. With my back to her I calmly replied, "I'm taking a leak."

"You can't do that here!" she cried dramatically. "This is where my Kim family is buried. My family is the Gyeongju Silla Kims!"

"Don't worry, I'm not hurting the tomb," I called.

Kim Heju sometimes takes the opportunity to remind me of her claim that her present Kim family clan in Daejeon are descendants of Silla King Gyeongsun's side of the family. King Gyeongsun ruled from AD 927 to 935. Three main families – Bak (often spelled Park), Seok and Kim – engendered Silla. Historians believe one tumuli in the park belongs to King Michu – reigning from AD 262 to 284 – the first Kim to sit on the Silla throne. Perhaps Heju did have blue blood, and all this time I should have been referring to her by her correct title: Your Silla Royal Highness. She would have appreciated that.

We exited at the rear of Big Tomb Park and walked on the path leading to more pastoral beauty, to expansive, grassy Wolseong Park, and scattered smaller tumuli. The landscape was green and pristine, not a whiff of concrete, not a vehicle in sight. Gyeongju officials had done a superb job in preserving the area. Next to a Silla palace we strolled by a large rock-rimmed pond, then stood riveted before Cheomseongdae, ("star-gazing tower") an astronomical observatory built about 1,300 years ago. Comprised of 365 exquisite, cut granite bricks – weathered and darkened by rain and wind over the centuries – it is almost 10-meters tall, like a mini Scottish castle tower. At night, the pond, observatory and tumuli are lit up.

We spent an entire day pleasurably ambling through the expansive area. It wasn't until dusk that we finally returned to the car. We drove across Taejong Road into Noseo-dong – a bustling, modern district with narrow lanes, bright lights and restaurants, including a McDonald's, Pizza Hut and KFC. The sudden leap from a bucolic, peaceful world two millennia old to 21st-century fast-food outlets was jarring.

We checked into a motel in Noseo-dong and relaxed. Famished, Heju declared, "I need chicken for dinner." A bit before 10:00 p.m., we walked under bright lights into a nearby KFC.

"Sorry, but we're closing now and out of chicken," a KFC staff said. Her Highness was understandably disappointed.

NORTHEAST

CHAPTER 21

Hahoe: A Village of Crusty Old Yangban

About seventy kilometers northeast of Gyeongju, in the Taebaek Mountains, is remote 1,122-meter Bohyeon Mountain. Via a series of switchbacks, the Scoupe — marginally, foot-by-foot — climbed the steep face of Bohyeonsan. Half way up, we stopped at the side of the road to allow the overheated little engine to cool down. In the late afternoon's white light — sitting on the road guard rail — we gazed far over a narrow agricultural plain surrounded by steep rocky eminences, a lonely homestead here and there. After forty-five-minutes, back in the car, we ascended the rest of the mountain and near the top parked at the Bohyeonsan Optical Astronomy Observatory.

We'd phoned ahead and arranged to meet the observatory's director, Mr. Kim, who greeted us in the large, empty staff quarters next to the observatory. We chatted about telescopes, space and stars. Mr. Kim told us this observatory was built in 1996 to replace the country's only other minor observatory. A group of astronomers, including Mr. Kim — from the Korean Astronomy and Space Science Institute — spent much of 1995 trekking numerous peaks through the peninsula seeking the ultimate location to put a 1.8-meter reflecting telescope. "We were looking for a mountainous area exposed to the least amount of man-made light from cities, with the most number of clear sky days annually," characteristics paramount for star-gazing, he said.

Remote Bohyeonsan was chosen, affording the most number of annual "clear days" — defined as minimal cloud cover and haze. "There are about 150 clear sky days annually here," said Mr. Kim. Just fifty kilometers south are Daegu's 2.5 million citizens. Daegu's lights affect night-time telescopic viewing at the observatory, he added. "But we're a small country, so it's hard to be far from any city."

As evening descended, the eerie blackness was absolute. Any light leakage from Daegu was undetectable to my naked eye. Mr. Kim took us inside the observatory, though unfortunately the telescope wasn't in use on this night. The image of Bohyeon Mountain observatory's telescope is on the back of South Korea's 10,000 won bill.

It was late evening when we descended the mountain. Thirty minutes later we found a motel standing alone on a county road in a secluded rural area on the edge of dense woods. Under a beautiful sky brimming with stars, I took a jog on the quiet road.

The following morning we continued north into the rugged, isolated Taebaeks in North Gyeongsang province. We passed a pebbly clear mountain stream and fruit orchards and wound slowly through woods. A couple of hours later, after stops for lunch and to view a scenic river, we arrived at noon at Andong Hahoe Folk Village west of the small city of Andong. Hahoe (pronounced Ha-Hway) is a secluded, 500-year-old traditional Joseon-era village, the most renowned of seven original inhabited villages in the country. About

1.7 million people visit Hahoe annually. In 1990, Queen Elizabeth II toured here. U.S. President George H.W. Bush and his wife Barbara visited in 2003.

Several days earlier in Busan, Heju and I had received a visit from a Seoul-based film-maker named Hwang Sung-yeon, who'd asked if I'd like to host a documentary he'd soon begin filming on traditional Korean homes or *hanok*. I'd met Mr. Hwang – a cheery, creative, rather unkempt sort – several months earlier on a Peter Bartholomew spring tour of Seoul Joseon architecture. In Busan, Mr. Hwang detailed his plan to tour the peninsula over the next several months and film the country's most renowned traditional homes. Hosting would be interesting and the role was paid. Why not, I thought. The first shoot was today in Hahoe.

A male cameraman and female assistant director were in Hahoe to meet us. Mr. Hwang was in Seoul on business, but he'd hired a Hahoe resident, Ryu Pil-seok, as our guide for the next twenty-four hours. Mr. Ryu was a slight man in his forties, a fifteenth-generation Hahoe Ryu (Ryu is today's spelling of Joseon's Yu).

"During Joseon, about 70 percent of Hahoe residents were Ryus," Mr. Ryu announced proudly. "The other 30 percent were servants. In the old days, we only wanted Ryus in Hahoe. They were *yangban* – very intelligent."

Hahoe has been administered by an extended Ryu clan since the 1500s. Of its 235 residents today, 85 percent are Ryus. In the 1590s, a Hahoe resident, Ryu Seong-ryong, was the prime minister of Korea. No less than Admiral Yi Sun-sin stopped by Hahoe to discuss the Imjin War.

Hahoe village – simple, rural and bucolic – appears rather like a Winslow Homer landscape. The hamlet has 126 thatched straw-and-shale-tile-roofed and red-clay-walled *hanok*. A path running through it is bordered by a low, dry crumbling wall of faded red clay. The community is nestled at a long, sharp U-turn on the sandy banks of the major Nakdong River, its genesis north in Gangwon province. The river here is dark, deep and languorous. On the far bank ascends vertically a tall, earthen red cliff. An appealing, wide pastoral swath of green agricultural plots and the odd small farm dwelling, bordered by low Taebaek foothills, spread out on the other side of the village. Modern development has thankfully escaped this little place. Not a paved road, shop or gas station disturbs the environment.

Mr. Ryu led our coterie on the path to the village's far corner, to stately upper-crust Yangjin House, where we knocked on the door. A tiny, rather bewildered ninety-three-year-old named Kim Myeong-kyo answered. Ms. Kim's wide grin exposed gums containing three teeth.

We introduced ourselves. The cameraman filmed. Ms. Kim volunteered brightly, "I married a Hahoe Ryu when I was fifteen and rode in a palanquin on my wedding day!" She said she'd attended the same public school as former President Park Chung-hee.

"How was President Park as a student?" I asked.

"He was tough. He liked to fight. He always had to win," she said.

After only several minutes we bade good bye to Ms. Kim. Back on the path under a hot, draining sun, we came to a large, handsome wood *hanok*, a wide veranda and courtyard in front. Sitting on the veranda was Hahoe's resident straw-maker — an elderly, unsmiling man with white hair and skin, who was wearing traditional, white baggy Joseon attire. He was using his hands and gnarled, yellow, callused bare feet to adroitly weave thick, raw strands of straw into bundles to replace old straw roofs.

"Mark, sit across from him," the assistant director instructed, so I did. The cameraman filmed. "Try weaving with your feet," she urged.

I removed my shoes and socks and was handed a thick strand of straw. The man showed me how to weave. I tried but wasn't very adept. My mentor had little patience for a neophyte and was soon uncharitably grumbling at me. We departed the unhappy grandfather and continued to more *hanok*.

In early evening we sat in a handsome home before another elderly, grim, unforgiving *yangban* – probably the brother of the straw-maker. This man tutored me on traditional tea-drinking protocol and how to be a gentleman, both of which I had no interest in learning. Silly proletarian me, I'd assumed drinking tea merely entailed bringing cup to mouth and gulping. Heavens no, this would never suffice for the vaunted, self-important *yangban*, who had strict social graces to uphold.

The cameraman filmed. The tea master ordered: "Sit cross-legged on the floor. Keep your back straight. Place the teacup at your stomach. Slowly bring it up to your mouth. Take a sip." In trepidation of being smacked by the wrathful fellow, I resolutely followed his instructions, and took such a dainty, meager sip that Queen Elizabeth would have been proud. The green tea was unsweetened, bland and tasteless. The tea master concluded, "Bring the cup back to your stomach and leave it there." I did so. All I really wanted was a tall, glass of cold soda to drain in one long gulp, then belch loudly, to spite my teacher. I was glad I hadn't been conceived in Joseon.

Next we were off to another *hanok* for a calligraphy lesson with another crusty, elderly *yangban*. (Was there any other kind?) Using a thick paint brush, I splashed black ink onto a long, narrow sheet of thick white paper. The cameraman shot. At about nine o'clock, filming finally concluded, we retreated, hot and exhausted, to Mr. Ryu's nearby *hanok*, and sat at a table in his garden enjoying a delicious dinner of beef, fried mackerel (*godeungeo-gui*) and rice.

After the meal the crew and Heju and I retired to a large separate *hanok* room in the yard. The *hanok's* thick clay walls were excellent absorbers of sound; a bazooka could have been fired outside and we wouldn't have heard it. It was surprisingly cool inside despite the oppressive humidity outside. With just one small window though, it felt like we were in a crypt. We unrolled thick, comfortable bed rolls and slept on the floor; the tomb-like silence and moderate temperature allowed for outstandingly sound and uninterrupted slumber.

My deep sleep came to a crashing halt at the ungodly hour of 8:00 a.m. when the cameraman wanted shots of me pensively gazing out the window. Then more shuffling and filming outside in the heat. We hiked up the rear section of the tall, steep, earthen cliff bordering Nakdong River's far shore. Then, in early afternoon, Mr. Ryu drove us in a van from the village a short way to picturesque Dosan Seowon Confucian Study Hall, built in 1572, surrounded by woods and hills by the Nakdong River.

A *seowon* was a private, Joseon-era, Confucian-based learning academy – often part of a large estate with slaves – for young *yangban* students. At one time, more than 700 *seowon* were scattered throughout Korea. In 1871, the government introduced the Seowon Abolishment Act, curtailing *yangban* authority, and many *seowon* were shuttered.

In recent years there's been a *seowon* renaissance of sorts. About 150 *seowon* have been refurbished. Weekend *seowon* retreats offer school students the experience of discovering life in old Joseon via lectures and workshops led by old, miserable tea, straw-making and calligraphy teachers. A photo accompanying a newspaper article I'd read showed a *seowon* retreat attended by a group of young students in traditional *yangban* garb sitting on the floor at low tables, being lectured on proper tea-drinking protocol by a resolute *yangban* master. The kids' eyes were collectively glazed over in a look of glum boredom.

Dosan Seowon was built on the lower slope of a wooded hill, its construction august, its wood units in a row forming a C-shape like a motel courtyard. A long porch running in front of the rooms was for students to study on. On the slope of a descending hill in front of the *seowon* was a grand wood gazebo with massive thick floor planks and beams. We wandered over and sat on the floor, its wood dry as a bone. A slight but refreshing breeze took the edge off the humidity. Tweeting birds darted in nearby woods. It was quiet and tranquil.

A sixtyish, formal, good-natured woman named Ms. Oh, who provided tours of the *seowon*, came over and joined us on the deck. Soon she and Heju were engaged in a spirited, tit-for-tat debate on the merits and demerits of Confucianism, a system of ethics, education and statesmanship taught by Confucius and his disciples. Confucianism stressed love for humanity, ancestor worship, reverence for parents and harmony in thought and conduct. It was – Joseon's ruling ethos and philosophy.

"I hate Confucianism," Heju confessed.

"But it brought peace and harmony to Korea," Ms. Oh countered politely.

"No, it didn't. Confucianism was about power and control over others. It brought fighting between the different classes of society," Heju rebutted.

Confucianism involved a rigid hierarchy closely mimicking military discipline, I contend. Every person in society had a defined role, and knew his or her place. The ethos determined whom one could marry, who received an education, one's position, where to reside, which clothes to wear and how to behave and speak in public. Submitting to elders and unquestioning obedience to authority were two decidedly undemocratic principles.

The *Analects of Confucius* state: "Let the ruler be a ruler, the subject a subject, a father a father and a son a son." It must not have been very pleasant living in Joseon if one didn't belong to the hereditary ruling *yangban* class. Most other people were low on the totem pole, under the oppressive yoke of teachers, bosses, officials, *yangban* and bitter tea masters – squashed, bossed, intimidated and belittled.

Even today, Confucianism is evident in Korea. Young men getting married bow low to parents, and university students bow to professors. Businesses and organizations favor vertical, top-town rather than horizontal decision-making. Using titles to honor those older than or "above" one is necessary in everyday interaction. Many elderly still expect unbending obedience from youngsters. Public school and *hagwon* educational systems are closely based on Confucian principles of teacher-dominated lecturing, rote memorization and constant testing. Had I been born in Korea in the Joseon Confucian era, I'd have departed on the first ship bound for anywhere, though the kingdom was so isolated, there were virtually no ships to board for travel outside the country.

Hahoe village's layout was hierarchical. Ruling *yangban* resided in the prime center; outside this zone was an area for second-tier, independent landowners; another parcel for third-string tenants; finally a tract for the least fortunate: merchants and artisans of the lowest class.

I'd read a published paper by a Korea University professor of English named Suh Ji-moon, who contended that *yangban* and British gentleman were comparable, the two lineages dating back more than 2,000 years. Both were expected to maintain high moral and refined personal standards, to uphold the structure of society, to guard their culture. *Yangban* were educated, well-versed in Confucian classics, awarded government posts and owned landed estates and serfs. Only they could live in large houses and wear luxurious garments. They established legal and social barriers and married among themselves, siring *yangban* children by concubines. Due to their haughty airs, idleness and sponging off relatives and society, they were collectively abhorred by common folk. "Deadly oppressors of the masses, they were in no small part responsible for the demise of Joseon," wrote Professor Suh.

Hangeul, the Korean alphabet invented in 1443 under the leadership of King Sejong, was simple to learn and write. *Yangban* insisted on using complicated and difficult Chinese characters for writing so the peasants remained illiterate. It wasn't until the 1970s that the government officially made Hangeul mandatory for writing in South Korea.

Isabella Bird Bishop disdained *yangban*. In her book she described a wintry day in Seoul at the end of the 19th century, standing atop a hill near Jongno, looking over a huge crowd of white-clad *yangban*, aimlessly drifting en masse, shuffling along pretending to be busy and to look important.

A Korean poll indicated about 70 percent of citizens believe they are of *yangban* blood. Quite impossible, considering only 15 percent of the population in Joseon were *yangban*.

We returned to Hahoe's entrance, to the modest outdoor coliseum-like stage, where Mr. Hwang had arranged for me to be taught the ancient Korean art of mask dancing. I'd seen Joseon-era photos of masks worn during rituals to keep evil spirits at bay. My mask-dance teacher today was Lee Sang-ho, a short wisp of a man in his seventies. Mr. Lee had performed on this stage for President George W. Bush and his wife, and for Queen Elizabeth II.

Mr. Lee handed me a wood mask, then demonstrated a few simple dance steps I was to imitate. Heju sat in the coliseum's bleachers, watching. The cameraman shot. Dancing was never my forte. At a grade-four class party at Norman Ingram Elementary School in Toronto, my cerebral classmate, Cathy Smith, asked me to dance. I reluctantly agreed. I wasn't sure what to do with my arms and legs, and gyrated mechanically like a mis-programmed robot gone haywire.

Cathy giggled and announced, "You dance like you're taking your pants off." I rarely voluntarily danced again.

I put on the mask, which resembled a 1960s-era fiberglass ice hockey goalie mask. This one had narrow slits for eyes that I could barely see out of. I attempted to shadow Mr. Lee's steps but unfortunately only managed to shuffle stiffly about like the Tin Man in *The Wizard of Oz*. I could hear Heju, sitting in the cheap seats, in the throes of uncontrollable and uproarious laughter.

Mr. Lee contemplated how a reasonably coordinated person could make such a mess of such basic steps. I couldn't disagree, but in my defense, mask dancing isn't as simple as it seems. Rather, it integrated a rather complicated series of half-shuffling, half-dance-like movements. Mr. Lee explained my lack of Fred Astaire smoothness was due to cultural differences.

"When Westerners dance they tap their feet and use the bottom half of their bodies," he said. "When Koreans dance they use their top half — shoulders and hands. Korean energy flows top to bottom, Western energy is bottom to top."

There you have it — no wonder I couldn't boogie.

It was mid-afternoon when *Dancing with the Stars* and filming concluded. We'd spent an intensive, exhaustive twenty-eight hours in the village. Heju and I said goodbye to the crew and our host and departed.

After my pan-Korea trip, I continued filming with Mr. Hwang and his crew. Over several months we engaged in a dozen, one-and-two-day passages, traversing thousands of kilometers, filming endless hours. Mr. Hwang's fifty-minute documentary titled: *Hanok: Korean Traditional House*, was released about a year later. When I viewed it, I was dismayed — most of my scenes had been left on the editing-room floor. I'd been on-screen for a grand total of about five minutes. I was an unheralded silent extra, a minion, a failed B-level thespian, my aspiring Hollywood career in tatters.

**

That night we stayed in the nearby old city of Andong alongside the Nakdong River's wide silty banks and flood plain. In the morning we headed north to the obscure mountain village of Baegam in North Gyeongsang province. A thousand years ago in Silla, Baegam was a remote hunting outpost. During the Japanese occupation in the 1900s, the colonizers built a hotel over one of Baegam's many natural hot springs. In the 1970s and 1980s, more above-ground spas were constructed and the town's popularity skyrocketed. Apparently, Baegam was the place-to-be for vacationers. Sadly, it fell out of favor and onto hard times. I was curious as to why.

From Andong we entered a lonely country road winding north through the Taebaeks. We passed beguiling rolling hills and woods, lush modest green farmland and verdant apple and pear tree orchards encompassed by steep hills. In one area the fragrance of blooming chestnut trees was overpowering. The terrain turned more rugged and wild as we slowly moved north. On the brow of a massive broad mountain was a wood café where we stopped to have tea – large windows offering an excellent panoramic over the arresting, expansive valley of dense thick woods reaching scores of kilometers to the horizon. One wouldn't want to get lost in that wilderness.

Back in the car, farther ahead in a narrow-wooded valley walled in by encroaching 1,006-meter-tall Baegam Mountain, we cruised down into the slim, tight, dreary village of Baegam, built on a short main street. No cars moved, no people were seen. On the road off to the side was worn Baegam Goryeo Hot Springs Hotel, connected to a large glass dome built over a large soaking pool. After parking in the empty lot we entered the lobby and were greeted by a friendly man,

Jeon Byung-tai, behind the counter. I guessed Mr. Jeon to be in his fifties. He said he'd been the spa's manager for six years.

"I was born in Baegam," he said. "When I was a boy, my friends and I swam in the hot springs," which are concentrated along a fissure in town. The water temperature is about thirty-five degrees Celsius in winter, forty-five in summer, he added.

Patricia Bartz explained that underground hot springs are usually associated with close volcanic activity. Since there hasn't been a volcanic eruption in Korea in recent history, she attributed the country's natural hot springs to the percolation of collected rain water in or near granite areas, under pressure by very deep fissures or faults.

In the late 1970s, the government allowed development of Baegam's natural hot pools, a process Mr. Jeon called unfair. "Locals didn't have the money to purchase the best land, so out-of-towners bought up every property with hot springs on them, and built a spa over each one. Every spa owner drilled down to get water for his own customers. The last time I saw an open natural hot pool here was in the 1970s. There are none now."

The Baegam Goryeo Hot Springs Hotel pool is fed by underground water percolating up at about fifty-four degrees Celsius — too scalding even for Koreans. The water is stored in a large tank and when it cools to about forty-five degrees, is released into the pool for customers.

When Mr. Jeon smiled, I noticed his teeth were brownish-yellow. He gladly volunteered the reason. "When I was a boy, my friends and I boiled hot spring water and drank it. It's heavy in sulfur. If you drink sulfur when you're five, six, seven-years-old — before your new teeth come in, they'll turn yellow. Sulfur gets in your gums. About forty or fifty people in town have the same problem I do."

In Baegam's heyday in the 1980s, Koreans flocked here. Professional deep-sea divers working off the east coast patronized the spas year-round. "The divers had big helmets with oxygen pumped into their suits," Mr. Jeon recalled. "They dove down to seventy meters, sometimes more. Water pressure affected their veins and muscles and damaged their blood circulation, so they came to Baegam for treatment. It helped their bodies."

In the 1980s there were five times more customers than his spa saw today. In the hour we'd been here not one customer had entered. Only two men were soaking in the pool now. "How many customers do you get these days?" I asked.

Mr. Jeon smiled and confessed, "It's a secret." I don't think many.

In the 1990s, after decades of Koreans' collective dedicated hard work had pushed the small country upward in terms of financial mobility, overseas vacations became in vogue and crowds stopped patronizing Baegam.

We thanked Mr. Jeon and drove to the nearby, modest Phoenix Hotel down the road in woods. We entered its small lobby. Two male employees were sitting at a coffee table intensely absorbed in a board game and didn't bother to glance up at Heju and me.

Back on the pavement we moved east on National Route 88 to the nearby port town of Hupo. Tomorrow was July 1. Heju needed to be back in Daejeon to resume teaching English at the academy she worked at after a four-month leave of absence. In Hupo, she'd board a bus for Daejeon.

In early evening we entered Hupo — a small, utilitarian town built on the coastal road below the Taebaek's parallel wall of a low, steep ridge. Hupo has a port area with several breakwalls. One breakwall formed a large square harbor where a fleet of fishing and squid trawlers was docked at a concrete wharf. A warehouse and a fish-processing facility were at one end of the wharf.

We parked at the harbor and strolled across the wharf to a docked squid-fishing boat — its powerful engine rumbling deeply. The captain was testing the high-powered lamps blazing bright and hot, hanging on two lines running the vessel's length. At night at sea these lights attract plankton, shrimp and small fish to the surface, in turn drawing squid – usually found between 75 and 600 meters down – into waiting nets. The energy generated from the ship's lights was so intense, we could feel the heat standing ten meters away. "What's the temperature on board?" we shouted to the captain over the din of the thundering engine.

"I don't know," he hollered, "but the lights are hot enough that they'll sunburn your face."

"How much does one lamp cost?" I called.

"Forty thousand won!"

"How long does it last?"

"About six months."

The total luminescence generated by the collective lights on a single vessel is equivalent to 3,000 individual 100-watt bulbs. Little wonder when these boats are at sea at night, satellite photos taken hundreds of kilometers above clearly show their brightness.

We returned to the car and puttered along the coastal road through Hupo. Several taxis sported large plastic squid signs that were fastened onto roofs. Stopped at a traffic light, a large orange-red tour bus pulled up behind us. Emanating from within were thudding and pulsating vibrations of amped-up Techno music. We looked back through the car's rear window to see the bus aisle crammed with stout, retirement-aged women with permed hair rocking to the beat. These are Korea's ubiquitous and notorious dancing *ajummas* – female friends on tour bus excursions who order hapless drivers to crank up the tunes. As the bus passed us, I noted a lone, seated elderly fellow – among a sea of gyrating women – plaintively staring out the window, his expression forlorn and desperate, like he'd just lost his last dollar.

***

The sky was steely gray, a steady drizzle falling as we motored up the coastal road in late morning to just outside town to the Hupo Bus Station. A lone ticket girl was in the small utilitarian building, a few chairs in front. We bought a ticket for the next southbound bus to Daegu. Heju would transfer onto another bus in Daegu and head northwest to Daejeon. As the crow flies, Daejeon is only about 200 kilometers almost due west of Hupo, so why travel south, then north to Daejeon? From the Hupo region there are basically no east-west routes due to the breadth and width of the Taebaek and Sobaek eminences standing squarely in the way. Driving through this topography is slow, challenging and nausea-inducing.

The bus pulled up, and we said our goodbyes. Without Heju's almost eleven total weeks on the trip, it wouldn't have been possible to converse with the numerous people we'd encountered. The bus pulled away and slowly rolled south on the narrow coastal road. I sat in the car, rain splattering the windshield. With Heju gone I wouldn't have anyone to blame now when I made a wrong turn or got lost.

But there was good news. In two days, I was scheduled to rendezvous 150 kilometers north in Gangneung with a Korean man who'd be arriving from Seoul. He'd answered my online ad and volunteered to accompany me for the final week of the trip in the northeast. I'd soon have someone to chide when I messed up. But frankly, I simply hoped he'd enjoy conversing, unlike the former translator, Sung-jai.

CHAPTER 22

Doma: North Korean Commandos; Taebaek: A City Up High

From the Hupo Bus Station, I drove north to the nearby coastal town of Uljin, where I headed inland and trekked into the long, humid, limestone Seongnyugul Cave, replete with yellow-brown stalagmites and stalactites. Near Uljin, I visited the interesting Hanul Nuclear Power Site Exhibition Center, which provided information on nuclear power and atoms.

After two days of slowly motoring up the coast from North Gyeongsang into Gangwon province, I arrived in Gangneung in early evening. In front of the Gangneung Train Station I met Park Tae-won, who'd driven from Seoul. "Call me T.W.," Tae-won said in excellent English. I did.

We sat in a utilitarian café across from the handsome, traditional one-story station. T.W. was in his late forties, with grayish-brown hair, a somewhat boyish face. He was a bit below medium height, calm and circumspect, and emitted a rather quiet, defeated air.

"I've been teaching English to kids for thirteen years," T.W. said wistfully. "My dream's to move to Mokpo and open a fishing charter business with my brother."

After forty-five minutes, we walked to my car in the parking lot. Standing next to the Scoupe, T.W. announced, "Why don't we use my car."

I was momentarily taken aback because I'd assumed he knew we'd be riding mine.

"No, it's better we take my car," I said, not considering anything else. "I have to constantly stop and start on the road to take notes, and if you're driving your car I wouldn't be able to do that."

T.W. benignly smiled and assuredly answered, "Mark, if we take my car you're the boss, I'll stop wherever you want. You order, I'll do it." He was persuasive.

I'd had a modicum of reservations when T.W. agreed to accompany me. It had to do with age and gender. In my experience, after a certain age, the Korean male species isn't particularly known for being the most celebrated of conversationalists. Stoicism and taciturnity are two words that spring to mind to describe this category, perhaps remnant characteristics from the Joseon *yangban* era.

It was easy now for T.W. to assure me he'd gladly pull over when I asked, but would he on the road? I had my doubts. Yet, for reasons I'm still unsure of to this day, I heard myself agreeing to ride shotgun in his car. Admittedly, it would be relaxing not having to direct my attention to the road, and simply sit back in the passenger seat. But the moment I acquiesced, a wave of uneasiness swept over me. In my gut I knew I'd erred.

I transferred a few essentials from my car into my gym bag and plunked myself down on the comfortable, well-padded passenger seat in T.W.'s almost-new Renault-Samsung SM-5 sedan. I left the trusty Scoupe in the train station parking lot. T.W. drove downtown to find a *jjimjilbang*.

I'd been to Gangneung a number of times before but had never warmed to it. Its core seemed drab and depressing and not defined by anything in particular. Once downtown, T.W. and I checked into a 24-hour *jjimjilbang*. I took a jog through the local neighborhood into a labyrinth of old back lanes lined with shops, small hidden drinking places and an outdoor market. When I returned to the *jjimjilbang*, I showered and placed my mat near T.W.'s and fell asleep.

Like Sung-jai, T.W. rose with the birds. I was in a deep sleep when I was awakened, T.W. sitting up. My watch showed 5:00 a.m. I returned to slumbering, but it was perfunctory; we were in the car to begin the day before eight o'clock.

We headed south down the coast a dozen or so kilometers to an area where, on September 16, 1996, a local taxi driver on his way home in pre-dawn darkness spotted a strange looking vessel just offshore and alerted police. The craft was a North Korean submarine that had run aground on a reef. When the ROK military opened the hatch, the sub was empty. It was concluded its North Korean crew had reached shore in an effort to scamper north back home through the rugged Taebaeks.

North Korean spies in the South aren't to be taken lightly. In 1999, an apartment surveillance video camera in Seoul captured a North Korean agent shooting a defector – a relative of North Korea's then-leader Kim Jong-il. The defector had been critical of Kim. In 2012, a North Korean operative was apprehended by authorities in Seoul moments before his planned poisoning of a defector.

Gangneung was soon buzzing with tens of thousands of ROK soldiers, commandos and special forces, the country's largest ever manhunt – even bigger in scale than the one still trying to apprehend me for dog-napping. When the sub was discovered, I'd been living in Korea for just over a year. For the next fifty days, the airwaves and newspapers provided constant daily reports and updates on the quest to capture the enemy.

The coastal road south of Gangneung we were driving along is bordered on the inland side by a low, rocky wooded ridge, on the seaboard by patches of exposed rocky shoals jutting above the waterline. The green-blue sea was choppy and swirling. In nearby Aninjin County was Gangneung Unification Park where the sub was on display, open for tours. First we stopped at the Unification Security Pavilion. I wasn't sure what to expect from the name. "Unification" evokes warm feelings while "security" denotes force and weapons.

In the modern, well-presented pavilion it was soon apparent the director had little interest in North and South ever uniting. In front of exhibits was provocative information castigating North Korea. Slowly moving through the halls, we read how North operatives had triggered a remote-controlled bomb onboard a Korean Air flight bound from Baghdad to Seoul on November 29, 1987. The plane had exploded in midair, killing all 104 passengers and eleven crew.

There were details of how in Rangoon, Burma (now Yangon, Myanmar), North Korean agents had planted a bomb targeting South Korean President Chun Doo-hwan on October 9, 1989, the detonation killing fourteen South Korean officials and four Burmese. In a glass case were items found in the beached sub, including a made-in-Canada, Browning nine-mm handgun and hand grenades. When we departed an hour later, I concluded a more apt title for the facility would be "Separation Security Pavilion."

Nearby, we pulled the car up to a narrow concrete wharf where a large South Korean Navy destroyer was docked. On dry dock at the wharf's far end was the dull green and rust-colored North Korean sub. In a small office by the sub we met the site manager, Kim Yong-bok, a rather humorless fellow to whom I put a number of questions about the 1996 incident. Mr. Kim refused to provide any information, pleading ignorance. He'd simply repeat, "I don't know," to queries.

He pointed to a sign at the sub, which stated: Sang-O-class, 325 tons, 32.5 meters long. "That's all we know ... what the sign says," he said. I was certain he knew more. His reticence stemmed from national security protocol ensuring classified information on North Korea wasn't released to the public. But I wasn't seeking secret files. Finally, Mr. Kim relented slightly and admitted the sub's crew had first headed from the wrecked vessel to Gwaebang Mountain.

"Where's Gwaebang Mountain?" I asked.

"I don't know," he said.

Of course he did.

"If you want to find out more, you'll need to phone the National Intelligence Service (NIS) and get permission," Mr. Kim insisted.

We weren't about to do that. I noticed a glossy pamphlet on his desk – on its cover a diagram of the route the North Koreans took from the sub to the mountains.

"May I take the pamphlet?" I asked.

"I'll have to check with NIS," Mr. Kim replied. He picked up his desk phone and dialed, I assumed, the local NIS office. He handed the phone to T.W., who conversed on the line a few moments, then hung up. "We can't take the pamphlet," T.W. announced. "If we want more information, we'll have to call the military."

This was getting ridiculous. I suppose it hadn't occurred to Mr. Kim that a government agency had printed the pamphlet on his desk for public use.

We entered the sub's claustrophobic interior – little space for twenty-six crew and commandos to move, sit, rest or sleep – no chairs or bunks. "Some crew may have slept in the empty missile tubes," Mr. Kim suggested. These were hardy North Koreans.

On our way to the car in the parking lot, T.W. confided that information he'd seen on the pamphlet in the office indicated the sub's crew had passed through Doma village. Checking the atlas, we found Doma on the map about twenty kilometers west of Gangneung. Well done, T.W., who was proving to be more valuable than what I was paying him. Not that I'd paid him. We'd head to Doma. Gwaebang Mountain, the same eminence Mr. Kim had insisted he didn't know where it was, was in the atlas too — one kilometer inland from our current position.

We were soon on the immediate western periphery of Gangneung driving north on a parkway. At this point — as the passenger, not the driver — I first regretted having relinquished the wheel to T.W. Not because Olivia Newton-John's greatest hits were being broadcast on the car speakers and I was now hostage to Olivia singing "Xanadu."

"We Koreans love Olivia Newton-John," T.W. said, swaying to the beat.

Rather, it was because we needed to exit at a nearby off-ramp to convey to a country road to reach Doma. But T.W. refused to take the ramp, even as I held open the atlas to the page clearly showing the exit was correct.

"The exit's farther ahead," he insisted. We spent the next twenty minutes driving north on the parkway, searching for his off-ramp. After a good many kilometers and unable to find his exit, he finally swung the car around and retraced the route back to where we started near the original off-ramp.

"I guess I went too far," T.W. concluded nonchalantly.

You don't say. Still not willing to exit at the correct ramp, he pulled into a nearby gas station and spent ten minutes in earnest conversation with the station's attendant, busily scribbling directions onto a scrap of paper on how to get to the correct exit. I percolated in the car.

"I got the directions!" T.W. triumphantly exclaimed on return.

Hallelujah!

Near the gas station, we exited at the off-ramp I'd pointed out an hour earlier, not a peep of contrition from the driver. On a more positive note, we'd just experienced an exhilarating, first-hand tour of Gangneung's famed, never-to-be missed parkway. As an added bonus, I'd heard every song that Olivia Newton-John's had ever recorded.

We drove west toward Doma through lonely backwoods. In isolated Wangsan County we turned onto a rural side road leading through a dominating quiet valley, a narrow, pebbly shallow river paralleling the road. On each side were heavily-wooded, 900-meter-tall mountain slopes. Overcast and foggy, ribbons of mist floated at the ridges' upper reaches. Across the river was a parallel narrow band of agricultural land and a few small farm dwellings. We parked on the side of the road, walked over a small footbridge spanning the river, approached a home and knocked on the front door. A man opened it.

Mr. Cho Bang-suk was a farmer, friendly and engaging. "Is this Doma?" we asked him.

"Yes," he said, acknowledging the North Korean submarine crew had passed though here.

Mr. Cho invited us in. We sat in his living room. He said Doma was the main military staging ground for ROK troops, a total of 42,000 soldiers joining the manhunt.

"A water canteen belonging to a guerrilla was found at the river," he said. "Thousands of soldiers pitched tents by the water." He recounted tracking dogs brought in and military helicopters flying overhead shining bright searchlights at night onto the mountains. "It was like a battle zone. Our homes shook from the usually five or six helicopters flying near the summit every night. It was scary. We couldn't sleep well, so we usually drank."

A day or two after the sub beached, Mr. Cho was ambling through Doma's narrow agricultural plots in the afternoon. He heard a dog barking, followed by multiple rapid gun shots fired from an automatic rifle. Dead in the hail of bullets was a young North Korean commando from the sub, Man Il-joon, who'd refused to surrender. Man's body was torn apart by bullets. "The military wouldn't allow villagers to see it," Mr. Cho said.

The sub's helmsman was captured wandering a field in Gangneung, and admitted the mission was espionage. Eleven crew members and fifteen commandos were in the sub. The dead bodies of eleven crew were found in local mountains, executed by their own men. Reports were the eleven had been eliminated for having slowed down the highly-trained commandos' effort to dash back home. Imagine shooting your own comrades. These North Koreans were Rambos on steroids, hearts of stone, veins of ice. No consciences. They were beyond dangerous – they'd refuse to be captured alive.

During the first two days of the search, seven of the fifteen commandos were killed by ROK troops, leaving eight of the original twenty-six North Koreans alive. In the following week, four more were tracked down and killed. Four enemy remained on the loose. About three weeks after the sub's incursion, three adults picking mushrooms locally in mountains near the village of Tapdong in Pyeongchang County – forty-five kilometers northwest of Gangneung – were found on October 9 shot to death. The trio had inadvertently crossed paths with two assailants. Three weeks later, seventy-five kilometers north of Doma, in the mountain town of Inje thirty kilometers south of the border, the trail of the two was picked up. A running firefight with the ROK military ensued. The North Koreans fired their weapons and tossed hand grenades, killing three ROK soldiers. The two commandos were also killed. The dragnet was finally over after forty-nine days. Of the remaining two enemy, one surrendered, the other was never caught. It was assumed the latter had successfully trekked back to his country. The death toll on the South side was eight ROK soldiers, four civilians, one policeman and one reservist.

(Two years later, in June 1998, a seventy-ton North Korean mini submarine got entangled in a fishing net in the sea east of Sokcho in Gangwon province. When the hatch was opened, the five crew and four commandos inside were found dead in an apparent murder-suicide.)

After talking with Mr. Cho for a couple of hours, we thanked him and said goodbye. Wandering alongside the hamlet's agricultural plots, we conversed with another villager. At dusk we departed Doma. Our next destination was Taebaek City, the highest of all cities in the country at more than 700 meters above sea level. Taebaek boasts several distinctions: home of the nation's highest elevation train station, and of the only casino where Koreans can legally gamble, and source of the country's two longest rivers. There is also a coal museum and Taebaek National Mountain Park. A lot to take in. It doesn't get much better than Taebaek.

While cruising the seventy-five kilometers south to Taebaek, I attempted to engage T.W. in conversation, but a couple of sentences at a time seemed to be his arbitrary limit; he wasn't one for extended dialogue. I was sure he was related to Sung-jai, and assigned to torture me. After ninety minutes of moving through wilderness, we were on a lonely stretch of blacktop just outside Taebaek City, wedged between two high, steep walls of rock face. In eerie blackness, the only illumination was from our car's headlights piercing the pavement ahead. We exited this narrow corridor of rock and abruptly met the bright lights of downtown Taebaek.

What a pleasant surprise. Along the inviting long main street were brightly-lit shops and restaurants appeared bustling and prosperous, pedestrians out and about, just how I imagined the mountain town of Aspen, Colorado. Later I learned the scene wasn't what it seemed. Taebaek and the local region were economically depressed. Numerous prosperous coal mines had been shuttered in the late

1980s and early 1990s, resulting in devastating unemployment.

On the downtown main road I spotted a *yeogwan* off to the side. "That looks like a good place to stay. Let's stop there," I said to T.W.

But he had other ideas. "No, I don't think it's good," he replied calmly. "I know of a nicer place outside town." He must have done some preplanning.

Had my backbone been operational, I'd have reminded him that the previous night at Gangneung Station, he'd clearly stated he'd honor my requests. Being a Canadian buttercup, not favoring confrontation, I instead chose silence and stewed. Big mistake. T.W. headed to his place of choice. Today was the first of our scheduled six days together. Heaven have mercy.

About sixteen kilometers southwest of Taebaek City, near Taebaek Mountain, in a remote woodsy area we pulled up to the Family Boseok Sauna where we'd stay tonight. I had a lot of things planned for the next day – it would be busy. T.W. would be earning his meal ticket tomorrow. He could be sure of that.

***

T.W. was awake early. I figured nine o'clock was a reasonable time to begin the day, and at that time we stepped out from Boseok Sauna to a gray, foggy morning, the alpine grandeur evident. I inhaled thin, cool air.

Not far off, we arrived at the base of the stalwart, wooded Taebaek Mountain, and strolled up a path on the lower slope to the modern, formidable Taebaek Coal Museum. I'd phoned ahead to arrange for a tour, and the museum's researcher, Chung Yun-soon, was waiting for us. Mr. Chung wore a spiffy suit, black hair thick and well-coiffed, his voguish attire surprising, considering a coal museum didn't seem the place for a fashion runway. Mr. Chung was a Taebaek native. In 1968, age 17, he was hired by a local coal mine to drill part-time. Mining was dangerous work and several of his colleagues died from black lung disease. Mr. Chung's monthly salary then was 13,000 won (equivalent to about U.S. $50). After taking time off from the mines to attend university, he returned to drill full-time and was later promoted to a front-office job.

Coal mining in Korea began with the Japanese in 1937. Twenty-two mines were dug in today's North Korea, thirteen in the South. Coal was shipped by rail to the east coast blue-collar city of Donghae, then by sea to Japan, which desired better quality coal for its warships than its domestic low-grade stuff.

Patricia Bartz wrote that toward the end of the Paleozoic period — around 250 million years ago — vegetable matter from fresh water deposits in inland seas and lakes in today's Taebaek region was later transformed into anthracite coal. This geological area is known as the Pyongan system. Surrounding it is the earlier Chosun system, or Great Limestone series. The latter consists of massive dark gray limestone which was deposited in a gradually deepening sea to a thickness of nearly 1,000 meters. Over time, after the sea receded, weathering occurred in the exposed limestone, forming holes and a series of caves. Seongnyugul Cave — where I'd trekked a few days earlier outside Uljin just southeast of Taebaek City — is Great Limestone series rock.

Coal mining flourished in the 1980s. At Taebaek's coal-mining peak, more than 60,000 miners were excavating 24 million tons of coal annually from hundreds of small mines. Most coal was converted into small, pressed briquettes or *yontan*, introduced in the 1920s to fuel stoves and heat homes. In the 1960s, there were about 400 *yontan* factories across the country. Today only fifty remain. As many as 250,000 households still rely though on *yontan* to cook and for heating. Every winter, newspapers print photos of volunteers going door-to-door delivering free *yontan* predominantly to the elderly.

Taebaek's and eastern Gangwon province's mining industry was crippled due to cheap Chinese coal flooding the country and from oil and gas replacing coal. By the late 1980s, 340 coal mines — many small and privately owned — had been permanently shuttered, and twelve-thousand miners were out of work. Taebaek City's population fell from 125,000 to 50,000. By 2003, only three million tons of coal were being excavated annually by 6,000 miners. Today, only five coal mines operate in the country.

Taebaek was forced to reinvent itself. It turned to eco-tourism and recreation, and constructed four golf courses, three ski resorts, a high-elevation sports training center and a casino. But first Taebaek needed to be bleached, scrubbed and rinsed.

"The city used to be black," Mr. Cho said. "School kids would draw pictures on the ground in the coal dust. They couldn't wear white because their clothes turned black. Even on sunny days we had to wear boots because of the coal dust. There weren't many trees either — farmers burnt them to make farmland and chopped them for firewood."

Streams were polluted, fish dying, roads unpaved. The metamorphosis has been remarkable, with little evidence of Taebaek's former unhealthy landscape.

Mr. Chung led us through the museum, then onto a mining elevator in the facility which we descended into a mine shaft. At noon, T.W. and I left the museum. The sun was finally peeking through clouds after a week of depressing grayness. Our next stop was the Daihan Coal Mine, the country's largest and oldest, established by the Japanese in 1936. We headed east from Taebaek Mountain, then south of Taebaek City through a series of pristine, wooded mountains. In Jangseong district we found the Daihan mine on the lower end of a very long wooded slope. Entering the mine's front office we met the mine manager, Kim Young-jin, who confessed Daihan's future was bleak.

"Our seventy-five-year production limit ends soon," he said. "Miners are digging deeper and deeper, making new shafts to get to coal, but it's getting scarcer to find."

Mr. Kim led us behind the office to the mine shaft entrance, where two rail tracks descended into darkness to a vertical depth of 900 meters. "There are 450 kilometers of underground tunnels," he said. Faint beams of light soon began to appear from deep within the recesses of the black tunnel and got brighter as they neared the entrance. A group of miners finally emerged into daylight, their headlamps on, faces black, caked in coal dust.

Back at the front office, Mr. Kim enthusiastically expounded on the merits of living 700 meters above sea level in Taebaek. "There are no mosquitoes and summers are cool," he announced. "If the temperature's twenty-nine degrees in Seoul, it'll be just twenty-one or twenty-two degrees here."

Driving back to Taebaek City, I put Mr. Kim's assertion to the test. I phoned Moonie, my friend in Seoul. "What's the temperature there?" I asked, of early July's oppressive heat.

"It's too hot ... thirty-four degrees," he complained lethargically. Moonie was feeling the effects in his apartment. With the humidity, the actual temperature was closer to thirty-eight degrees. I checked my thermometer — twenty-three degrees, moderate and comfortable in Taebaek. Mr. Kim was right!

In downtown Taeback, T.W. spent twenty minutes navigating numerous back streets seeking a suitable place to park.

"How about this one?" I suggested, motioning to an open space on the side of the road — one of numerous available parking spots, long enough to fit a sixteen-wheel long-haul truck.

"No, I don't think there's enough space," T.W. answered. After more searching, he gingerly and carefully angled his car into an open lot.

We entered a nearby small noodle restaurant for lunch. T.W. wasn't in the mood for dialogue so we mostly ate in silence. The TV on the wall was tuned to a comedy, or gag show, a staple of Korean television. This particular gag featured a famous Korean female pop singer and dancer, Lee Hyo-ri. When Ms. Lee recited the wrong words to a nursery rhyme, a light-weight tin plate fell from above onto her head. Maybe the most moronic program in television history.

After lunch, we strolled on the main street to nearby Hwangji Park, where a spring is the source of the mighty Nakdong River. The Nakdong meanders 525 kilometers in a broadly southerly direction, emptying at the sea just west of Busan. Through a gate we entered the small green park, dotted with leafy trees. Rays of late afternoon sunshine slanted through tree branches. On several benches sat and lay homeless men, their lives squandered by alcoholism. As we walked past them, T.W. muttered condescendingly under his breath. I was surprised because he'd admitted he'd once struggled with an overindulgence of *soju*.

In the park's center is a large, circular pool of bright bluish-green, crystal-clear water. In the middle a little stream of bubbles percolates up from an underground spring.

A sign stated: "This is the starting point of the Nakdong River. The temperature of the pond is always fifteen degrees. Every day, five thousand tons of water flow from the spring. The pond has a diameter of a hundred meters. The altitude is seven hundred meters (2,300 ft)."

How this minuscule trickle morphed into the grand Nakdong River was beyond me.

Just ten kilometers west is the spring of the country's second-longest river — the 514-kilometer Han. We returned to the car and drove west to Mt. Hambaek to find the spring. At the base of the lonely, bulky wooded eminence, we parked and rambled on a lovely trail rising gradually through a modest deciduous forest and a small pretty meadow, and sloshed across a creek. The early evening summer sunlight flickered through tree branches. Twenty minutes later, on the lower side of a wooded hill, the path ended at a tiny limestone pool, Geomryongso Pond – the size and shape of a round bathtub.

A sign announced: "This is the Han River, producing two thousand tons of water a day at a constant nine degrees Celsius."

Sliding down the exterior of the rock pool was a tiny dribble of water that flowed downhill, soon converging with a separate trickle of flowing water, the combined gush the Han River's genesis. Although Taebaek City is less than twenty miles from the coast, both the Han and Nakdong's routes are blocked from moving to the East Sea due to the Taebaeks. Instead, the Han flows west and the Nakdong south.

We next drove northwest of Taebaek City to Chujeon Station, one stop west of Taebaek Station. At 855 meters, snow falls at Chujeon as late as April. We parked on a lonely stretch of a country road, then trudged up a knoll, emerging at a long rail platform. At the far end was a red-brick station house. Across the tracks is a steep green mountain heavy with woods. The rail line disappears in both directions behind tall wooded slopes. On the platform, two young fellows, station employees, were playing catch with a baseball. A sign trumpeted: "Welcome to the Station Closest to the Sky."

T.W. and I entered the station house, the lone occupant the station manager, Lee Su-hyeong, a fortyish, stoic man to whom words did not come easily. We sat at a coffee table. Mr. Lee reluctantly volunteered short answers to questions.

"Chujeon Station isn't busy," he admitted. "Only one passenger train stops here every morning, at nine o'clock."

"Do passengers get off the train?" I asked.

"Rarely."

"Do they get on?"

"No one."

"Is it lonely here?"

"Yes."

Chujeon Station is on the single-track Taebaek Line, linking the small mountain town of Jecheon ninety kilometers west to Baeksan Station one stop east of Taebaek City. Chujeon Station wasn't always a minor player. Up until the mid-1980s it had been a critical cog for shipping coal.

"We used to load about 100,000 tons of coal a month and had fifteen full-time employees," said Mr. Lee. Times were so auspicious, locals had a saying: "Even dogs wander around town with 10,000-won bills in their mouths."

"Now we have only three employees and load just 10,000 tons of coal a month," he said.

In darkness, we departed and scooted onto a nearby parkway to whisk us west to the day's final destination: Kangwon Land Casino. We were soon at the tall, white, concrete, steel-and-glass casino, which included a hotel, restaurants and movie cinema — totally incongruous with the surrounding greenery, woods and mountains. We entered the casino, jam-packed with predominantly middle-aged Korean men. We could barely move. We attempted to find an empty seat at a blackjack table to wager a few dollars but couldn't even get close to one. Every table was surrounded by phalanxes of punters seven rows deep, every seat holding a warm body.

An empty chair at a blackjack table here is apparently rare. Patrons reserve seats well before their arrival. They hire local professional seat-sitters to occupy their chair for when they need a washroom, food or rest break to retain their coveted place at the table for hours, even days at a time.

It was dispiriting looking into the blank stares of these hard-core gamblers. I was employed as a sports reporter in 1984–85 at the *Tahoe Daily Tribune* in Lake Tahoe on the California-Nevada state line, and would occasionally pop into a local casino and spend a couple of hours wagering $10 total on $2 minimum blackjack bets. Groups of retirees bussed in from Oakland and San Francisco played the slot machines all day, repeatedly pulling leavers, their hollow gazes differing little from patrons here at Kangwon Land Casino.

T.W., downcast and lethargic, wandered off alone into the crowd. We hooked up forty-five minutes later, now ten o'clock. "I hate this place," he said wearily. "I'm exhausted. I want to go." He'd been awake since 5:00 a.m. He'd earned his paycheck today.

We drove onto the parkway, and a short way along T.W. turned onto a deserted, dark lonely road winding up the side of a mountain.

"There's a *jjimjilbang* here I want to stay at," he said, information he hadn't shared with me. "I think this is the way."

We slowly climbed into silent blackness. After fifteen minutes, well up the mountain, surrounded by woods, I proffered, "I don't think there's any place here."

Undeterred, T.W. continued up. We finally dead-ended at the mountain's pinnacle at a chair lift, at the top of a grassy ski hill.

"I guess I took the wrong turn," he conceded.

I guess so.

We headed down, reentered the parkway, and steered south to the base of Hambaek Mountain, where we found a rustic, handsome *jjimjilbang* standing alone adorned in neon lights. After showering and a soak in the hot tub, T.W. and I had a late meal at the snack bar, then threw down mats in the sleeping area. T.W. lay down and began watching the big-screen TV. It was near midnight and he was fatigued. I suggested he get some sleep.

"Not yet," he said. "I have to wait at least an hour after dinner before I sleep to digest my meal."

"Why an hour?"

"Because scientists say that you should wait at least forty minutes after a meal before you sleep."

"But can you sleep instead of watching TV?" I asked, puzzled.

"No, because when I watch TV, I lay sideways with my head on my elbow, like this," he said, indicating his body was on an angle. "Food digests faster this way. But when I sleep I lie flat and my food digests slower."

I was dog-tired and when my head hit the mat, I was out like a light on my stomach – to heck with correct digestion.

CHAPTER 23

Haean: The Punch Bowl;
Seoul: Home Sweet Home

During the third and final year of the Korean War – from spring 1952 to July 1953 – ROK and UN allied troops were locked in bitter, bloody close fighting against Chinese and North Korean soldiers along the 38th parallel dividing South and North Korea. Soldiers on both sides were in mortal combat dying over essentially a hilltop, a ridge, a few hundred meters of real estate. "Protracted purgatory" was how one war historian described the battles. A village, Haean, on the border in Gangwon province, became synonymous with this war of attrition.

Haean lies on a plain encircled by mountain ridges. U.S. soldiers referred to it as the Punch Bowl due to its shape and the moniker stuck. Other local battle grounds included Heartbreak Ridge, Bloody Ridge and Pork Chop Hill. Villagers sometimes find the bones of soldiers who perished fighting there.

In the Punch Bowl is a ROK military observation post high on a mountain ridge overlooking the DMZ. Under the mountain is the

Fourth Invasion Tunnel dug by the North into the South, discovered in 1990. Tours of the post and tunnel are available. We were on our way.

The morning was smashing — bright and hazy, the sky white, mountain air fresh. About to depart our Hambaek Mountain digs to begin the 150-kilometer jaunt north to the Punch Bowl, T.W. suddenly announced he wanted to visit Yeongwol sixty kilometers west of Taebaek. "I've got a priest friend there I'd like to see," he said. He'd mentioned he'd overcome an over-reliance on *soju* with counseling from a priest. I had nothing against Yeongwol or priests, but T.W. was making a habit of springing surprises on me.

From Taebaek we entered National Route 38, an enchanting road we had exclusively to ourselves, moving west through rugged, arresting terrain in a long, narrow valley sandwiched between low, vertical granite eminences. A shallow, pebbly river paralleled sections of the road.

We soon were passing the town of Sabuk, a grim reminder of the long-gone halcyon days of mining. There are rows of old, abandoned, low-rise apartment blocks and rusty buildings with grimy walls and shattered windows. A coal mine elevator shaft rises high in the sky. When the area's mines were shuttered, some communities were largely abandoned, giving way to shantytowns like Sabuk. Decaying concrete contrasted with a handful of new apartment buildings.

On No. 38, sections of the Taebaek rail line move in and out of tunnels burrowed through mountain granite. At one juncture, the track conveys over an old iron rail bridge — buttressed by stone girders — connecting two close, low, rocky vertical mountains. Along the road, construction was ongoing to build a freeway. My concern was No. 38 — a peaceful, slow route — would be forever jettisoned, replaced by a new band of pavement whisking motorists twenty minutes faster to Yeongwol. Who cared about rocketing anywhere in this pristine, beguiling area of Gangwon province.

Yeongwol is a pretty, slow-paced mountain town on the banks of the Han River. We spent a couple of hours at the priest's house, T.W. talking alone with him. After, we entered National Route 31 — its 628 total kilometers connecting Busan in the south up to the border. No. 31 north from Yeongwol was lonely and bereft of vehicles. We passed the sparsely populated alpine county of Pyeongchang, the main site of the February 2018 PyeongChang Olympic and Paralympic Winter Games. The Olympic sports venues are spread out across the county east to Gangneung. Snow commonly falls between late November and late February, averaging about two meters in the Pyeongchang region — where mountains ascend to 1,600 meters.

North of Pyeongchang we traversed vast tracts of wilderness so remote, there weren't even the requisite tiny villages that commonly dot the roadside every few kilometers in rural areas. The car's repetitive herky-jerky motion — resulting from ascending and descending hills and swinging around roads shaped like coiled serpents — made me nauseous. We stopped for an hour near the top of at a remote mountain rest area where several tented stalls were managed by a few women selling snacks.

T.W. told me he'd been a platoon leader in his compulsory two-year military duty. "In the old days, soldiers used to hate being assigned to the mountains in Gangwon province," he said. "Roads weren't paved and it took all day to hike down from an outpost to pick up supplies and return."

South of Inje City, thirty-five kilometers from the border, we paralleled the lovely Naerin River, flowing through tight, enchanting Naerin River valley, the water clean, dark green and littered with big boulders. The Naerin River and the first half of the Guem River in the southwest are the only two waterways in the country to flow north. We reached Inje City, where the Naerin converges with the south-moving minor Inbuk River, the confluence producing the west-flowing Soyang River. A tall, narrow bridge crosses to Inje City over the volatile watery junction. On the far side of the bridge in Inje City, I could see hints of the town's buildings.

We continued north on Route 453, the only road in and out of Haean, and we were soon in the Civilian Control Zone: a 250-kilometer-long swath south of DMZ under military jurisdiction, civilian access restricted. We were stopped at a roadside ROK military guard, the soldier checking our intentions for entering the zone.

It was early evening and still sunny when we finally entered the Punch Bowl. I was flabbergasted at its size, and immediately realized I'd totally misjudged its scope. I'd envisioned the bowl similar in size to a large football stadium. It is actually about seven kilometers wide and the same distance long: fifty square kilometers of a green agricultural plain surrounded by an almost circular wall of rather distant mountain ridges. Viewed by satellite, the Punch Bowl — once an active volcano — is an almost perfect circle. On the plain there wasn't a single apartment or commercial unit, only a scattering of mostly small dwellings and farmhouses. We slipped into "downtown" Haean; if you blink you miss it. The main street is a mere hundred meters long, not a person or car around, just a couple of restaurants, a *yeogwan*, a mom-and-pop shop and two hardware stores.

Having spotted a small homestead — Punch Bowl Minbak — entering the plain, we doubled back and stopped there. The car's odometer read 300 kilometers added since departing Taebaek this morning. The *minbak* owners were a kind, retirement-aged farming couple who earned extra money renting a side room attached to the house.

After showering and dining on the usual bread and slices of processed cheese in the room, I embarked on a late-night jog on the road into Haean. The night was pitch black, except for Gachil

Peak's ridge on the Punch Bowl's edge. Bright military floodlights shone eerily into the DMZ, back-lighting the mountain. The unusual illumination reminded me of a scene from the 2005 movie, *War of the Worlds*, where Tom Cruise's character and his son are on a hill alongside soldiers, on the other side attacking alien tripods, the night sky lit up with bursting explosions.

***

We were out of the *minbak* in the car at 9:00 a.m., on our way to a nearby mountain base, to sign up for a government-run tour of the Fourth Tunnel and the Eulji Observatory military post. Hot and hazy, an ominous band of thick fog hovered low over the far ridge line and was slowly drifting toward the observatory. I worried the shifting fog might hinder our view from the Eulji ridge post, across the DMZ into the North.

We stopped on the road at a military guard post. The guard explained the official order of the tour was tunnel first, observatory post second.

"T.W., do you mind asking if it's possible to visit the observatory post first and tunnel second?" I tried. "It looks like the fog will be over the ridge soon. If we can see the post first, we can beat the fog."

T.W. made the overture to the guard, then informed me: "The guard says we have to go in order of tunnel first, observatory post second."

I asked T.W. to try again, but he bristled, and was silent and stone-faced. I waited a few moments, then added, "I'm only asking you to try one more time."

T.W. reluctantly mumbled a few words to the guard, who responded with the same answer and waved us through. T.W., now seething, slowly and clearly enunciated for me: "In the Korean military there are strict rules we must follow." From that moment, I was persona non grata, I'd crossed his line, I'd pay the price – he wouldn't speak to me unless he had to.

In a large hall at the base of the mountain we signed a document to the effect that if stray North Korean bullets strike us while at the DMZ post, the government bore no responsibility for our deaths. We, and a modest gaggle of visitors, were shown into the auditorium to view a documentary on the DMZ. T.W. sat apart from me. After the viewing, our group boarded a shuttle bus for the short drive to the Fourth Tunnel, where we trundled 145 meters down a wide shaft into the mountain's bowels, then rode a mini-train a short way on a track through the two-meter-wide, two-meter-high tunnel. Hacked through rock, the train tunnel was claustrophobic and shadowy.

Back on the bus, we climbed the steep, twisty road to the Eulji observatory at the ridge where ROK guards were manned with machine guns and there were three layers of wire fencing. A large information center with a wide expansive deck faces north to the four-kilometer-wide DMZ. Despite some fog partially obscuring the horizon, the view was outstanding. Over a vast, overgrown valley of wilderness seemingly reaching forever, is rolling ridge after rolling ridge of a sea of lush dense green. Human habitation has been entirely absent in the DMZ since it became a buffer zone in 1953. Nature certainly flourishes when devoid of people.

To take a closer look into the DMZ, I retrieved my binoculars from my backpack. A nearby ROK solider mistook them for a camera and ordered I put them back.

"It's not a camera … they're binoculars," I explained, and he permitted me to use them.

After an hour on the deck, we headed back to the mountain base to the car. T.W. said he wanted to see a war monument and fort about twenty kilometers southwest of Haean. First we stopped in Haean to talk with a resident — introduced to us by the *minbak* couple — who'd been living in the Punch Bowl for more than fifty years. In the elderly man's house, he told us he originally hailed from the city of Wonju, east of Seoul, and grew up dirt poor. During the Korean War he'd volunteered to carry U.S. soldiers' equipment in exchange for food. In 1960, he learned the Korean government was handing out free parcels of land in Haean. He applied, received a plot of land, and has farmed here since. The only catch was that Haean, being a security area, residents have to stay in their homes at night with doors and windows locked.

We took No. 453 west out of town and quickly ascended into formidable, rugged dry hills rippling all around. The terrain is rough and barren with shrub-like vegetation and few trees, reminding me of Salinas Mountains' dry foothills in California. A remote ROK military barrack was off the side of the road. Several dozen young soldiers were training on a dirt field in front. We stopped at its roadside guard post, where two young Koreans in uniform on guard duty were armed with rifles. One told us: "I'm from Seoul. I was assigned to Gangwon province for my two-year military service."

The road began to arch south. After rolling along for forty-five minutes, and no sign of the monument or fort, we doubled back to Haean. Near the Punch Bowl Minbak was a small war museum I wanted to see. T.W. parked in the museum lot.

"Would you like to go in?" I asked.

"No, I'll stay in the car," he replied. I entered alone. My mind was on T.W., not the museum. If he wasn't going to converse, there didn't seem much point to continue the trip with him. We needed to iron things out.

After five minutes in the museum, I exited and found T.W. standing in the parking lot. "Can we talk?" I asked.

"Okay," he said tersely.

"I know you're upset about what I said at the guard post. I know you don't want to talk..."

T.W. interjected, "I want to finish the trip now. I'm going back to Seoul!" He immediately turned and stalked back to his car, opened the front door and sat in the driver's seat waiting for me to retrieve my stuff.

I was livid for having been abruptly ditched without transportation in the middle of nowhere. I marched over to T.W.'s car, stood between him and the open door — so he couldn't drive off — and gave him a piece of my mind.

"You're angry because I questioned the military," I stated heatedly. "Tough luck ... that's how Western journalists operate. Maybe Korean journalists are polite and don't push back, but that's not how we do it in the West. My job's to get the facts, and that's what I'm going to do!" (Never mind that I wasn't a journalist, nor with the media, nor employed.) I told him giving me the silent treatment was childish. Not exactly culturally sensitive commentary, but at the moment I didn't care.

T.W.'s gaze remained down at his mobile phone. He fiddled with it. "Yeah, Koreans have to do what the U.S. tells us," he replied sarcastically, evoking resentment about ostensibly being under the yoke of imperial America and U.S. soldiers.

I grabbed my bag from the back seat and strode back into the parking lot. T.W. quickly reversed the car, threw it into drive and barreled onto the country road. We'd been together four days. I knew I should have driven my Scoupe. I wasn't having much luck with translators.

I sat on a bench at the edge of the parking lot pondering what to do next, the mid-afternoon sun beating down like a hot laser. For some time I soundly cussed T.W. After a while, I realized I could continue castigating him and take up residency in Haean, or find a bus and head to Gangneung to retrieve my car. I preferred the former but chose the latter and trudged onto the road to find a bus stop. I decided that Gangneung would now be my final destination, scuttling my original plan to explore the isolated border region on the way back to Seoul. The trip was essentially over. A wave of relief flooded over me. I found a nearby bus stop and waited. Twenty minutes later, an old public county bus squeaked to a halt.

"Where are you heading?" I called to the driver through the open bus door.

"Inje," he said.

Good enough. I hopped aboard and greeted my fellow passengers – a half dozen rural folk. An hour later, at the Inje Bus Station, I approached the ticket window and asked the clerk when the next bus was due for Gangneung. In ninety minutes, she said. I bought a ticket and scurried into downtown Inje. What a revelation! I'd mistakenly envisioned Inje to be slow and sleepy. After all, vast Inje County had just 34,000 people, the lowest population density in the country. Inje City is sandwiched on a narrow slice of land between the Soyang River and a low, steep rock face. The busy main street bustled with cars, the sidewalks with throngs of pedestrians. Three and four-floor commercial buildings housed restaurants, shops, mobile phone stores and PC rooms tight against each other. Downtown Inje could have passed for a fashionable mini Gangnam in Seoul.

I searched for a PC room to check my emails and entered one brimming with scores of young soldiers in uniform playing military video games. Every computer was in use, the large room reverberating with the deafening cacophony of computer-generated machine-gun fire and commandos barking orders. I hastened to another PC room, but it too was crammed with young servicemen playing military-themed computer games. At a third, also full of soldiers, I found a single unused computer and sat down. Inje was obviously a popular draw for soldiers posted in the region serving their mandatory two-year military duty. It occurred to me that today being Saturday and apparently troops' weekly day off, if North Korea's leader Kim Jong-un in Pyongyang desired to launch an invasion of the South, Saturday might be a propitious day to do so; every ROK soldier across the country apparently is holed up in PC rooms.

Back at the bus station, I boarded a country bus destined for Gangneung. My six fellow passengers were young women in their late teens and early twenties, dolled up for having met their soldier beaus in Inje.

The bus headed east on National Route 44, bound for the coastal town of Yangyang and south to Gangneung. We entered Seorak Mountain National Park's 373 square kilometers. The tallest of the park's steeple-like granite ridges is 1,708-meter Daecheong Peak. The word Seorak doesn't simply refer to a single mountain, rather to a broad area that includes the Inner Seorak Mountains west of Inje and the Outer Seorak Mountains near the coast.

No. 44 in sections is impossibly twisty and narrow and moves past arresting blocks of vertical, sky-high granite rising on each side of the road. We entered Hangye Valley, a V-shaped wedge squeezed between walls of rock, next to the road flowing a narrow mountain stream with huge boulders. The occasional small roadside stand offered light meals to visitors hiking the river. The little tables and chairs on the road's narrow shoulder were frighteningly close to traffic. Our bus squeezed past them, just a meter of space to spare.

Our speed was limited to thirty kilometers per hour on tight turns and curves. The driver constantly shifted and ground the gears, and accelerated and braked, making me nauseous. One moment it was sunny and clear with a blue sky, the next instant we were enveloped in solid white cloud, visibility reduced to near zero. Ten minutes later, just as quickly, we were out of the soup and back in bright sunshine.

We arrived at the Gangneung Bus Station in early evening. I took a taxi to the train station to retrieve the Scoupe, then found a nearby *yeogwan*. I took a shower, then a long evening stroll through old downtown. To celebrate the journey's conclusion I treated myself to dinner at McDonalds and walked some more. A substantial load had been lifted from my shoulders. The expedition was over.

***

The next day was a rainout, so I spent all of it indoors, relaxing and dozing at a *jjimjilbang*. The following early afternoon — the sun shining in a deep blue sky — I drove to Gyeongpo Beach, one of the country's most popular. I walked on the soft, yellow sand extending indefinitely in both directions. The sea was a sparkling, expansive deep blue, the intense color the result of the East Sea's formidable depth. A row of restaurants and motels line the road behind the beach. On this perfect July day, the entire beach was curiously bereft of a single beach-goer. I had a kilometer-long stretch of sand to myself. I was in heaven.

I spread my towel out on a narrow sliver of shade next to an empty lifeguard stand, lay down and stretched out. Immediately, I fell into a most welcome, luxurious deep sleep and dreamed that Lee Hyo-ri — Korea's glamorous pop singer — was feeding me expensive Chilean green grapes. I awoke with a start. I checked my watch — four o'clock. I'd been out cold for a couple of hours and was also no longer in the shade, strips of my skin now bright red. I decided to cool off, and fit my swim goggles over my head, then skipped down to the surf. No one was in the water.

The sea was just bracing enough so it took a couple of minutes to ease my way in. I swam out a bit then made a series of shallow dives in crystal clear water to the sandy bottom, though the water quickly descended to dark depths where a great white shark or lurking sea monster could end my life. About fifteen meters from shore, I began swimming parallel to the beach, but after only a few minutes I became aware of a series of repetitive shrill whistle blasts. I stopped swimming, treaded water and looked toward the beach. A young lifeguard, maybe eighteen-years-old, was standing with a group of friends and frantically gesturing at me. I wondered what he was so riled up about.

There was no exposed fin of a prowling great white shark in the water ready to devour me, so that couldn't be it. I wasn't drowning, and if I was, I hoped the lifeguard wouldn't be standing there like a moron, instead valiantly rushing to me with a life jacket. I wasn't ogling female swimmers; there were none to ogle. Then it suddenly dawned on me: I was guilty of swimming too far out from shore. You see, to Koreans, ten or fifteen meters from the water's edge might as well be halfway across the Pacific Ocean.

Visit any popular beach on summer vacation, and within five meters of the length of the shoreline you'll invariably witness a long, narrow parallel band of water where throngs of bathers relax and float on blown-up inner tubes and other inflatable devices. The bathers are content in the knowledge that the sandy bottom is easily touchable by foot. No one actually swims, certainly not past this imaginary line five meters from shore where the bottom deepens to more than a person's height. Koreans seem to have an irrational fear of water deeper than two meters.

The lifeguard wouldn't be pacified unless I got out of the water. Not feeling like arguing, I complied, went to my towel and slept some more.

I woke up ninety minutes later, the early evening light fading. I gathered my stuff and returned to the car. Thoroughly relaxed and groggy, I opted to extend my indulgent mini-vacation for another night. Not far along the beach road, I found a large, airy *jjimjilbang* devoid of customers and stayed the evening.

Early the next afternoon I departed Gangneung for Seoul. Three hours later I was back in Myeongil-dong. The Scoupe's odometer showed about 8,000 kilometers had accumulated since the road trip began April 7. Today was July 10. Those clicks were equivalent to driving twice across the United States. This pleased me. The journey's conclusion seemed a bit of a letdown — no ticker-tape parade through Myeongil-dong, no confetti floating down from rooftops, no boisterous crowds welcoming home their adapted son. Instead, I slipped into my small flat and slept some more. One thing was for certain — I wouldn't be driving tomorrow.

CHAPTER 24

A Kiwi Treks the Baekdu-Daegan Trail

A sense of normalcy began to prevail after the trip. I returned to teaching English as a second language to Korean kids in Myeongil-dong. That fall through early winter — about one weekend each month — I was on the road crisscrossing the peninsula filming *hanok* for the documentary with Mr. Hwang and his crew.

In the autumn I attended a Royal Asiatic Society lecture given by a New Zealander, Roger Shepherd, who'd accomplished quite a feat. Beginning at Jiri Mountain — the terminus of the Sobaek range near Gurye in the south — Roger had trekked 735 kilometers northeast on mountain ridges to the border. Had there not been the DMZ to halt his ten-week expedition, he'd have continued into North Korea.

Roger had tackled what's known as the Baekdu-Daegan Trail (Baekdu referring to Mount Baekdu; Daegan meaning Trail Ridge). Mount Baekdu is an extinct, 2,744-meter-high volcano in North Korea near the Chinese border — the tallest peak in the two Koreas. From Jiri Mountain to Mount Baekdu is about 1,500 kilometers. Koreans believe Mount Baekdu to be spiritual.

In the RAS lecture hall at a downtown Seoul hotel, Roger stood before a standing-room-only audience of about three hundred. On a good night, lectures draw perhaps a hundred people. Topics range from Korean Buddhism and tea-drinking to national history and renowned Koreans. The Baekdu-Daegan Trail wasn't very well known among the expat community. RAS membership is mainly Western and European teachers, professors, business people and diplomats.

Lean, tall, bearded and in his late thirties, Roger talked in that straightforward, no-nonsense New Zealand style. He'd been a police officer in New Zealand and had taken time off from his job to travel in Korea and teach English. He fell in love with the mountains and settled here.

Roger presented a slideshow of photos he'd snapped on the Baekdu-Daegan Trail from atop ridges and peaks, the panoramic vistas seemingly in clouds. He'd undertaken the adventure with his friend, Andrew Douch, and along the route they'd slept in tents, casual alpine huts, *minbak* and outdoor traditional gazebos. "Hospitality from locals was amazing," Roger recounted, villagers sharing bottles of *soju* and food. The trail moves mostly along ridges ranging from a low of 200 meters above sea level to a high of 1,900 meters. There is sort of a path, but unlike the renowned, well-marked Appalachian Trail in the eastern United States, this one isn't as easily identifiable. Taking detailed notes and recording names of villages, flora and fauna and landmarks as he trekked, Roger published a book, *Baekdu Daegan Trail: Hiking Korea's Mountain Spine*.

The Kiwi would go on to hike thousands of kilometers in mountains in North Korea, including at Mount Baekdu. He led a group of New Zealand motorcyclists south from Siberia through North Korea to South Korea's south coast. Roger started his own business – Hike Korea – leading foreigners on excursions into interior mountains.

During his lecture, Roger mentioned he'd soon be riding a motorbike along the Baekdu-Daegan Trail for a couple of weeks to do follow-up research. Temperatures at 1,500 meters in the fall can be chilly. Since my Scoupe was sitting idle, I introduced myself to Roger after his talk and offered its use. He gladly accepted.

Several weeks later, I was heading southeast from Seoul to meet Roger in Mungyeong, a village on the Sobaek Mountains' northern boundary. The Sobaeks divided the peninsula northwest and southeast, and Mungyeong is close to the country's geographical midpoint. For millennia, Koreans had trekked the Mungyeong Pass, which ends in Goseon thirty-five kilometers northwest of Mungyeong.

In early evening I arrived at Mungyeong's sparsely populated village, enveloped by a wall of looming, dominating darkly foreboding eminences that were blocking the descending sun rays. The long slopes are so close, I felt as if I could reach out and touch them. At this broad, wooded base I met Roger. We rented a room in a nearby *yeogwan* and spent the evening in conversation. After hearing a bit about his life as a former cop in New Zealand, I concluded he wasn't one to suffer fools gladly.

The next morning — gray, misty and chilly — Roger began retracing his route on the trail through the Mungyeong Pass. I tagged along. He wasn't in a verbose mood; rather, deep in thought, diligently jotting information in his notebook. Focused and engrossed, he barely said a word. After ninety minutes I thought it best to let him continue alone. We returned to the *yeogwan* and we drove to the nearby Mungyeong Bus Station, where I caught a bus back to Seoul. Roger would be using the Scoupe for the next couple of weeks.

***

Earlier that fall I'd embarked on my own short hike in Jirisan National Park in South Jeolla province, driving from Seoul to the park and rendezvousing with an RAS friend. We enjoyed a sunny day ambling up a broad, lovely eminence, the earthen path moving under foliage by little mountain homesteads and small fields.

Jiri Mountain isn't just a single peak. Rather, it consists of scores of ridges and peaks in Jirisan National Park's massif: 472 square kilometers extending into North and South Jeolla and South Gyeongsang provinces. The park's tallest eminence is 1,915-meter Cheonwang Peak, the country's second-highest after 1,950-meter Mount Halla on Jejudo, the island province sixty miles off the south coast.

After the hike, I perused my road atlas to seek a more varied route back to Seoul. I eschewed freeways. I discovered National Route 19, established in 1971. It begins in the south on Namhae Island, then parallels the Sobaek's spine and ends 497 kilometers north in obscure Hongcheon County in Gangwon province. The route warranted exploring.

Just west of Jirisan National Park, I found No. 19, bereft of vehicles. Almost immediately it began to ascend on a series of switchbacks tightly snaking up the side of a broad green mountain. At the wide summit was a treat: under a noon blue sky stretched a fabulous panoramic vista north over a section of the vast Sobaek range, nothing but rounded ridge after rounded ridge of long, bullish green slopes. The sheer scope was arresting. Roger referred to the Sobaeks as largely "unexplored." He wasn't kidding.

From the broad crest the road began pitching down a series of long sweeping switchbacks. To my immediate left is a long, steep drop-off to the valley floor far below. I decided to have a bit of fun and coast, slipping the automatic gearshift from drive into neutral. This may not come as a surprise to those who aren't morons, but on a steep descent a coasting car quickly gains momentum. In mere seconds the Scoupe was rocketing down like a bat out of hell. Immediately, of course, I applied the brakes. To my dismay they had almost no effect on slowing the car — something to do, I supposed, with the transmission being in neutral. I pumped the brakes harder, to no avail. My heart rate doubled, matching the car's acceleration. I had a fleeting, troubling vision of hurtling across the road and plunging to the bottom of the valley. I thrust the gearshift back into drive and thankfully the brakes reengaged. The moral of the story is don't be a dotard and tinker with a car's driveshaft when descending a steep mountain slope — if you enjoy living.

What a pleasure to cruise the several hundred kilometers on No. 19. I passed a varied environment of secluded green valleys, hamlets, villages and pretty meadows, and went up and down and around lush hills. My speedometer never got north of sixty kilometers per hour, which was fine, because I wasn't in a hurry. I was content to simply watch rural life slowly unfold.

It took the entire afternoon to early evening to drive from Jirisan to near Wonju — about a hundred kilometers southeast of Seoul. At Wonju, I bade goodbye to the route and reluctantly veered northwest to Seoul. If someone was to ask me how to best experience the peninsula's unspoiled rugged interior, I wouldn't hesitate to recommend a long, leisurely cruise on No. 19.

***

After dropping off the car at Mungyeong, and returning to Seoul by bus, my pan-Korea trip was essentially over. I couldn't measure it against the hardships stalwart adventurers like Isabella Bird Bishop and Mark Napier Trollope, and other pioneers experienced slogging on foot through this rough land more than a century earlier. More recently, Simon Winchester and Roger Shepherd had trekked major swaths of terrain. Compared to the challenges these brave souls faced, my pilgrimage was a cakewalk.

But I too suffered for my art. I believe I'd shrunk from sitting behind the car wheel for sometimes up to ten hours a day for more than three months. Slouching in the bucket seat, it felt as if my chest and stomach had seemingly fused into one. I now had difficulty ascertaining where my chest began and my stomach ended.

It was satisfying to view the many sites in four months and to meet notable people, including Lee Byeong-hee — the former Seodaemun prisoner — and blue-blood Yi Seok. Despite the country's modest size, it would take ages to see everything, and we'd barely scratched the surface. I find it ironic hearing Koreans talk about traveling the length of the country.

"Oh my, driving from Seoul to Busan. Better pack a lunch, compass and rescue flares. It's a long way."

Those 500 kilometers, north to south, only equal the distance from say, New York City to Washington or Toronto to Ottawa. On a map of North America, that span barely registers.

Imagine the limitless possibilities for overland travel when that baneful DMZ is eradicated, and South and North are on compatible terms. Simply hop in your car in Seoul, head north, turn left at Pyongyang and continue 10,000 uninterrupted kilometers west to Paris. Not a fan of foie de gras? No worries. Cruise from Pyongyang to Beijing, then southwest to India, and partake of some hot curry. With that oppressive DMZ border, there are now only three ways off the peninsula: plane, boat or swim.

That barbed wire will be gone one day; the Berlin Wall was razed overnight. But the country may face a more pressing future issue. South Korea has one of the world's lowest birthrates of less than one child per woman, due to exorbitant private education and housing costs. The government is forecasting only about 35 million South Koreans will remain on the peninsula in 2060, down from the current 52 million. I realize I'm in the minority, but would fewer Koreans in an overcrowded, small nation be a bad thing? I think not: less cars on the road, more available seats on the subway, fewer K-Pop boy bands.

On his 1816 voyage south along Korea's west coast, British captain Basil Hall described Koreans as wearing white garments and straw shoes, laboring as farmers and fishermen, living simply in villages and grouped by bloodlines. Today, businessmen don suits and ties and women wear designer, name-brand clothes, but underneath the sartorial polish, I believe they're the same audacious, salt-of-the-earth folk as in centuries past. I'm not sure this modern, urban, fast-paced lifestyle living in high-rise apartments and working in office towers — all study and work — suits them.

Hall wrote that Koreans were aggressive forces of nature. They still are. No matter how quiet, deferential and unassuming they may outwardly appear, they won't be dismissed, forgotten or ignored. They are hard-charging, hard-working and hard-living.

Sometimes they try too hard — their energy, drive and will unstoppable. Forgive them for this, for they are Korean — failure is not an option. Their collective sheer will power, tenacity and fortitude have propelled the country from one of the world's poorest after the Korean War to the eleventh wealthiest. A remarkable achievement; not by chance. I know of no other country that has accomplished so much in so little time. Yet, this ambition has resulted in a sort of pan-Korean stress. Studies show the country is one of the world's most sleep-deprived and a global leader in hard liquor consumption.

Having lived in South Korea for about twenty years, between 1995 and 2022, I'm not much further ahead in understanding the people than when I first arrived. I sometimes feel their psyches are impenetrable, their character camouflaged. Koreans are still an enigma to me — Korea exotic and mysterious. It shouldn't be any other way.

The peninsula became my second home and captivated me. I was attracted to the people, to their sense of innocence, to their hospitality, to their unique ability to find humor in the most insignificant thing. Yet, there is a fierceness to them. Were I in a foxhole, the enemy perilously close, I'd choose a Korean as my partner; definitely an *ajumma* — they take no prisoners. I'd skip the Buddhist monk and nun — they'd negatively comment on the size of my stomach. Not that it's all that big. But you know what I mean.

ACKNOWLEDGEMENTS

I'm indebted to Kim Heju for accompanying me on our travels through the country and for translating – an exhausting task. Heju spent many months and countless hours after the trip contacting government and tourism offices, guides, temples, museums, professors and historians, to confirm information and facts. Without Heju the book wouldn't have seen fruition.

Many thanks to Park So-yeon at Hollym Publishing, who without her much-appreciated and enthusiastic initiative, the book wouldn't have seen the light of day in South Korea. To Hollym's editor, Hahm Minji, gratitude for her great effort and patience during a long editing process. I'm grateful to veteran journalist Donald Kirk, who has covered South Korea since 1972 for the *Chicago Tribune*, *International Herald Tribune*, CBS Radio, *USA Today*, *Christian Science Monitor*, *The Daily Beast*, and *Forbes Asia* – author of four books on South Korea – for his expertise in editing the manuscript.

My appreciation to the many Koreans – including city hall and tourism office employees, tour guides and strangers — who kindly offered assistance during four months traversing South Korea. Thanks to Park "T.W." Tae-won and Sung-jai for translating portions of the trip.

In Memoriam

Peter Bartholomew arrived in South Korea in 1968 at age 23 as a member of the U.S. Peace Corps. Peter went on to become one of the foremost authorities on traditional and historical Korean grand architecture. I took his informative walking tours of Seoul palaces and other grand architecture. I observed his keen and active involvement at Royal Asiatic Society - Korea meetings in his role as past president. In Seoul courts, Peter fought developers' plans to demolish old traditional clay and wood homes, known as *hanok*, to build high-rise buildings in their places. After 53 years in his beloved adopted South Korea, Peter sadly passed away in his Seoul *hanok* from apparent heart failure at age 76 on May 13, 2021.

Mark Dake

BIBLIOGRAPHY

Adams, Edward B. *Through Gates of Seoul: Trails and Tales of Yi Dynasty*, Vol. 1. Seoul: Sahm-bo Publishing, 1970.

Allen, Horace N. *Things Korean: A Collection of Sketches and Anecdotes, Missionary and Diplomatic*. New York: Fleming H. Revell Company, 1908.

Barris, Ted. *Deadlock in Korea: Canadians at War, 1950-1953*. Toronto: Macmillan, 1999.

Bartz, Patricia M. *South Korea*. Oxford: London Clarendon Press, 1972.

Bird, Isabella L. *Korea and Her Neighbours*. New York: Fleming H. Revell Company, 1898.

Bryson, Bill. *A Walk in the Woods: Rediscovering America on the Appalachian Trail*. New York: Broadway Books, 1998.

Carlson, Lewis. H. *Remembered Prisoners of a Forgotten War: An Oral History of Korean War POWs*. New York: St. Martin's Press, 2002.

Clark, Donald N. *Living Dangerously in Korea: The Western Experience, 1900–1950*. Norwalk, CT: EastBridge, 2003.

Cook, Harold F. *Pioneer American Businessman in Korea: The Life and Times of Walter Davis Townsend*. Royal Asiatic Society, Korea Branch: 1981.

Diamond Sutra Recitation Group. *King Sejong the Great: The Everlasting Light of Korea*, Vol. 2. Korean Spirit and Culture Series. Pohang, Korea: Yong Hwa Publications, 2007.

Eckert, Carter J., Ki-baik Lee, Young Ick Lew, Michael Robinson, and Edward W. Wagner. *Korea Old and New: A History*. Seoul: Harvard Korea Institute, 1990.

Ellis, Richard, and John E. McCosker, *Great White Shark*. Stanford, CA: Stanford University Press, 1991.

Ha, Tae hung. *A Trip Through Historic Korea*. Vol. 2, Korean Cultural Series. Seoul: Yonesei University Press, 1960.

_____. *Behind the Scenes of Royal Palaces in Korea (Yi Dynasty)*. Seoul: Yonsei University Press, 1983.

Hall, Basil. *Voyage of Discovery to the West Coast of Corea and the Great Loo-Choo Island*. London: J. Murray, 1818.

Hamel, Hendrik. *Hamel's Journal and a Description of the Kingdom of Korea, 1653-1666*. Translated by Br. Jean-Paul Buys. Seoul: Royal Asiatic Society, Korea Branch, 1994.

Hanley, Charles J., Choe Sang-Hun, and Martha Mendoza. *The Bridge at No Gun Ri: A Hidden Nightmare from the Korean War*. New York: Henry Holt and Company, 2001.

Hawley, Samuel. *The Imjin War: Japan's Sixteenth-Century Invasion of Korea and Attempt to Conquer China*. Seoul: Royal Asiatic Society, Korea Branch. Berkley, CA: Institute of East Asian Studies, University of California, 2005.

Ilta, Zen Master. *Everyday Korean Buddhist Practices. Translated by Brian Berry*. Seoul: Hyorim Publishing, 2009.

Kang, Chol-hwan, and Pierre Rigoulot. *The Aquariums of Pyongyang: Ten Years in the North Korean Gulag*. Translated by Yair Reiner. New York: Basic Books, 2001.

Kim, Agnes Davis. *Unrealized Challenge*. Seoul: Yonsei University Press, 1982.

Kim, Myong-taek, ed. *Korea Tour-Road Atlas (Chinese-English Edition)*. Seoul: Chung-ang Atlas Co., 2007.

Kirk, Donald, and Choe Sang-Hun. *Korea Witness: 135 Years of War, Crisis and News in the Land of the Morning Calm*. Seoul: EunHaeng Namu, 2006.

Kirkbride, Wayne A. *Panmunjom: Facts about the Korean DMZ*. Seoul: Hollym International Corp., 1986.

_____. *DMZ: A Story of the Panmunjeom Axe Murder*. Seoul: Hollym International Corp., 1984.

Nahm, Andrew C. *Korea: Tradition and Transformation: A History of the Korean People*. Seoul: Hollym International Corp., 1988.

_____, ed. "Korea Under Japanese Colonial Rule: Studies of the Policy and Techniques of Japanese Colonialism [Proceedings of the Conference on Korea, November 12-14, 1970.]" Center for Korean Studies, Western Michigan University, 1973.

Nilsen, Robert. *Moon Handbooks: South Korea*. Emeryville, CA: Avalon Travel, 2004.

Oberdorfer, Don. *The Two Koreas: A Contemporary History*. New York: Basic Books, 1997.

Palais, James B. *Views on Korean Social History*. Seoul: Yonsei University Press, 1998.

Russ, Martin. *Breakout: The Chosin Reservoir Campaign, Korea 1950*. New York: Penguin, 2000.

Sands, William Franklin. *Undiplomatic Memories: The Far East 1896-1904*. London: John Hamilton, 1904.

Shepherd, Roger, and Andrew Douch. *Baekdu Daegan Trail: Hiking Korea's Mountain Spine*. Seoul: Seoul Selection, 2011.

Sonjae, Br. Anthony An. *Discovering Korea at the Start of the Twentieth Century*. Seoul: The Academy of Korean Studies Press, 2011.

Spencer, F. Robert. *Yogong: Factory Girl*. Seoul: Cheng and Tsui, 1988.

Steers, Richard M. *Made in Korea: Chung Ju Yung and the Rise of Hyundai*. New York: Routledge, 1999.

Tucker, Spencer C., ed. *Encyclopedia of the Korean War: A Political, Social, and Military History*, Vol. 1. Santa Barbara, CA: ABC-CLIO, 2000.

Underwood, Horace G. *Korea in War, Revolution and Peace: The Recollections of Horace G. Underwood.* Seoul: Yonsei University Press, 2001.

Underwood, Lillias H. *Underwood of Korea.* New York: Fleming H. Revell Company, 1918.

Vol. XLI of Transactions. Seoul: Royal Asiatic Society, Korea Branch, 1964.

Vol. 68 of Transactions. Seoul: Royal Asiatic Society, Korea Branch, 1993.

Vol. 80 of Transactions. Seoul: Royal Asiatic Society, Korea Branch, 2005.

Vol. 85 of Transactions. Seoul: Royal Asiatic Society, Korea Branch, 2010.

Winchester, Simon. *Korea: A Walk Through the Land of Miracles.* London: Grafton Books, 1988.

Yi, Sun-sin. *Nanjung Ilgi: War Diary of Admiral Yi Sun-sin.* Translated by Tae-Hung Ha. Seoul: Yonsei University Press, 1977.

ABOUT THE AUTHOR

Mark Dake grew up in Toronto, Canada, playing ice hockey and tennis and hoping to make the big leagues. Not nearly proficient enough in either sport, he was forced to get a real job. He coached tennis in Canada, Austria, Germany, Qatar and the U.S., and was a newspaper sports reporter in Lake Tahoe, California. He generally didn't stay in one place for long.

In 1995, living in Long Beach, California, Dake answered an ad in the *Los Angeles Times* seeking Westerners to teach English in South Korea. Three weeks later he was in Seoul. He discovered that Koreans are energetic and hard charging, and Seoul vibrant and pulsating – the city never sleeps. He taught young Korean students at an after-school academy beginning at 2:00 p.m. daily, so he got to sleep in late. Life didn't get much better than this.

Dake has spent parts of three largely enjoyable decades living and teaching in this ancient, mountainous land. He also served as a copy editor at *The Korea Herald* and *Yonhap*, the national news agency. He occasionally spends summers teaching tennis in Toronto. He's visited thirty-seven countries but still hasn't figured out where to settle down.

Mark Dake's contact: interstate400@gmail.com